WOLF PACK

The Story of the U-Boat in World War II

OSPREY
PUBLISHING

The Author

Gordon Williamson was born in 1951 and currently works for the Scottish Land Register. He spent seven years with the Military Police TA and has published a number of books and articles on the German forces of World War II.

He has long been fascinated by the U-boat world and has spent many years researching the men and craft that formed this elite fleet.

WOLF PACK

The Story of the U-Boat in World War II

GORDON WILLIAMSON

First published in Great Britain in 2005 by Osprey Publishing Ltd.
This paperback edition published in 2006 by Osprey Publishing Ltd,
Midland House, West Way, Botley, Oxford OX2 0PH, United Kingdom.

Email: info@ospreypublishing.com

Previously published as New Vanguard 51: *Kriegsmarine U-boats 1939–45 (1)*;
New Vanguard 55: *Kriegsmarine U-boats 1939–45 (2)*; and Warrior 36: *Grey Wolf*.

© 2005 Osprey Publishing Ltd.

CIP data for this publication is available from the British Library.

ISBN 10: 1 84603 141 9
ISBN 13: 978-1-84603-141-0

Design: Ken Vail Graphic Design, Cambridge, UK
Artwork by Ian Palmer and Darko Pavlovic
Index by Alan Thatcher
Originated by The Electronic Page Company, UK and PPS Grasmere Ltd, UK
Printed and bound by Bookbuilders

06 07 08 09 10   10 9 8 7 6 5 4 3 2 1

FOR A CATALOGUE OF ALL BOOKS PUBLISHED BY OSPREY PLEASE CONTACT:

NORTH AMERICA
Osprey Direct c/o Random House Distribution Center,
400 Hahn Road, Westminster, MD 21157, USA
E-mail: info@ospreydirectusa.com

ALL OTHER REGIONS
Osprey Direct UK, P.O. Box 140, Wellingborough,
Northants, NN8 2FA, UK
E-mail: info@ospreydirect.co.uk

www.ospreypublishing.com

EDITOR'S NOTE
All photographs, unless indicated otherwise, are courtesy of the U-Boot Archiv.

FRONT COVER IMAGE
The Type XXIII U-2336, returning from her last mission of the war on 14 May
1945. (Artwork by Ian Palmer © Osprey Publishing Ltd)

CONTENTS

ACKNOWLEDGEMENTS

This book and those individual volumes that preceded it would not have been possible without the gracious assistance of Horst Bredow, founder of the U-Boot Archiv. Herr Bredow has been a most gracious host on my visits to Cuxhaven, allowing me not only access to the Archiv, but to reside in the Archiv building during my trips. He has provided much help and encouragement and has made available the photographic collection of the Archiv for use in this work. The Archiv is the world's foremost repository of information and photographs on the subject not only of the U-boats of the Kriegsmarine but also of their forerunners in the Kaiserliche Marine of Imperial Germany.

Noted U-boat historian Jak P. Mallmann-Showell has also offered his encouragement and help in correcting and revising material for this and other related projects.

I would also like to express my grateful thanks to the following individuals for their assistance with this project: Chris Boonzaier, Malcolm Bowers, Josef Charita, Thomas Huss, Michel Legrand, Kevin Matthews, Detlev Niemann, François Saez and Mark Wood.

The U-Boot Archiv

The majority of photographs in this book were kindly provided by Horst Bredow, founder and director of the U-Boot Archiv in Cuxhaven-Altenbruch.

A former U-boat officer who served on U-288, Herr Bredow was spared the fate of his crew-mates when he was sent to hospital for treatment of wounds and missed the last sailing of his boat, which was lost with all hands during an attack on Convoy JW58 on 3 April 1944.

Herr Bredow has dedicated his life to researching the fates of all of Germany's U-boats and in the process has assembled the world's finest archival collection of photographs, documents and historical artefacts relating to the U-boats, not only of the Kriegsmarine, but also of their predecessors of the Imperial Navy of the Kaiser's day.

Maintaining and expanding this wonderful collection is a major undertaking. The Archiv receives no official funding and is a registered charity depending on donations from visitors and those who use its research facilities. For further details, contact Horst Bredow, U-Boot Archiv, Bahnhofstrasse 57, 27478 Cuxhaven Altenbruch, Germany, enclosing two International Reply Coupons.

To support the Archiv, membership is available for the Freundeskreis Traditionsarchiv Unterseeboote e.V, or FTU (the Circle of Friends of the U-boat Archive). An annual subscription allows members the use of Archiv research facilities at preferential rates as well as a substantial yearbook containing specially selected material on the U-boat war not generally or easily available elsewhere.

Readers interested in supporting this worthy cause can obtain further information from: Jak P. Mallmann-Showell, 3 Sandpiper Road, Hawkinge, Folkestone, Kent CT18 7TA, UK. Please include an SAE if in the UK, or if outside the UK, two International Reply Coupons.

INTRODUCTION

Few forms of combat in modern history have grabbed the imagination of the public to the degree that has been the case with submarine warfare. There is, to many, something innately sinister about any weapon which can operate unseen and whose arrival is first heralded by a huge explosion and eruption of flame as the victim it has been stalking is sent plunging into the depths.

The German submariner has, in popular Western culture, usually been portrayed as some sort of Nazi fanatic, revelling not only in the destruction of enemy ships, but also in the death of their crews. The reality of course was somewhat different. The German Navy was fiercely traditional and made every effort to ensure that it remained as free as possible from political interference. For a long time, membership of any political party was frowned upon, even after the Nazis came to power. The Commander-in-Chief U-Boats, Karl Dönitz, who of course ultimately became the commander-in-chief of the entire navy, made strenuous efforts to ensure that so-called 'National Socialist Leadership Officers', somewhat analogous to the political commissars employed by the Soviets, were kept well away from the U-boats.

Many of those military formations throughout history that have become perceived as 'elite' have held a fascination for those with an interest in military matters. The German Armed Forces of World War II have many such formations, the fighter arm of the Luftwaffe, the Fallschirmjäger, the Afrikakorps, the Panzerwaffe and the Waffen-SS to name but a few. Of all the branches of the Wehrmacht, however, few were so successful, and came so near to bringing the enemy to its knees, as the 'Grey Wolves' of the U-Bootwaffe under Karl Dönitz.

From the very first day of war to the very last, the U-boats and their crews performed with great distinction. Despite beginning the war with only a fraction of the number of boats intended, Dönitz and his submarines achieved phenomenal results.

The German U-boat designs were immensely successful. They were relatively small in comparison with some of the Allied models. Despite the intensely uncomfortable conditions and privations suffered by the crews, the Type VII which formed the backbone of the U-boat fleet was responsible for sinking more

ships than all of the Allied types put together. The larger Type IX boats had immense range and roamed from German waters all the way to the Far East, operating from bases controlled by the Imperial Japanese Navy. In the second half of the war, the technical innovations incorporated into the Type XXI, Type XXIII and the so-called 'Walter' boats were years ahead of their time, and although too late to affect the course of the war at sea, directly influenced much of post-war submarine development.

The Germans were world leaders not only in constructing these boats, but also in building the special protective bunkers to house them in occupied ports. The great bunkers erected in occupied France in particular were to prove virtually impregnable to attack. Even the massive bunker-busting 'Tallboy' bombs developed specially for use against such targets could inflict only superficial damage on these massive structures. So strong were they that the cost of demolishing them after the war was seen as prohibitive and many of them stand to this day, testament to the abilities of their German constructors.

In many ways, the U-Bootwaffe was unique amongst German military formations. Its level of success was achieved despite fighting its war in a manner which was acknowledged even by its enemies as far 'cleaner' than the manner in which they themselves had fought. Apart from the solitary incident involving the killing of the survivors of the *Peleus* by Kapitänleutnant Eck, the U-boats were distinctive not so much in the number of atrocities committed but rather for the number of occasions on which U-boat commanders went out of their way to try to aid the survival of the crews of ships they had sunk. A significant number of successful U-boat commanders went on to join the post-war West German Navy and served again with great distinction, reaching high rank in NATO working alongside their former foes.

As can be seen in this 1940 photograph of U-551, a Type VIIB, although the net cutters were removed from many boats by the outbreak of war, a few carried them for much longer, though they were rarely required to fulfil their original purpose.

A rare shot of the 2cm gun fitted to the pedestal, here on U-24. Note the rather overcrowded conning tower. This boat survived 21 operational missions before being scuttled owing to damage sustained in a bombing raid on her base.

In 1981, the release of the movie *Das Boot* played a major part in altering the perceived image of the U-boat crewmen. For the first time they were shown as being human, with the same hopes and fears as their counterparts in any other navy, living in cramped, uncomfortable conditions with the prospect of an extremely horrifying death their constant companion.

Despite facing a rapid rate of development in Allied anti-submarine measures, the U-boats were adept at developing fresh tactics to face each challenge. From the original 'stand-off' attacks engaging enemy convoys from a distance with spreads of torpedo shots to attacking at close range on the surface at night; from hunting in pre-arranged 'packs' on the lookout for convoys to the more effective 'patrol-lines' where the U-boat locating the convoy then called up support from other boats; and of course in the spectacular solo successes such as Prien's attack on the *Royal Oak* at Scapa Flow, Guggenberger's sinking of the *Ark Royal* and Tiesenhausen's destruction of the *Barham*, German U-boat commanders were to prove themselves masters of submarine warfare. All this was achieved despite the Allies having cracked the German naval codes following the capture of an example of the naval version of the 'Enigma' coding machine, and in the face of almost overwhelming Allied air superiority.

Today, surviving examples of U-boat memorabilia are much sought after and fetch extremely high prices, leading to widespread faking of such items.

This book is intended to give the reader a good grounding in all aspects of the U-boat war. It includes detailed descriptions and technical specifications of the boats themselves; the construction of the massive U-boat bunkers and their ultimate fates, including details of those that survive and may still be visited today; information on life as a U-boat crewman covering recruitment, training, pay and conditions, uniforms and insignia; a brief review of the U-boat war itself, the operations and tactics; and additional information on further research resources, including online facilities and recommended reading.

CHRONOLOGY

1 October 1933	Unterseebootsabwehrschule founded.
29 June 1935	The launch of U-1.
27 September 1935	1. Unterseebootsflotille *Weddigen* commissioned by its first chief, Fregattenkapitän Karl Dönitz.
1 January 1936	The appointment of Kapitän zur See Karl Dönitz to the post of Führer der Unterseeboote.
4 August 1938	The first Type IX U-boat commissioned.
4 September 1939	Liner *Athenia* sunk by U-30.
14 October 1939	Battleship *Royal Oak* sunk at Scapa Flow by U-47 under Kapitänleutnant Günther Prien in the U-Bootwaffe's first major success.
7 March 1941	Günther Prien killed in action around this date (exact date not known).
17 March 1941	Joachim Schepke killed in action and Otto Kretschmer captured. Germany has now lost three of its top aces.
9 May 1941	U-110 captured intact by the British.
14 November 1941	Aircraft carrier *Ark Royal* sunk by U-81.
15 November 1941	Launch of U-459, the first Type XIV tanker U-boat, or so-called *Milchkuh*.
25 November 1941	Battleship *Barham* sunk by U-331.
13 January 1942	Operation *Paukenschlag* offensive against shipping off the American coast begins. The start of the second 'Happy Time'.
5 July 1942	Convoy PQ17 decimated by combined U-boat/air attacks.
12 September 1942	U-156 sinks the passenger liner *Laconia* and is attacked by Allied aircraft while rescuing survivors, resulting in a prohibition of future rescue attempts.
30 January 1943	Karl Dönitz appointed Grossadmiral and Supreme Commander-in-Chief of the Navy.
20 March 1943	Largest-ever convoy battle, with wolf pack attacks on HX229 and SC122.
24 May 1943	Scale of U-boat losses prompts Dönitz to withdraw all U-boats from the North Atlantic.
17 April 1944	Launch of the first Type XXIII U-boat.
12 May 1944	Launch of the first Type XXI.

PART I

THE DEVELOPMENT OF THE KRIEGSMARINE'S U-BOATS

Amongst the many onerous terms of the Armistice that Germany signed in 1918 was a demand that all German U-boats were to be surrendered to Britain and additionally that all boats still under construction were to be destroyed or dismantled. Germany was also prohibited from building any other submarines, to include merchant vessels, in the future. These demands were subsequently ratified in terms of Articles 188, 189 and 191 of the Treaty of Versailles signed on 28 June 1919. Existing U-boats at the time of signing were distributed to Britain, the United States, France, Italy and Japan, where they were the subject of intensive study.

Fortunately for Germany, the Allies, though demanding the surrender of all U-boats, seem to have overlooked the huge repository of technical expertise and knowledge represented by the documentary records of the German submarine construction industry. Although the Allies had demanded the surrender of all records and information, the high levels of knowledge and experience remained.

A Type II in dry dock. This shot gives a good view of the saddle tanks, and in particular of the torpedo tube arrangement. Two upper tubes were fitted side by side with a third below on the boat's centre line.

Before long, though prohibited from actually building submarines, Germany was actively marketing her expertise in this field, selling U-boat designs to Japan and working in cooperation with shipyards in Argentina, Italy and Sweden. In order to avoid political problems that might come from being seen to be acting against the spirit of the Versailles Treaty, a cover firm, NV Ingenieurskanntor voor Scheepsbouw (IvS), was set up in Holland in July 1922. Although legal technicalities prevented the opening of the company's office in The Hague until 1925, the firm was run until that time directly from Germaniawerft's office in Kiel.

Secretly funded by the German Navy, IvS manufactured two submarines for Turkey, the design of which was closely based on the Type UBIII of the Kaiserliche Marine. Both were launched in 1927, with the contracts worded in such a way that IvS personnel were involved with crew selection and training and were permitted to take part in the boats' service trials. The Germans thus gained first-hand knowledge of how their design behaved in practice.

In 1932, the Germans decided on a reconstruction programme designed to provide the nation with a modern navy. This programme included provision for a small fleet of eight medium-sized (500-ton) submarines, though this number was later increased to 16. A year later, in 1933, a school for training U-boat crews was established, ironically under the title of 'Anti-Submarine Defence School' (Unterseebootsabwehrschule) at Kiel.

Three minelaying submarines were also ordered by Finland, again based on an earlier design, this time the Type UCIII, but greatly improved. The boats were built in Finnish shipyards, but with intensive involvement of German technicians who once again participated in their sea trials. Two further orders were received from the Finns, one for a small 115-ton vessel, and one for a larger 250-ton boat, very similar to what would become the MVBII. The last of these, the *Vesikko*, launched in May 1933, had her handover to the Finnish Navy deliberately delayed until January 1936 so that she could be used for the purpose of training future U-boat crews. The *Vesikko* is still preserved today.

Germany now began to develop designs for submarines for her own navy. These projected designs, for the purpose of subterfuge, were referred to as *Motorenversuchsboote* (MVB) or 'Experimental Motor Boats'. Deutsche Werke in Kiel was selected to build the new boats, and a new U-boat base was to be constructed at Kiel-Dietrichsdorf.

Component materials began to be surreptitiously gathered at Deutsche Werke's Kiel base, ready for the order to begin production. The programme envisaged the following types being built:

An exterior view of a Type II tower, in this case U-10. The inverted horse-shoe-shaped object above the painted boat number is a life-preserver, and just astern and below this is the boat's starboard navigation light housing.

1934	two large 800-ton boats and two small 250-ton boats
1935	four small 250-ton boats
1936	two large 800-ton boats and six small 250-ton boats
1937	two large 800-ton boats and six small 250-ton boats

Each small boat was costed at between 1 and 1.5 million marks, including preparation costs, and each large boat at between 4 and 4.5 million marks. The larger boats were designated as MVBIA and the smaller as MVBIIA.

The Anglo-German Naval Agreement of 1934 had agreed a proportional parity of 3:1 between the two countries. With Britain's submarine fleet totalling just over 50,000 tons, this would allow Germany (had the construction of U-boats been permitted at all) a fleet totalling around 17,500 tons. This was initially perceived as being 20 of the MVBIA type and six of the smaller MVBIIA type.

In fact, however, naval theory favoured large numbers of the smaller type as being more effective than a smaller number of large boats. A figure of around ten of the larger boats and 18 of the smaller was arrived at, still leaving Germany well within her theoretical tonnage allowance.

All of this was somewhat academic, however, as Germany still was not in a position where she was allowed to build submarines of any type. Hitler, who had come to power in January 1933, still harboured hopes of an accord with Britain and did not wish his political plans to be upset by any discovery that Germany was building prohibited U-boats. Permission to begin construction was therefore withheld for the time being.

Meanwhile, the Unterseebootsabwehrschule continued with its theoretical training for future U-boat crews, and design work on other models also progressed. An improved version of the MVBII, the MVBIIB, was designed, with a lengthened hull to provide additional fuel bunkerage and thus extended endurance. With three approved designs, it was clear that Deutsche Werke alone could not build sufficient numbers rapidly enough to meet demands, and the decision was taken to distribute the various types to additional shipbuilders. Deutsche Werke at Kiel would build the MVBIIA, Deschimag-AG Weser the MVBIA and Germaniawerft the MVBIIB. By the autumn of 1934 sufficient materials and components had been stockpiled for construction to begin, but still Hitler held back, not approving the commencement of work until 1 February 1935.

Further models had been considered, including the MVBIII, a large development of the MVBIA, which would serve as a minelayer as well as carrying two motor torpedo boats; the MVBIV, which would be a seagoing workshop/supply/repair submarine serving the main combat units of the U-boat fleet; the MVBV, which was to have a new propulsion system designed by Dr Helmuth Walter; and finally the MVBVI, which was to have a new design of steam-driven engine. All of these types were ultimately rejected in favour of the MVBVII, a medium 500-ton design destined to become the Type VII, the backbone of the U-boat fleet during World War II. Once again, this latest model was to be based upon the successful UBIII design of World War I.

Although the MVBII was subsequently further developed to produce the IIC and IID variants, its further development potential was limited. The MVBVII, basically an enlarged MVBII, was a far more versatile design and was further transformed into a bewildering number of variants and sub-variants through the course of World War II. The first orders for the building of the MVBVII type were issued in January 1935, just two months before Hitler formally repudiated the terms of the Treaty of Versailles and rearmament began in earnest. Around this time the 'MVB' prefix was dropped.

THE TYPE I

In terms of volume production, this was one of the least successful of U-boat designs: only two Type IAs were ever built. The decision not to produce more, however, seems to have been dictated by political decisions rather than by any major inherent faults in the design, although Admiral Godt later agreed that, although very good boats, they could be difficult to handle. Constructed by the Deschimag yard, U-25 and U-26 were to be the only boats of their type, though this model was a direct forebear of the later, much more successful, Type IX.

OPERATIONAL USE

The two boats of this type were used predominantly on training duties until 1940 when the general shortage of available boats required their use in combat. In fact, both boats were relatively successful in terms of their combat successes.

U-25 carried out a total of five war cruises, sinking eight enemy ships totalling some 50,250 tons. Her first (pre-war) commander was Korvettenkapitän Eberhardt Godt who was eventually to become Chief of U-Boat Operations in the late stages of the war. His successor as commander was Korvettenkapitän Viktor Schütze, who would become one of Germany's top U-boat 'aces' with a total of 35 ships (180,000 tons) sunk. Passing through a recently laid enemy minefield on 3 August 1940, she struck one of the mines and sank with all hands.

U-26 carried out eight war cruises. On her first cruise, she was employed on minelaying duties, and was rewarded by the sinking of three merchant ships and the damaging of one British warship by mines laid by her. On her second cruise she became the first U-boat of the war to enter the Mediterranean, though the remainder of the cruise was uneventful. Her third cruise saw her add a further three merchant ships to her score in a brief sortie into the Atlantic. The fourth cruise saw her being used for transport duties during the Norwegian campaign, though she sank a 5,200-ton merchantman during her return trip from one of her transport sorties. After three more uneventful patrols, U-26 set off on her eighth war cruise on 20 June 1940. Three merchantmen were sunk on 30 June, and on

U-26, one of only two boats of Type I. She and her sister, U-25, actually performed reasonably well, but this large type never received the high-level political support it needed to go into large-scale production.

the next day an attack damaged a further merchant ship. The attack was followed by a severe depth-charging from two British warships that forced U-26 to the surface where she was bombed by a Sunderland flying boat. The crew were forced to scuttle her, the majority being rescued by their attackers.

Despite both boats having relatively successful, if short, combat careers, they were technically not particularly good sea boats, especially considering that they were intended as ocean-going rather than coastal vessels. Their stability was poor, their diving speed slow, and their manoeuvrability under water unimpressive. Nevertheless, with 13 war cruises and 18 ships sunk between them, the Type IAs had acquitted themselves well when in the hands of experienced skippers.

THE TYPE II

The Type II was a natural enough progression from the UB coastal types of the Kaiserliche Marine in World War I. Small, cheap and easy to build, they could be produced in a remarkably short time. Based on the CV-707 export design produced for Finland between the wars, the Type II made excellent training vessels but, owing to their small size, very cramped interiors and tendency to roll

This pre-war photograph of U-3, a Type IIA, shows a torpedo being loaded on board. The red/white stripes to the warhead indicate that this is a training torpedo. The diminutive size of the Type II is evident here.

heavily when on the surface, they were rather contemptuously referred to as *Einbäume* or 'canoes' by the Germans. Nevertheless, several of this type acquitted themselves well in combat operations as well as in training, and a number of variant types were produced. All carried just three bow torpedo tubes in an unusual inverted triangle arrangement with one each to port and starboard and a third below them on the boat's centre line.

TYPE IIA

A total of just six Type IIAs were built.

SPECIFICATIONS

Length:	40.9m
Beam:	4.1m
Draft:	3.8m
Displacement:	254 tons surfaced, 301 tons submerged
Speed:	13 knots surfaced, 6.9 knots submerged
Endurance:	2,000 nautical miles surfaced, 71 nautical miles submerged
Powerplant:	2 × 350 bhp MWM diesels coupled with 2 × 180 bhp electric motors
Armament:	3 bow torpedo tubes, 6 torpedoes carried
	1 × 2cm flak gun
Crew:	25

TYPE IIB

The Type IIB was basically a lengthened version of the IIA, the additional hull capacity allowing a greater fuel load to be carried, thus enhancing the boat's

Another shot of U-3, this time looking down into the bridge. Note the open hatch into the interior. As can be seen, there was very little space on the bridge of these small coastal boats.

The tower was later modified, as shown here on U-121, by the addition of a spray deflector halfway up the tower. This gave some small modicum of protection to the bridge crew in heavy seas. Note also the D/F loop.

endurance. Five seconds were also shaved off the critical time taken to dive the boat, a reduction from 35 to 30 seconds. A total of 20 Type IIBs were built, the largest number of any sub-type.

SPECIFICATIONS

Length:	42.7m
Beam:	4.1m
Draft:	3.8m
Displacement:	279 tons surfaced, 329 tons submerged
Speed:	13 knots surfaced, 7 knots submerged
Endurance:	3,900 nautical miles surfaced, 71 nautical miles submerged
Powerplant:	2 x 350 bhp MWM diesels coupled with 2 x 180 bhp electric motors
Armament:	3 bow torpedo tubes, 6 torpedoes carried 1 x 2cm flak gun
Crew:	25

TYPE IIC

Once again, this boat was simply a lengthened version of its immediate predecessor, with increased bunkerage. The Type IIC also had a lengthened control room and a second periscope. The Type IIC can easily be identified on photographs by the flush front to the tower, rather than the stepped front found on the IIA and IIB. Only eight Type IICs were built.

SPECIFICATIONS	
Length:	43.9m
Beam:	4.1m
Draft:	3.8m
Displacement:	291 tons surfaced, 341 tons submerged
Speed:	12 knots surfaced, 7 knots submerged
Endurance:	4,200 nautical miles surfaced, 71 nautical miles submerged
Powerplant:	2 x 350 bhp MWM diesels coupled with 2 x 205 bhp electric motors
Armament:	3 bow torpedo tubes, 6 torpedoes carried 1 x 2cm flak gun
Crew:	25

This fine shot of U-61, a Type IIC, gives an excellent view of the typical bridge configuration of this type. As well as the cast bronze national emblem being removed, the tower numbers were painted out on the outbreak of war.

TYPE IID

The Type IID, but for its small size, might almost pass for a Type VII with its enlarged conning tower with rear flak platform, together with its distinctive saddle tanks. It also had greatly increased range.

The bridge configuration on this Type IIB is unusual, this set-up with its distinctive guard rails being common for Type IIDs, but fitted to only a tiny number of Type IIBs.

SPECIFICATIONS

Length:	44.0m
Beam:	5.0m
Draft:	3.9m
Displacement:	314 tons surfaced, 364 tons submerged
Speed:	12.7 knots surfaced, 7.4 knots submerged
Endurance:	5,680 nautical miles surfaced, 71 nautical miles submerged
Powerplant:	2 x 350 bhp MWM diesels coupled with 2 x 205 bhp electric motors
Armament:	3 bow torpedo tubes, 6 torpedoes carried 1 x 2cm flak gun
Crew:	25

This Type IID, U-139, is shown in training. The large 'X' on the side of the tower is a tactical mark indicating her status as a *Schulboot*. This boat spent most of her life with 22. U-Flotille in Gotenhafen as a training boat.

THE TYPE VII

GENERAL DESCRIPTION

The Type VII was a single-hulled boat, the pressure hull in places forming the outer hull of the boat. It differed principally from earlier designs in that its bunkerage was contained within the pressure hull rather than in saddle tanks, giving additional protection to the precious fuel. A single central ballast tank was provided, together with bow and stern ballast tanks outwith the pressure hull and two large saddle tanks on either side of the hull. Outside the pressure hull was a streamlined external casing, the area between the two being free-flooding. Between the deck and the top of the pressure hull a considerable amount of ducting and trunking was fitted, as well as the mounting for the deck gun,

Type VIIA U-boats. Particularly distinctive of this type is the external stern torpedo tube. On later models this was moved inside the boat and was fired out through the space between its twin rudders/propellers.

THE SURVIVORS OF A U-BOAT ATTACK

During the early part of World War II, many merchant ships still travelled alone. Escorts were in short supply and air cover was restricted, so several U-boats took the time to question the survivors in an attempt to confirm the identity of the sunken ship, knowing that the chance of the enemy appearing was slight.

Here, a Type VIIA has just sunk a merchantman and the crew watch as survivors are beckoned over by the captain. Space on a Type VII U-boat was extremely restricted, so the taking on board of survivors was a rarity. In several recorded cases, U-boat captains would check to ascertain if any of the survivors were wounded or needed medical attention, and were known to provide the survivors with the odd

bottle of brandy and a course for the nearest safe landfall before disappearing under the surface again.

As the war progressed and anti-submarine measures grew in their effectiveness, few opportunities for such niceties would occur, as any boat coming to the surface put itself in the greatest danger. After the *Laconia* incident, when U-506 was bombed despite clearly having a number of survivors, including women and children, on her decks and towing several lifeboats, Grossadmiral Dönitz as Commander-in-Chief U-Boats ordered that no U-boat commander should put his boat and its crew at risk by attempting to rescue survivors. This order, however, was occasionally disobeyed. (Artwork by Ian Palmer © Osprey Publishing)

ready-ammunition locker for the deck gun, a small dinghy and, ultimately, storage for spare torpedoes. All could be accessed via hatches or by removal of deck plating. An 8.8cm naval gun was fitted on the foredeck just in front of the conning tower and a 2cm flak gun just aft.

TYPE VIIA

The first variant to be produced was the Type VIIA, of which ten were completed. These were allocated the numbers U-27 through to U-36. Four were

built by Germaniawerft and six by AG Weser. Construction began in February 1935 with the first boat of the type, U-33, launched on 11 June 1936.

One of the most instantly recognisable visual characteristics of the Type VIIA was the hump of the external stern torpedo tube, clearly visible on the aft decking.

SPECIFICATIONS

Length:	64.5m
Beam:	5.8m
Draft:	4.4m
Displacement:	626 tons surfaced, 745 tons submerged
Speed:	16 knots surfaced, 8 knots submerged
Endurance:	4,300 nautical miles surfaced, 90 nautical miles submerged
Powerplant:	2 × 1,160 bhp diesels coupled with 2 × 375 bhp electric motors
Armament:	5 torpedo tubes, (4 bow, 1 stern)
	1 × 8.8cm gun
	1 × 2cm gun
Crew:	44

TYPE VIIB

The Type VIIB was a marked improvement over the initial variant. It was given twin rather than single rudders to allow for the external stern torpedo tube of the VIIA being brought inside the pressure hull and firing out between the two rudders. The boat was given an increase in length of 2m to provide additional bunkerage, and additional fuel was now also carried in special fuel cells within the saddle tanks. These cells were self-compensating – as fuel was drawn from the top of the tank, sea water entered at the bottom, compensating for the loss in weight. Compensating tanks were also installed to help prevent the boat rolling when on the surface. Finally, turbochargers were fitted to the diesel engines to provide a modest increase in speed. All of these changes increased the size and weight of the boat significantly.

A total of 24 Type VIIBs were built: the first seven (U-45 to U-51) by Germaniawerft, a second tranche of four, also from Germaniawerft, and a third tranche consisting of four boats each from Germaniawerft and Vulcan, with five from Flenderwerft.

SPECIFICATIONS

Length:	66.5m
Beam:	6.2m
Draft:	5.7m
Displacement:	753 tons surfaced, 857 tons submerged
Speed:	17.2 knots surfaced, 8 knots submerged
Endurance:	6,500 nautical miles surfaced, 90 nautical miles submerged
Powerplant:	2 x 1,400 bhp diesels coupled with 2 x 375 bhp electric motors
Armament:	5 torpedo tubes, (4 bow, 1 stern)
	1 x 8.8cm gun
	1 x 2cm gun
	15 mines
Crew:	44

This view of a Type VII on the slipway gives a good view of the bulbous external saddle tanks typical of this type. The drain holes for the free-flooding area over the pressure hull differed in configuration between the many shipyards which constructed Type VIIs.

TYPE VIIC

The third and most significant variant of the Type VII was the 'C'. It was originally proposed as a vessel for the new sonar search equipment known as the Such-Gerät (S-Gerät), with an increase in length to both the control room and the conning tower to accommodate the necessary equipment. Other smaller, but nevertheless welcome, modifications were also incorporated. A small buoyancy tank was fitted, within the saddle tanks, which could also be flooded to improve diving time. A new filtration system for the diesel engines, a new diesel rather than electric-powered compressor for the air tanks – to ease demands on the electrical system – and more modern electrical switching systems were all added to this model.

BELOW LEFT

This shot shows the conning tower of U-73 as originally built, with the typical small platform at the rear to carry the 2cm flak gun. This was the standard configuration on all early Type VIIs, often referred to as Turm I.

BELOW RIGHT

This particularly sharp view of U-212 shows the various handrails typical of vessels of this type. Note the rails on, above and below the lower spray deflector, and the removable wire guides which ran between the forward and aft fixed handrails.

SPECIFICATIONS

Length:	67.1m
Beam:	6.2m
Draft:	4.8m
Displacement:	761 tons surfaced, 865 tons submerged
Speed:	17 knots surfaced, 7.6 knots submerged
Endurance:	6,500 nautical miles surfaced, 80 nautical miles submerged
Powerplant:	2 × 1,400 bhp diesels coupled with 2 × 375 bhp electric motors
Armament:	5 torpedo tubes, (4 bow, 1 stern)
	1 × 8.8cm gun
	1 × 2cm gun
Crew:	44

TYPE VIIC/41

The first major sub-variant of this type was the VIIC/41. This variant featured extensive replacement of existing electrical equipment by newer, more compact models. The weight thus saved (some 11 tons overall) was utilised in thickening the steel plate used for the pressure hull by a further 2.5mm, thus allowing an increase in diving capabilities from a maximum depth of 250m to 300m. The bow was also lengthened slightly to increase seaworthiness. One major improvement was the fitting of flexible bearings, joints, etc. Rigid mounts (e.g. for the engines) tended to suffer badly when the boat was shaken by the detonation of depth charges.

An aerial view shows the degree of modification made to U-73's tower during subsequent refitting. The flak platform or *Wintergarten* has been extended significantly to accommodate further anti-aircraft armament, though in this view she still carries only a single 2cm gun.

SPECIFICATIONS

Length:	67.2m
Beam:	6.2m
Draft:	4.8m
Displacement:	759 tons surfaced, 860 tons submerged
Speed:	17 knots surfaced, 7.6 knots submerged
Endurance:	6,500 nautical miles surfaced, 80 nautical miles submerged
Powerplant:	2 x 1,400 bhp diesels coupled with 2 x 375 bhp electric motors
Armament:	5 torpedo tubes, (4 bow, 1 stern)
	1 x 8.8cm gun
	1 x 2cm gun
Crew:	44

TYPE VIIC/42

This projected sub-variant was an attempt to improve speed further by adding additional turbochargers, coupled with an increase in length to give greater fuel storage capabilities. Armour-plate was to be used rather than normal steel for the pressure hull, taking the maximum depth possible up to 500m. None of this type was ever completed.

TYPE VIIC/43

Another design that got no further than the drawing board, this was essentially a Type VIIC/42 with armament upgraded to provide six rather than four bow torpedo tubes.

TYPE VIID

This version of the versatile VII design was a minelayer. The hull of the basic Type VII was extended by almost 10m, just aft of the control room, to provide five vertical mine shafts. Additional benefits of the extension in hull length included space for additional fuel and longer trim tanks. These boats also had the luxury of refrigerated food storage. The full torpedo and gun armament of the standard Type VII was retained. On the downside, the additional weight and length, to say nothing of the raised decking required for the mine shafts, reduced overall speed and handling qualities, though overall endurance was increased.

SPECIFICATIONS

Length:	76.9m
Beam:	6.4m
Draft:	5.0m
Displacement:	965 tons surfaced, 1,080 tons submerged
Speed:	16 knots surfaced, 7.3 knots submerged
Endurance:	8,100 nautical miles surfaced, 69 nautical miles submerged
Powerplant:	2 x 1,400 bhp diesels coupled with 2 x 375 bhp electric motors
Armament:	5 torpedo tubes, (4 bow, 1 stern)
	1 x 8.8cm gun
	1 x 2cm gun
	15 mines
Crew:	44

TYPE VIIE

A design project only, this version was to have been fitted with a new type of two-stroke V12 lightweight diesel engine made by the Deutz firm. The project was abandoned before any could be built.

TYPE VIIF

The Type VIIF was a modification of the basic Type VII design similar to that of

U-552, the famous 'Red Devil Boat', commanded by Erich Topp, returns to port after a mission. Note the prancing red devil emblem painted on the front of the tower. It was common for returning boats to be welcomed back by a crowd of well-wishers. Here a number of female auxiliaries are visiting the boat, one of whom can be seen climbing onto the flak platform.

the VIID, in that a 10.5m additional length of hull was inserted just abaft the control room. This allowed an extra 24 torpedoes to be carried, as well as additional refrigerated food storage and two extra crew members. The VIIF was to act as a resupply boat, delivering additional supplies of torpedoes to bases that were running low on supplies.

Only four of this type were eventually built (U-1059 to U-1062), all produced by Germaniawerft.

The crew of U-1061 pose with the shipyard management on the day of her commissioning. She was one of only four Type VIIF boats manufactured and used as re-supply boats, their additional 10.5m length giving them much greater carrying capacity.

29

SPECIFICATIONS

Length:	77.6m
Beam:	7.3m
Draft:	4.9m
Displacement:	1,084 tons surfaced, 1,181 tons submerged
Speed:	16.9 knots surfaced, 7.9 knots submerged
Endurance:	9,500 nautical miles surfaced, 75 nautical miles submerged
Powerplant:	2 x 1,400 bhp MWM diesels coupled with 2 x 375 bhp electric motors
Armament:	5 torpedo tubes, (4 bow, 1 stern)
	1 x 8.8cm gun
	1 x 2cm gun
Crew:	46

TYPE VIIC VARIANTS

Of all of the Type VII models, none saw as much modification and improvement to the basic design as did the most common model of all, the Type VIIC. The variants mentioned above relate principally to internal modifications, which would not be obvious from photographs of the boats themselves. However, one major series of modifications that became necessary during the course of the war, and which drastically altered the appearance of each type, was made to the conning tower.

As Allied anti-submarine measures improved, the use of aircraft against U-boats took on a considerable significance and it quickly became apparent that the single 2cm anti-aircraft gun carried on the basic Type VII was woefully

Instead of the 3.7cm flak, some boats carried the 2cm *Flakvierling* on the lower platform. This four-barrelled weapon was capable of putting up a substantial hail of fire. The upper platform weapons on this boat seem to be single-barrel 2cm pieces rather than *Zwillinge*.

The Type VIIB bridge was modified soon after introduction, to accommodate a large air intake trunk up the outside of the tower. Most Type VIIBs had the spray deflector fitted at the mid-point of the tower and this type also saw the 2cm flak gun moved up from the afterdeck.

The bridge of the Type VIIC Turm 2 conversion saw the addition of a second round platform, on a lower level, to the rear of the upper platform. It also carried a single 2cm flak gun.

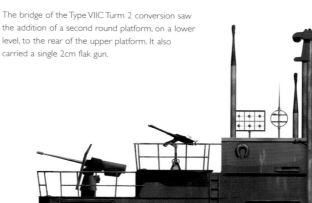

The Type VIIC Turm 4 was the bridge configuration found on most late-war Type VIIs. The wide upper platform featured two twin 2cm flak guns side by side, whilst the lower, lengthened platform featured a single 3.7cm flak gun or occasionally a quadruple 2cm *Flakvierling*.

(Profiles by Ian Palmer © Osprey Publishing)

inadequate. In fact, no matter how much the flak armament was beefed up, few U-boats would risk taking on aircraft (although in several recorded cases, when left with no option but to remain on the surface, U-boats did take on aircraft and succeed in shooting them down).

The first major attempt to beef up flak defences was to widen the platform somewhat, and replace the single 2cm flak gun with two twin 2cm machine gun mounts. The various conning tower configurations, beginning with the basic circular platform to the rear of the tower, with its single 2cm flak gun, were given numeric codes, the basic configuration being known as Turm 0:

Turm 1 – This design was to see a second, lower, platform fitted to the rear of the conning tower (generally known to U-boat men as the *Wintergarten*) on which would be fitted a twin 2cm flak. This design was approved in June 1942.

Turm 2 – Owing to problems with the supply of the new weapons required for the Turm 1 design, a second new tower configuration was introduced in which the original round upper platform was joined by a similar lower platform, both of which were fitted with a single 2cm flak gun. Installation of this type commenced in December 1942.

Turm 3 – This little-used configuration saw two single 2cm flak guns mounted side by side on the upper platform and was used only on the Type VIID.

Turm 4 – This, destined to become the most common configuration, had two twin 2cm guns fitted on a widened upper platform, and a single four-barrelled 2cm flak gun, the *Flakvierling*, on the lower. The *Flakvierling* was gradually replaced by a single-barrelled 3.7cm flak gun.

Turm 5 – An experimental model, fitted to only one U-boat (U-362) this configuration had two twin 2cm flak guns on the upper platform, a single twin 2cm flak gun on the lower, and a fourth twin 2cm gun on a special platform built on to the front of the tower.

Turm 6 – Another little-used model, only two boats receiving this modification. This configuration had a single-barrelled 3.7cm flak gun on the lower platform, two twin 2cm flak guns on the upper, and a single twin 2cm in front of the tower on a separate pedestal. Only U-673 and U-973 were so converted.

Turm 7 – A 'concept' only and never actually built, this tower would have seen twin 3.7cm flak guns on platforms both to the rear and in front of the tower.

Flak Boats

Seven boats were ordered to be converted into Flak Boats, and given heavy anti-aircraft armament to allow them to take on enemy aircraft on relatively even terms. U-441 was given a *Flakvierling* on a mount in front of the tower, another on the upper platform at the rear of the tower, as well as a 3.7cm flak gun on the rear lower platform. Although U-441 succeeded in shooting down a Sunderland

This shot taken from a dockside vantage point gives a good view down onto the extended flak platforms of a heavily armed Type VIIC with two 2cm flak *Zwillinge* and a 3.7cm flak.

Some boats carried an extremely heavy flak armament in an attempt to give adequate defence against Allied aircraft. As well as the two 2cm flak *Zwillinge* on the upper platform, this boat has had two twin machine gun mounts fitted.

flying boat, the adverse effect of the new bridge structure on diving times and handling, combined with the heavy armament now being installed on standard boats, saw the order cancelled with all Flak Boats to be reconverted back to Turm 4 configuration.

INTERNAL DESCRIPTION

The 'core' of any submarine is, of course, its pressure hull. In the case of the Type VII this was of circular section, tubular in the centre section, and then tapering slightly towards the bow and stern. The pressure hull was made from welded rolled steel up to 2.2cm thick. The whole consisted of six sections, plus a bow and stern end cap. On top of this pressure hull was built the external casing, an area which was free-flooding and was used to accommodate ventilation trunking and for storage.

Starting from the bow, the first compartment was the forward torpedo room, into which the four bow torpedo tubes penetrated by some 4m. To the ceiling was attached a hoist used for manoeuvring the torpedoes into the tubes, and the angled torpedo loading hatch. To the rear of the compartment were located three sets of two-tier bunks on each side. Compressed air cylinders were located below the bottom bunk, as were collapsible tables for the use of the junior ratings who occupied this compartment. Under the decking there was storage space for two additional torpedoes and, under these, the bow trim tanks.

After passing through the first bulkhead, the next compartment in line was the senior non-commissioned ranks' accommodation, comprising two sets of two-tier bunks each side. A further bulkhead followed before reaching the

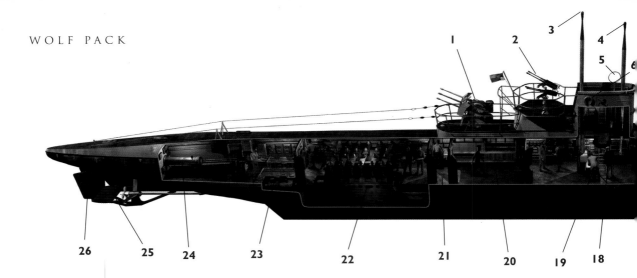

INTERIOR LAYOUT OF A TYPE VIIC/42

1 Quad 2cm flak gun
2 Twin 2cm flak gun
3 Navigating periscope
4 Attack periscope
5 Direction finding loop
6 Lifebelt
7 Commander's accommodation
8 Officers' accommodation
9 Senior NCOs' accommodation
10 Watertight containers for inflatable life rafts
11 Capstan
12 Anchor
13 Bow hydroplanes
14 Bow torpedo tubes
15 Forward torpedo room
16 Junior ratings' accommodation
17 WC
18 Commander's attack position
19 Control room
20 Petty officers' accommodation
21 Galley
22 Diesel engines
23 Electro-motors
24 Stern torpedo tubes
25 Stern hydroplanes
26 Rudder

(Artwork by Ian Palmer © Osprey Publishing)

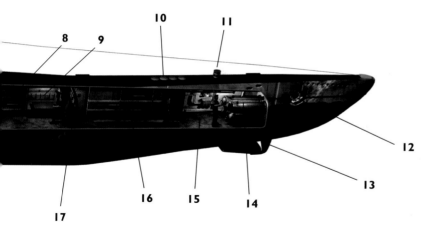

officers' accommodation. Again, two sets of two-tier bunks were provided but as only three officers were normally carried, one of these was usually stowed. A small table was provided on the port side.

Then came the commander's bunk. He was the only man on board afforded a modicum of privacy, provided by a simple curtain at the entry to his 'quarters'. Directly across the walkway were located the radio room and sound detector room, giving the operators of these essential pieces of equipment instant access to the commanding officer. Under the decking of this area were stored the forward batteries as well as, under the radio room, ammunition for the deck gun.

Reaching the central portion of the boat, the hub of activity was the control room, or *Zentrale*, with a heavy pressurised bulkhead at either end. On the port side, from the bow end, were located the boat's main helm, the diving planes, the navigator's table and the auxiliary bilge pumps. On the port side were the periscope motor, the main vent controls, the main bilge pump and a drinking water tank. In the centre of the compartment were the periscope tubes, the main optics for the sky, or navigation, periscope being located in the control room.

Above the control room was the conning tower. In it was a tiny space, the commander's attack station. Within this compartment were the optics for the attack periscope, the attack computer, the repeater compass and the exit hatch to the exterior of the conning tower. Under the decking of the *Zentrale* were fitted ballast tanks and fuel bunkers.

Passing through the rear control room bulkhead, the next compartment was the junior non-commissioned ranks' accommodation, consisting of two pairs of twin bunks each side. Towards the rear of this compartment, on one side was the boat's tiny galley and on the other the aft WC and food storage pantry. The aft batteries were stored under the deck plates of this area.

This shot gives a good view of the beefed-up flak armament on U-995, the restored Type VIIC now on display by the naval memorial at Laboe. Note the twin 2cm flak guns and the 3.7cm flak on the lower *Wintergarten*.

The next bulkhead led through to the engine room. Within this small space were located the boat's two diesel engines on their massive founds, with only a narrow passageway in between. A further bulkhead allowed passage into the motor room in which were located the boat's two electric motors, coupled to the same shafts as the diesels. Also contained in this compartment were a compressor for the boat's modest refrigerated storage, the main electrical control panels and the stern torpedo tube, which fired out between the boat's twin rudders. Beneath the deck plating in this area were the stern trim tanks.

EXTERNAL FITTINGS

The U-boat's external decking was covered in wood or steel planking, with a 1cm gap between planks to allow for drainage. Wood was used to avoid the degree of icing up that would have been encountered in winter conditions with metal decking.

The area between the outer casing and pressure hull was free-flooding, and along the side of the outer casing of any Type VII were numerous draining slots. The exact number and positioning of these varied from manufacturer to manufacturer. In the area between pressure hull and outer casing, in the forward portion of the boat, was located a storage tube for a spare torpedo. On some boats this was replaced by a series of watertight containers for life-rafts.

Moving away from the bow, there was an angled torpedo loading hatch leading from the outer deck to the pressure hull. This allowed the torpedo to be taken into the boat nose first, facing the tube into which it would be loaded. Beyond the torpedo loading hatch was a watertight storage container with a small amount of ammunition for the deck gun. This allowed the gun to be brought into action swiftly, while the remainder of the ammunition was brought up through the boat from the ammunition storage under the radio room.

On the outer decking itself at the forward point some early boats still had the serrated net cutter fitted to World War I boats, but by the outbreak of World War II most of these had been removed. Retractable bollards were fitted near the bow and stern, with additional pairs, port and starboard, approximately mid-way between the bow/stern and the conning tower. A removable capstan winch and retractable hydrophone array were also mounted on the foredeck.

The conning tower, as has already been discussed, was one of the areas in which considerable differences may be found from boat to boat and at different stages throughout the war. In general, the front and sides of the tower were screened up to a height of some 1.6m to give the crew some measure of protection against the elements. The rear of the bridge was open, leading onto the aft platform which was surrounded by a safety railing. On the bridge itself were the mounts that supported the periscopes, a pedestal mount for the UZO (*U-Bootzieloptik*) torpedo-aiming device, a binnacle and, on the starboard wall of the tower, a slot to house the retractable direction-finding loop. Later examples of the Type VII had the *Schnorchel* fitting mounted on the port side of the tower.

The afterdeck was relatively featureless. Apart from the small stern torpedo-loading hatch, the space under the rear decking was devoted almost entirely to trunking. The trunking, which passed through the free-flooding area under the afterdeck, led up through the conning tower casing to the rear outer tower wall. Types VIIA and VIIB had large trunking running up the outside face of the tower, but by the VIIC model this was contained within the tower casing.

This wartime shot shows the same flak configuration as fitted to U-995. Note, however, the slab-sided plating to the side of the conning tower of this boat, giving any bridge crew some additional protection from enemy aircraft fire. The 2cm flak gun crews on this boat had no such protection.

A single thick antenna cable ran from the most forward point of the bow to just before the conning tower, where it split, one fork running to a locating point either side of the top of the tower wall. From here, one antenna cable ran down to an anchor point on each side near the stern.

CONSTRUCTION DETAILS

Deschimag, Bremen
VIIA U-27 to U-32	6 boats

(This firm concentrated on the Type IX)

Germaniawerft, Kiel
VIIA U-33 to U-36	4 boats
VIIB U-45 to U-55	11 boats
VIIB U-99 to U-102	4 boats
VIIC U-69 to U-72	4 boats
VIIC U-93 to U-98	6 boats
VIIC U-201 to U-212	12 boats
VIIC U-221 to U-232	12 boats
VIIC U-235 to U-250	16 boats
VIIC U-1051 to U-1058	8 boats
VIIC U-1063 to U-1065	3 boats
Total	*80 boats*

Bremer Vulcan, Vegesack
VIIB U-73 to U-76	4 boats
VIIB U-77 to U-82	6 boats
VIIC U-132 to U-136	5 boats
VIIC U-251 to U-300	50 boats
VIIC U-1271 to U-1279	9 boats
Total	*74 boats*

Danzigerwerft, Danzig
VIIC U-401 to U-430	30 boats
VIIC U-1161 to U-1172	12 boats
Total	*42 boats*

Flenderwerft, Lübeck
VIIB U-83 to U-87	5 boats
VIIC U-88 to U-92	5 boats
VIIC U-301 to U-330	30 boats
VIIC U-903 to U-904	2 boats
Total	*42 boats*

Nordsee Werke, Emden
VIIC U-331 to U-350	20 boats
VIIC U-1101 to U-1110	10 boats
Total	*30 boats*

Flensburger Schiffsbau, Flensburg
VIIC U-351 to U-370	20 boats
VIIC U-1301 to U-1308	8 boats
Total	*28 boats*

Howaldtswerke, Kiel
VIIC U-371 to U-400	30 boats
VIIC U-651 to U-683	33 boats
VIIC U-1131 to U-1132	2 boats
Total	*65 boats*

Stülcken Sohn, Hamburg
VIIC U-701 to U-722	22 boats
VIIC U-905 to U-908	4 boats
Total	*26 boats*

Many operational flotillas used a variety of different U-boat types through the course of the war, where others seemed to use a specific type predominantly, if not exclusively. The following flotillas are those in which use of the Type VII predominated:

1. Unterseebootsflotille   Types VIIB, VIIC and VIID
3. Unterseebootsflotille   Types VIIB and VIIC
6. Unterseebootsflotille   Types VIIB and VIIC

A typical Type VIIC running on the surface, again with net cutter still fitted. Note the narrowness of the foredeck compared with the roomier Type IX. Sailors needed to be sure-footed to keep their balance on such a narrow space in anything much more than a moderate swell.

7. Unterseebootsflotille	Various Type VIIs
9. Unterseebootsflotille	Types VIIC and VIID
11. Unterseebootsflotille	Type VIIC
13. Unterseebootsflotille	Type VIIC
14. Unterseebootsflotille	Type VIIC

With just over 700 examples built, the Type VII was, in terms of volume production, by far the most successful of all the U-boat types. It fitted well with the decision taken that Germany would build a large fleet of small to medium-sized boats rather than a small fleet of large boats. Despite its modest size and relative ease of construction, it proved itself a reliable design capable of operating throughout the Atlantic, its capabilities restricted only by the amount of fuel and munitions it could carry.

The Type VII had a faster diving speed than the larger Type IX, a critical factor that endeared it to its crews, as did its capability of diving, on occasion, much deeper than its recommended safe maximum depth without mishap. The biggest 'downside' for the crews was the extremely cramped interior. Space was at an absolute premium and conditions within these boats could become extremely uncomfortable very quickly. However, to many U-boat men, even though the Type IX was more spacious and thus more comfortable, its slow diving speed and thus greater vulnerability when caught on the surface made it a relatively less 'safe' boat than the Type VII.

Without doubt, the Type VII in its many guises was by far the most influential submarine in the U-boat war. Through the course of the war, over 2,600 war cruises were undertaken in the Type VII boats. During the course of these cruises, around 1,365 enemy ships were sunk, that total including 190 warships. From the total of just over 700 Type VIIs that were built, over 400 were sunk by enemy action. In the great majority of these cases, the boats were lost with all hands. Of the total of approximately 30,000 U-boat men who lost their lives in World War II, around 22,000, or 73 per cent, were serving on the Type VII.

THE TYPE IX

The Type IX U-boat was a direct development of the unsuccessful Type IA (of which only two, U-25 and U-26, were built). Although the bulk of U-boat construction for the Kriegsmarine concentrated on the medium, sea-going Type VII, there was still a need for a larger ocean-going boat capable of operating in distant waters. The Type VII, of course, was perfectly capable of operating all the way across the Atlantic and into American waters, but larger submarines with far greater range were required if Germany was to be capable of operating further afield, far into the South Atlantic and even into the Indian Ocean. The result was the Type IX.

As with the Type VII, the design reached its optimum with the 'C' variant, which represented 141 out of the total number of 194 Type IXs built. The Type IX design was not without its drawbacks, which will be discussed later, but it was

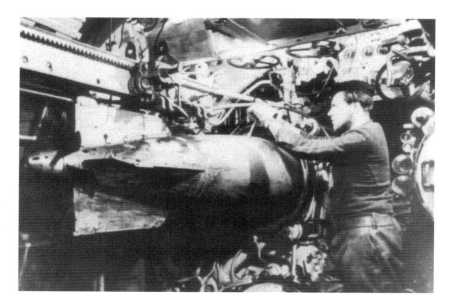

The close confines of the *Bugraum* or bow torpedo compartment of a Type IX as an 'eel' is loaded into one of the four tubes. Note the twin, contra-rotating propellers on the torpedo, which ensured its ability to run in a straight line.

an excellent sea boat, capable of operating at great distances from its base, and was far more spacious and comfortable than the cramped Type VII.

BASIC DESCRIPTION OF TYPE

Although, with the exception of the lack of saddle tanks as fitted to the Type VII, the Type IX resembled its smaller cousin, particularly after both types had received the Turm 4 conning tower conversions, the Type IX was significantly different in its internal layout. The engine room was much larger and the junior NCO accommodation was moved to the forward part of the boat. Without the bulky external saddle tanks typical of the Type VII, the Type IX was a much sleeker-looking boat and had greater fore and aft deck space. Its bigger size, however, meant that its diving speed was rather lower than the Type VII's.

Beginning at the bow, the first compartment was the torpedo room with its four torpedo tubes. Along each side of the compartment were three upper and three lower bunks, which could be folded up to give more space when not in use. Folding tables were also provided. Owing to the 'hot bunking' system used, these 12 bunks were effectively home to 24 sailors. Under the decking plates was storage for additional torpedoes, and at the rear of the compartment a hatch through the pressure hull onto the upper decking allowed fresh torpedoes to be taken on board.

Through the first bulkhead was the main accommodation area. Forwardmost was the junior non-commissioned ranks' area. On the port side was a WC compartment and two sets of bunks, whilst on the starboard were three sets of bunks, giving accommodation for ten men. Next followed the senior non-commissioned ranks' area containing accommodation for six senior ranks. Under the deck plates of the accommodation area were stored the boat's batteries. Just beyond this accommodation area, separating the non-commissioned ranks from the officers, were the refrigerated storage lockers on the port and starboard sides of the small galley. The boat's ammunition magazine was located under the deck plates of this area.

Through the next bulkhead was one officer's bunk on the port side, separated from the commander's 'compartment' by the sound room. To starboard were two officers' bunks and the radio room, directly opposite the commander. The commander's 'compartment' was a simple bunk area with a curtain that could be drawn to afford a modicum of privacy. The commander's bunk area was slightly more spacious than any other and also had the benefit of a small washstand with a folding lid to convert it into a table. As with the Type VII, the sound and radio rooms were deliberately placed next to the commander's area to allow immediate access to him should important messages be received or enemy ships detected. Further battery storage was located under the deck plates of this area.

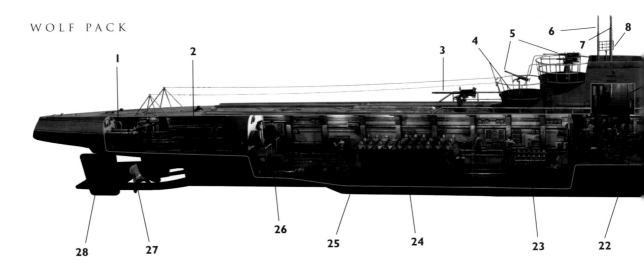

INTERIOR LAYOUT OF A TYPE IX

1 Stern torpedo room
2 Junior Ranks' accommodation
3 3.7cm flak gun
4 *Wintergarten* platform
5 2cm flak guns
6 Navigation periscope
7 Attack periscope
8 Radar
9 Conning tower
10 Commander's attack position
11 10.5cm deck gun
12 Retractable bollards
13 WC
14 Retractable capstan
15 Bow torpedo room
16 Junior Ranks' accommodation
17 Petty Officers' accommodation
18 Warrant Officers' accommodation
19 Galley
20 Officers' accommodation
21 Commander's bunk
22 Control room
23 Electro-motors
24 Diesel engines
25 Keel
26 Propellor shaft
27 Propellors
28 Rudders

(Artwork by Ian Palmer © Osprey Publishing)

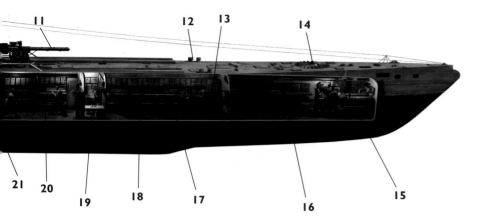

The hub of the boat was the control room or *Zentrale*. Here were the ship's helm, the diving planes, navigator's table, main ballast pump controls and periscope tubes. A ladder led up into the conning tower, which contained the commander's attack position, and on up to the main exit hatch to the bridge.

Aft of the *Zentrale* was the Type IX's large engine room. First came the two massive diesel engines, with only a small passageway between. Aft of the main engines were the electric motors used for powering the boat underwater. On the starboard side was the large compressor used to recharge the boat's compressed air supply.

The aftermost compartment was the stern torpedo room. This contained the aft WC, followed by two sets of upper and lower bunks each side, accommodating up to 16 men, as well as the two stern torpedo tubes and the emergency helm.

An engine-room mechanic can be seen here tending to one of the huge MAN diesels in a Type IX. A narrow passageway ran the length of the engine room between two banks of diesels. The noise in the engine room when the diesels were running was cacophonous.

Crew members service the 3.7cm deck gun on a Type IX which, by the relaxed attitude of her crew, must be sailing in safe waters. Fitted to most early Type IX boats, this after deck gun was omitted in many later boats as larger, extended *Wintergarten* platforms were fitted to the rear of the conning tower.

TYPE IXA

The Basic Type IXA was a well-armed, long-range boat, but only eight were constructed (U-37 to U-44) before the next, improved model was introduced.

SPECIFICATIONS	
Length:	76.5m
Beam:	6.5m
Draft:	4.7m
Displacement:	1,032 tons surfaced, 1,153 tons submerged
Speed:	18.2 knots surfaced, 7.7 knots submerged
Endurance:	8,100 nautical miles surfaced, 65 nautical miles submerged
Powerplant:	2 x MAN 2,200 bhp MWM diesels, 2 x SSW 500 bhp electric motors
Armament:	1 x 10.5cm deck gun forward, 1 x 3.7cm deck gun aft
	1 x 2cm flak gun on conning tower platform
	6 torpedo tubes (4 bow, 2 stern)
	22 torpedoes carried
Crew:	48

TYPE IXB

The Type IXB was almost identical to its predecessor, with a small increase in fuel bunkerage giving it a slightly increased operational range, with its additional weight only causing a very slight reduction in its submerged top speed. The forward deck gun was also relocated to a position slightly nearer to the conning tower. Fourteen Type IXBs were constructed.

SPECIFICATIONS

Length:	76.5m
Beam:	6.8m
Draft:	4.7m
Displacement:	1,061 tons surfaced, 1,178 tons submerged
Speed:	18.2 knots surfaced, 7.3 knots submerged
Endurance:	8,700 nautical miles surfaced, 64 nautical miles submerged
Powerplant:	2 × MAN 2,200 bhp MWM diesels, 2 × SSW 500 bhp electric motors
Armament:	1 × 10.5cm deck gun forward, 1 × 3.7cm deck gun aft
	1 × 2cm flak gun on conning tower platform
	6 torpedo tubes (4 bow, 2 stern)
	22 torpedoes carried
Crew:	48

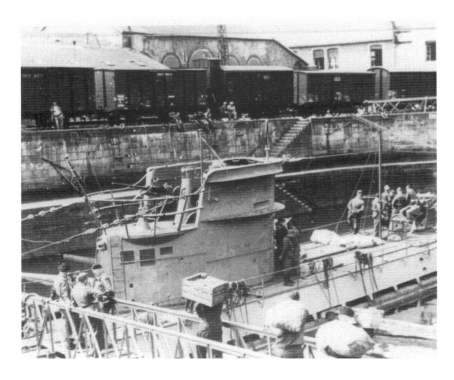

U-65, a Type IXB, is re-provisioned in port. This view shows the standard early tower configuration, very similar to that of the Type VII. Despite the greater space on board a Type IX, provisioning still meant substantial amounts of food, supplies and ammunition being laboriously loaded into the boat's interior through narrow hatches.

The view down into the mid-section of U-163, a Type IXC, shows how much more space was available on the bridge of these larger vessels. Considerably greater deck space was also a feature of these boats, early examples of which carried a 3.7cm gun aft of the tower as well as the 10.5cm forward deck gun.

TYPE IXC

The Type IXC was very slightly longer than the previous models, the principal improvement in the type being the provision of additional fuel bunkerage giving greatly extended operational range. Fifty-four Type IXCs were commissioned.

SPECIFICATIONS

Length:	76.8m
Beam:	6.8m
Draft:	4.7m
Displacement:	1,120 tons surfaced, 1,232 tons submerged
Speed:	18.3 knots surfaced, 7.3 knots submerged
Endurance:	11,000 nautical miles surfaced, 63 nautical miles submerged
Powerplant:	2 x MAN 2,200 bhp MWM diesels, 2 x SSW 500 bhp electric motors
Armament:	1 x 10.5cm deck gun forward, 1 x 3.7cm deck gun aft
	1 x 2cm flak gun on conning tower platform
	6 torpedo tubes (4 bow, 2 stern)
	22 torpedoes carried
Crew:	48

TYPE IXC/40

The Type IXC reached its zenith in the IXC/40 sub-type. Once again, minor tweaking of the design allowed a marginally increased fuel bunkerage, giving a further modest extension to the operational range. Eighty-seven of this model were produced, more than any other Type IX variant.

SPECIFICATIONS

Length:	76.8m
Beam:	6.9m
Draft:	4.7m
Displacement:	1,144 tons surfaced, 1,257 tons submerged
Speed:	18.3 knots surfaced, 7.3 knots submerged
Endurance:	11,400 nautical miles surfaced, 63 nautical miles submerged
Powerplant:	2 × MAN 2,200 bhp MWM diesels, 2 × SSW 500 bhp electric motors
Armament:	1 × 10.5cm deck gun forward, 1 × 3.7cm deck gun aft
	1 × 2cm flak gun on conning tower platform
	6 torpedo tubes (4 bow, 2 stern)
	22 torpedoes carried
Crew:	48

TYPE IXD1

The Type IXD was a considerably enlarged variant, fully 11m longer than the original design. Though the operational range was reduced somewhat, this variant could achieve a highly respectable top speed in excess of 20 knots. This was achieved by substituting six Daimler Benz MB501 diesels, of the type used on the Kriegsmarine's E-boats, for the standard MAN diesels. Three of the MB501s were coupled to each shaft. Though fine in theory, in practice the experiment was not a success. Only two of this variant were completed, U-180 and U-195, and both experienced considerable technical problems with the engine arrangement, including overheating and the production of excessive exhaust smoke, which made the boat much easier for the enemy to spot when running on the surface. Both boats were reconverted to produce the next, cargo-carrying sub-variant.

SPECIFICATIONS

Length:	87.6m
Beam:	7.5m
Draft:	5.4m
Displacement:	1,610 tons surfaced, 1,799 tons submerged
Speed:	20.8 knots surfaced, 6.9 knots submerged
Endurance:	9,900 nautical miles surfaced, 57 nautical miles submerged
Powerplant:	6 × Daimler Benz MB 1,500 bhp diesels, 2 × SSW 500 bhp electric motors
Armament:	1 × 10.5cm deck gun forward, 1 × 3.7cm deck gun aft
	1 × 2cm flak gun on conning tower platform
	6 torpedo tubes (4 bow, 2 stern)
	24 torpedoes carried
Crew:	55

TYPE IXD1 (CARGO)

Converted from the original Type IXD1 specification, U-180 and U-195 had their Daimler Benz fast diesel motors replaced by conventional Germaniawerft submarine diesels. Also, the torpedo tubes were removed to provide additional cargo-carrying capability.

SPECIFICATIONS

Length:	87.6m
Beam:	7.5m
Draft:	5.4m
Displacement:	1,610 tons surfaced, 1,799 tons submerged
Speed:	15.8 knots surfaced, 6.9 knots submerged
Endurance:	9,900 nautical miles surfaced, 115 nautical miles submerged
Powerplant:	2 x Germaniawerft bhp diesels, 2 x SSW 500 bhp electric motors
Armament:	1 x 3.7cm deck gun aft
	2 x 2cm flak gun on conning tower platform
Crew:	55

TYPE IXD2

This interesting and relatively successful variant, the penultimate Type IX, used a twin-powerplant system. As well as its powerful supercharged MAN diesels, its lengthened hull allowed it to carry two additional diesel engines that could be used for cruising on the surface whilst the supercharged diesels were switched on to free-spinning mode to recharge the boat's batteries rapidly. A total of 28 of this variant were produced.

Twin 3.7cm flak guns were relatively unusual, the majority of boats carrying either twin or quadruple 2cm or single 3.7cm guns. This twin 3.7cm set is mounted on an unidentified Type IX.

SPECIFICATIONS

Length:	87.6m
Beam:	7.5m
Draft:	5.4m
Displacement:	1,616 tons surfaced, 1,804 tons submerged
Speed:	19.2 knots surfaced, 6.9 knots submerged
Endurance:	23,700 nautical miles surfaced, 57 nautical miles submerged
Powerplant:	2 x MAN supercharged 9-cylinder 2,200 bhp diesels, 2 x SSW 580 bhp electric motors
Armament:	2 x 2cm flak guns on upper conning tower platform
	1 x 3.7cm or 2cm *Flakvierling* on lower platform
	6 torpedo tubes (4 bow, 2 stern)
	24 torpedoes carried
Crew:	57

TYPE IXD2/42

The flip side of the Type IXD1 concept, where the emphasis was on high speed, was the IXD2/42, in which the emphasis was on extending operational range to the maximum possible. Only one of this variant was produced.

SPECIFICATIONS

Length:	87.6m
Beam:	7.5m
Draft:	5.4m
Displacement:	1,616 tons surfaced, 1,804 tons submerged
Speed:	19.2 knots surfaced, 6.9 knots submerged
Endurance:	23,700 nautical miles surfaced, 57 nautical miles submerged
Powerplant:	2 × MAN supercharged 9-cylinder 2,200 bhp diesels, 2 × SSW 500 bhp electric motors
Armament:	1 × 10.5cm deck gun forward, 1 × 3.7cm deck gun aft
	1 × 2cm flak gun on conning tower platform
	6 torpedo tubes (4 bow, 2 stern)
	22 torpedoes carried
Crew:	57

FLOTILLAS

Although most U-boat flotillas contained a number of different U-boat types over the course of the war, there were certain flotillas in which a particular type predominated. The following flotillas are those that made heavy use of Type IX vessels:

2. Unterseebootsflotille
10. Unterseebootsflotille
12. Unterseebootsflotille
33. Unterseebootsflotille

CONSTRUCTION DETAILS

Type IXA **Deschimag, Bremen**		Type IXC **Deschimag, Bremen**	
U-37 to U-44	8 boats	U-66 to U-68	3 boats
Total for type	*8 boats*	U-125 to U-131	7 boats
		U-153 to U-160	8 boats
Type IXB **Deschimag, Bremen**		U-171 to U-176	6 boats
		U-841 to U-846	6 boats
U-64 to U-65	2 boats	U-853 to U-858	6 boats
U-103 to U-111	9 boats	U-877 to U-881	5 boats
U-122 to U-124	3 boats	U-889 to U-891	3 boats
Total for type	*14 boats*	*Total*	*44 boats*

Type IXC cont.	
Seebeck, Wesermünde	
U-161 to U-166	6 boats
Total	*6 boats*
Deutsche Werft, Hamburg	
U-501 to U-524	24 boats
U-1221 to U-1238	18 boats
Total	*42 boats*
Total for type	*92 boats*
Type IXC/40	
Seebeck, Wesermünde	
U-167 to U-170	4 boats
U-801 to U-806	6 boats
Total	*10 boats*
Deschimag, Bremen	
U-183 to U-194	12 boats
Total	*12 boats*

Deutsche Werft, Hamburg	
U-525 to U-550	26 boats
Total	*26 boats*
Total for type	*48 boats*
Type IXD1	
Deschimag, Bremen	
U-180, U-195	2 boats
Total for type	*2 boats*
Type IXD2	
Deschimag, Bremen	
U-181 to U-182	2 boats
U-196 to U-200	5 boats
U-847 to U-852	6 boats
U-859 to U-864	6 boats
U-871 to U-876	6 boats
U-883 to U-886	4 boats
Total for type	*29 boats*

THE TYPE XIV

SPECIFICATIONS

Length:	67.1m
Beam:	7.3m
Draft:	4.9m
Displacement:	1,688 tons surfaced, 1,930 tons submerged
Speed:	14.4 knots surfaced, 6.2 knots submerged
Endurance:	9,300 nautical miles surfaced, 67 nautical miles submerged
Powerplant:	2 x 1,400 bhp diesels coupled with 2 x 375 bhp electric motors
Armament:	No torpedo tubes
	2 x 3.7cm guns, one forward and one aft of the tower
	1 x 2cm gun on the conning tower platform
Crew:	53

With the opening of the U-boat campaign in US waters, and into the South Atlantic, the need for a special resupply U-boat became more and more marked. A U-boat returning from a war patrol in far-off waters would occasionally rendezvous with another whose fuel or torpedo load was running out, and would transfer whatever it could of its remaining stock before heading for its home port, an extremely difficult and hazardous task in anything but the calmest of waters. Whilst this certainly helped, the amount of supplies which could be transferred would be extremely limited.

This shot shows U-461, one of the large 1,930-ton Type XIV *Milchkuh* vessels. She carried out six war cruises during which she refuelled/resupplied a total of 61 U-boats before being caught and sunk when outward bound from Bordeaux on her seventh war patrol.

The solution to this problem was seen to be the construction of large supply boats capable of transporting significant amounts of fuel and other essentials to those boats operating on extended patrols in distant waters. The result, designated the Type XIV, was known to the Germans as the *Milchkuh*, or Milk Cow. The Type XIV could carry up to 400 tons of additional fuel as well as four torpedoes and substantial amounts of fresh food. It even had its own bakery so that boats being supplied could be treated to the luxury of freshly

U-461, a Type XIV *Milchkuh*, is approached by a Type VIIC seeking refuelling. The refuelling pipes can be seen coiled on her after deck casing. Such operations were extremely risky, the boats being particularly vulnerable to attack whilst transferring fuel.

baked bread. A total of ten such boats were constructed, six by Deutsche Werke in Kiel (U-459, U-460, U-461, U-462, U-463 and U-464) and four by Germaniawerft (U-487, U-488, U-489 and U-490).

Initially, these boats were highly successful and played a significant role in keeping more boats than would otherwise have been possible on station in the western and south-western Atlantic. Gradually, however, Allied intercepts of German signals, thanks to the cracking of the Enigma codes, allowed the Allies to set up ambushes in many of the designated rendezvous points, and thus, one by one, the vulnerable Milk Cows were attacked and sunk.

The first to be sunk, U-464, was attacked on 21 August 1942 just seven days into her first cruise when she was attacked on the surface by a US Catalina flying boat. Although the boat was lost, her crew was rescued by an Icelandic fishing boat. U-490 was next to be lost when, also on her first cruise, she was attacked en route to the Indian Ocean by a combination of US aircraft and warships. Fortunately, all but one of her crew were rescued by her attackers. U-463 succeeded in carrying out four war cruises before being attacked by a British Halifax bomber and sunk with all hands on 10 May 1943 during her fifth cruise. Whilst running on the surface to charge her batteries on 22 July 1943, U-489 was attacked by an aircraft. She was spotted by a Sunderland flying boat and, although the flying boat was shot down, the submarine was so badly damaged that it had to be abandoned. Most of the crew was rescued. Disaster struck the U-tanker programme in July 1943 when four boats, U-459, U-461, U-462 and U-487, were all attacked on the surface and sunk by Allied aircraft. Between them, however, they had carried out 21 war cruises, replenishing combat U-boats at sea. Of Germany's two remaining U-tankers, U-460 was sunk on 4 October 1943 when she was caught by enemy aircraft on the surface along with three U-boats she was refuelling. U-488 was detected whilst submerged and attacked by enemy warships west of the Cape Verde Islands on 26 April 1944; she was never seen again.

THE TYPE X

Broadly analogous to the large ocean-going UE (U-117) Class minelayers of the Kaiserliche Marine, the Type X was produced specifically to handle the newly developed Sondermine A (SMA) anchored mine. The initial design, the Type X, was to provide dry storage for its complement of SMA mines, which required the detonators to be individually, manually, adjusted prior to launch, so that wet storage was impossible. This boat was projected to have displaced up to 2,500 tons: a very large vessel indeed. A further variant, the Type XA, was projected, in which the main mine chamber would be supplemented by additional mine shafts in the saddle tanks. In the event, neither type was ever produced.

Close-up of the tower of a Type XB as the *Reichskriegsflagge* is raised during her commissioning. Although she carries two 2cm *Zwillinge* on her upper platform, her lower one has only a single 2cm gun. This may well have been a temporary measure, later replaced with a 3.7cm flak, or a 2cm *Flakvierling*.

THE TYPE XB

A total of eight boats of the Type XB Class were produced, the mine chamber of the Type XA projected designs being replaced by six vertical wet storage shafts in the forward part of the hull. The boat could carry up to 18 mines in these shafts (three per shaft) plus an additional 48 mines (two per shaft) in a series of 12 shafts set into the saddle tanks on each side – six just forward and six aft of the conning tower position. The Type XBs were large boats, with a very distinctive narrowing of the foredeck between the bow and conning tower area, designed to help speed up the boat's diving time.

SPECIFICATIONS

Length:	89.8m
Beam:	9.2m
Draft:	4.7m
Displacement:	1,763 tons surfaced, 2,177 tons submerged
Speed:	16.4 knots surfaced, 7 knots submerged
Endurance:	14,450 nautical miles surfaced, 188 nautical miles submerged
Powerplant:	2 x Germaniawerft 9-cylinder supercharged 2,100 bhp diesels, 2 x AEG 550 bhp electric motors
Armament:	2 x 2cm flak gun on upper conning tower platform
	1 x 3.7cm flak gun on lower platform
	66 mines carried
	2 stern torpedo tubes
	5 torpedoes carried
Crew:	52

CONSTRUCTION DETAILS

Germaniawerft, Kiel

U-116 to U-119	4 boats
U-219 to U-220	2 boats
U-233 to U-234	2 boats
Total for type	*8 boats*

The Type XB was a large, minelaying, submarine. This shot shows U-233 and her size is evident from the scale of the figures visible on her tower. She carried a 10.5cm deck gun as well as the usual enhanced flak armament.

The commissioning of U-219, another of the large minelaying types. The circular mine-carrying tubes can be seen along her flanks. These were extremely large vessels, displacing some 2,177 tons submerged compared to around 860 tons for a Type VII.

Of the eight boats produced, six (U-116, U-117, U-118, U-119, U-220 and U-233) were sunk by enemy action. Of the 312 crewmen this represents, 45 survived the sinkings.

U-219 was docked in Jakarta when Germany surrendered and was subsequently seized and used by the Imperial Japanese Navy. The most interesting Type XB of all, and one of the most interesting of all the U-boats, was U-234. This boat was en route to Japan at the war's end, carrying a number of high-ranking military and scientific staff, two Japanese officers, 260 tons of cargo, secret blueprints for advanced weapons, and containers of uranium oxide probably for use in atomic research. On hearing of the German surrender and orders for U-boats to give themselves up to the Allies, the Japanese officers committed suicide. U-234 was snatched by the Americans, who spirited away the uranium oxide in considerable secrecy. Much of the information regarding this boat and its fascinating final journey is still shrouded in mystery.

Given the large number of U-boats which never sank a single enemy ship, the Type XB was not unsuccessful as a class, many of the class did achieve some successes sinking or damaging enemy ships with both torpedoes and mines:

U-116   One enemy ship sunk (4,300 tons) and one damaged.
U-117   No enemy ships sunk, but two damaged by mines.
U-118   Three enemy merchants sunk (14,000 tons total), one enemy corvette sunk and three enemy ships damaged.

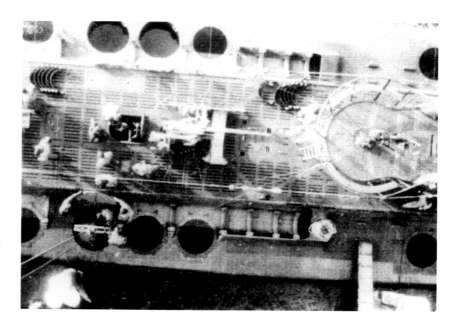

This interesting shot of U-117 clearly shows the wet storage of the mine-carrying tubes. At bottom left, a mine can be seen being lowered into its tube. Some 66 mines could be carried, giving these boats an awesome potential for destruction.

U-119	One enemy ship sunk (2,940 tons) and one damaged, both by mines.
U-219	No enemy ships sunk.
U-220	Two enemy ships sunk (7,200 tons total).
U-233	No enemy ships sunk.
U-234	No enemy ships sunk.

THE TYPE XXI

Of the boats previously used by any navy, none could be considered a true 'sub-marine'. In effect, all were submersible boats. None was capable of remaining submerged for a significant length of time owing to the extremely limited life of the batteries used to power the boat when submerged. Early submarines had to surface to run the main engines in order to recharge their batteries and replenish their compressed air supplies before diving again, and all suffered from severely reduced speed when submerged. In most cases, submarines had to position themselves carefully to allow the target to pass by them in order to achieve the optimum firing position for their torpedoes. The speed of most surface vessels exceeded that of a submerged submarine. In fact, the speed of many vessels on the surface exceeded the top speed of a submarine running on its main diesel engines. Once a target had slipped past a submarine, it would often be impossible to catch up with the intended victim.

With the advent of the Type XXI, the Germans had made a quantum leap in submarine design and manufacture. This amazing vessel was the first to be mass-produced in modular form. In order to take advantage of manufacturing capacity throughout the Reich, actual manufacture of components and of these components into sub-assemblies was carried out in various parts of Germany, often well inland rather than at traditional coastal shipbuilding locations. Sections of hull were fabricated, had internal components fitted and were even painted, before being transported to assembly yards at Blohm & Voss, Hamburg, AG Weser, Bremen and Schichau at Danzig. At these yards, the various hull sections were carefully aligned and welded together. The theoretical total build-time for a Type XXI was estimated at 176 days.

U-2511, commanded by Adalbert Schnee, one of only two Type XXIs that actually carried out a war cruise. (Artwork by Ian Palmer © Osprey Publishing)

Type XXI boats were of modular construction, sections being fabricated at various factories and transported to the shipyards where they were assembled. This shot gives a good view of the inner, pressure hull and its surrounding outer casing.

The Type XXI was fully streamlined, with no extraneous external fittings to produce unwanted drag. All periscopes, *Schnorchel* pipes, radar masts, etc. were fully retractable, and even the flak guns were built into streamlined rotating turrets and the forward and rear edges of the tower.

The large, roomy hull, which had all of its six torpedo tubes mounted in the bows, could take a much larger complement of batteries to power its vastly improved electric motors, greatly improving its underwater endurance. As well as new and extremely powerful turbo-supercharged diesel engines, the Type XXI was provided with a special 'creep' motor to allow silent running, and a whole host of improved electrical gear.

The streamlined shape of the Type XXI hull is seen to good advantage here. The tower and its two twin-flak gun turrets were also enclosed within a streamlined casing, reducing drag to a minimum and giving the Type XXI a top speed of up to 17 knots, faster than some of the escort vessels it might encounter.

The Type XXI could achieve a top speed of 17 knots submerged, more than double that of the Type IX, and could run under water on its batteries for up to 75 hours, around 50 per cent longer than the Type IX. The streamlined shape and silent running capability also made it a much harder target for the enemy to detect. The Type XXI was the first submarine to have a faster speed submerged than when running on the surface.

SPECIFICATIONS

Length:	76.7m
Beam:	6.6m
Draft:	6.3m
Displacement:	1,621 tons surfaced, 1,819 tons submerged
Speed:	15.6 knots surfaced, 17 knots submerged
Endurance:	11,150 nautical miles surfaced, 285 nautical miles submerged
Powerplant:	2 x MAN turbo-supercharged 2,200 bhp diesels
	2 x SSW 2,500 bhp electric motors
	2 x SSW 320 bhp 'creep' motors
Armament:	2 x twin 2cm turret-mounted flak guns on conning tower
	6 bow torpedo tubes
	23 torpedoes carried
Crew:	57

INTERNAL DESCRIPTION

There were several significant differences in the internal layout of the Type XXI as compared to the Type IX, not the least of which was the greater amount of space. The hull of the Type XXI was, as stated, of modular construction, made up of nine separate units: the stern section containing the WC and workshop, the electric motor room, the diesel motor room, the aft crew accommodation, the control room, the forward accommodation, the torpedo storage area, the bow cap with torpedo tubes and the conning tower unit.

Beginning at the bow end, the bow cap was pierced by six torpedo tubes rather than the four common to most previous types. Immediately aft of this was the torpedo storage area containing the boat's payload of torpedoes. Then followed the forward crew accommodation area. This was much roomier than on previous types. On most other models, a central walkway separated two rows of bunks attached to the interior hull side. On the Type XXI, however, a double row of bunks separated by a further narrow walkway was set up on the port side, whilst to starboard was the forward WC and to the rear of this, accommodation for the three ship's officers.

Moving aft, the second part of this section had, once again to port, a double row of bunks separated by a narrow walkway, accommodating the senior

A view looking back from the bow of a Type XXI accentuates its cigar-shaped hull. There are no extraneous protruding components, or railings on the hull or tower. Everything was done to decrease drag when moving underwater.

non-commissioned ranks, whilst to starboard was the chief engineer's quarters – a fairly spacious sleeping accommodation/office.

Moving aft again, on the port side was the commander's cabin, which was much more spacious than on earlier boats. Directly across the central walkway was the radio/sound room. The heart of the boat was the control room or *Zentrale* which, as on most boats, contained the diving plane controls, main switchboard, periscope controls and navigator's table.

Aft of the control room was the food preparation area. To port was the galley itself with its electric cooker, whilst on the starboard was the pantry, which boasted a freezer compartment to keep fresh foods from rotting in the damp, humid atmosphere.

Abaft this area was the main crew accommodation. To both port and starboard of the main walkway were double rows of bunks, each separated by a further narrow walkway. The 12 bunks provided on each side could accommodate a maximum of 48 men, using the 'hot-bunking' system, where two men shared a bunk, one occupying it whilst the other was on watch.

Next came the main diesel motor room with one of the huge MAN turbo-charged diesels either side of the central walkway. This was followed by the electric motor room with, on each side, a 2,500 bhp electric motor and 320 bhp 'creep' motor coupled to each shaft.

There were no stern torpedo tubes on the Type XXI. The stern compartment featured the stern WC to starboard and, to port, a small workshop area provided with a lathe to allow repair work to be undertaken.

Most of the space available under the floor plates of the Type XXI was taken up with storage for the boat's large complement of batteries.

The Type XXI, externally, was highly streamlined with no bulging saddle tanks, no deck armament and all bridge works contained in a single hydrodynamic tower to reduce drag. On both forward and aft ends of the tower were located twin 2cm flak guns, in streamlined turrets. Periscopes, *Schnorchel* and Hohentwiel radar array could be retracted into special housings. Everything possible was done to reduce drag and thus increase underwater speed.

On the underside of the bow, the Type XXI was equipped with a sonar array known as GHG or Gruppenhorchgerät. This provided a basic all-round listening device. On the front face of the tower a further active sonar array was installed, the Nibelung SU(R), which provided direction/range-finding capabilities. The combination of this equipment allowed the Type XXI commander to detect enemy ships, estimate their range and course and launch his torpedoes all without recourse to the use of the periscope and the risk of the betrayal of his position that periscope use entailed.

CONSTRUCTION DETAILS

Blohm & Voss, Hamburg
U-2501 to U-2552   52 boats

Deschimag, Bremen
U-3001 to U-3051   51 boats

Schichauwerft, Danzig
U-3501 to U-3530   30 boats
Total   *133 boats*

THE TYPE XXIII

Probably the least well-known of the operational U-boat types in World War II, the Type XXIII was, ironically, one of the best. Developed in 1943, the Type XXIII was intended to provide a modern replacement for the obsolete Type II for operations in coastal waters and also, at the insistence of Grossadmiral Dönitz, for use in the relatively shallow waters of the Mediterranean and Black Sea.

As with its larger relative, the Type XXI, it was intended that the boat be constructed in sections, with various modules being manufactured by subcontractors. In the event, Germany's battlefield reverses, shortages of steel and Allied bombing of construction facilities meant that construction was severely delayed and was ultimately concentrated at Germaniawerft in Kiel and Deutsche Werft in Hamburg.

The boat was kept as simple as possible. It had a single hull of all-welded construction, with the small conning tower as its only external structure above the waterline. The Type XXIII featured a single propeller and single rudder. Only two torpedo tubes were fitted and, owing to the small size of the boat, no reloads were carried. The torpedoes were loaded into the boat in a rather ingenious fashion. Floated out to the boat on a barge or raft, they were inserted into the tubes manually, from the exterior. In order to facilitate this, the boat had to be ballasted so that it became stern heavy, lifting the bow tubes clear of the water.

A close up of U-2329's tower. Although a relatively large tower, space on the bridge was extremely limited as can be seen here. The white recognition bands around the conning tower indicate that the boat is still in training.

Intended for operation on patrols of relatively short duration (with only two torpedoes available) in coastal waters and with a *Schnorchel* breathing device fitted, it was assumed that these boats would spend most of their time submerged. No exterior decking was therefore provided, and this in turn assisted in the streamlining of the boat and a substantial reduction in drag. Set into the forward face of the conning tower was a small watertight container that held an inflatable life-raft.

Only a modest single 630 bhp diesel was fitted but, like its larger cousin the Type XXI, this boat had a significantly better battery capacity than earlier boats. This, coupled with its *Schnorchel* facility, enabled it to remain submerged for extended periods.

The Type XXIII had a particularly fine standard of seaworthiness, being fast for its size and extremely manoeuvrable. It also had a very fast crash-dive time, of just nine seconds. This brought its own problems, however, and any ingress of water into the boat could cause disaster. Both U-2365 and U-2331 were lost to accidents when water entered the boats and caused rapid sinking. It was also discovered that the assumed maximum depth before hull failure could be expected had been grossly overestimated at some 250m. In fact, the maximum safe operating depth was eventually established at just 80m.

For the first time ever on an operational U-boat, the torpedoes left the tubes under their own power rather than being ejected solely by compressed air.

The Type XXIII was constructed from just four basic hull modules. The bow compartment contained only two torpedo tubes, with no provision for reloads. Aft of this was the crew accommodation. To port were two sets of bunks followed by a tiny galley and to starboard were three sets of bunks, allowing a total crew accommodation for 20 men. Abaft the main crew accommodation was the *Zentrale* with the commander's space followed by the sound room and radio room, all to port, and the diving planes, main electrical and pump controls to starboard. Further astern was the diesel motor room with its single MWN diesel, followed by the electric motor room. With no stern torpedo tubes, the aftermost compartment contained the boat's tiny WC. Only a single periscope was fitted to the Type XXIII, along with a *Schnorchel* mast.

The first Type XXIII, U-2321, was launched at Deutsche Werft on 17 April 1944. A total of 62 Type XXIIIs entered service before the end of hostilities, of which only about six actually had the opportunity to carry out operational war cruises. During these, however, four enemy ships were sunk, and no U-boats lost. The first Type XXIII to carry out an operational war patrol was U-2324, which set off from Kiel on 18 January 1945. Although she survived the war, no sinkings were achieved. The first Type XXIII to achieve combat success was U-2322, under the

The Type XXIII U-2336, under the command of Kapitänleutnant Emil Klusmeier, returning from her last mission of the war on 14 May 1945. Her final victim was the freighter *Avondale Park*, the last boat to be sunk by submarine action in World War II. (Artwork by Ian Palmer © Osprey Publishing)

command of Oberleutnant zur See Fridtjof-Heckel. Setting off from her Norwegian base on 6 February 1945 she encountered a convoy near Berwick on the Scottish coast and sank the small coaster *Egholm* on 25 February. U-2321, also operating from the same Norwegian base as U-2322, sank the coaster *Gasray* on 5 April 1945 off St Abbs head. More successful was U-2336, under Kapitänleutnant Emil Klusmeier, which sank two ships, the 1,790-ton *Sneland* and the 2,880-ton *Avondale Park*, also off the Scottish coast, on 7 May 1945. These were the last two ships to be sunk by U-boat action during World War II.

After the end of the war, two scuttled Type XXIIIs (U-2365 and U-2367) were raised and restored. These boats, commissioned into the West German

Bundesmarine as the *Hai* (Shark) and *Hecht* (Pike), respectively, provided the nucleus of the second rebirth of the U-Bootwaffe.

SPECIFICATIONS

Length:	34.7m
Beam:	3.0m
Draft:	3.7m
Displacement:	234 tons surfaced, 275 tons submerged
Speed:	9.7 knots surfaced, 12.5 knots submerged
Endurance:	4,450 nautical miles surfaced, 285 nautical miles submerged
Powerplant:	1 x MWN 6-cylinder 630 bhp diesels
	1 x AEG 35 bhp electric motor
	1 x BBC electric manoeuvring motor
Armament:	2 bow torpedo tubes
Crew:	14

CONSTRUCTION DETAILS

Deutsche Werft, Hamburg

U-2321 to U-2331	11 boats
U-2334 to U-2371	38 boats
Total	*49 boats*

Germaniawerft, Kiel

U-2332 to U-2333	2 boats
Total for type	*51 boats*

THE WA201

This was an experimental design intended to utilise the revolutionary new propulsion system developed by Dr Helmuth Walter. Hydrogen peroxide was

The experimental Wa201, a Type XVII powered by the revolutionary Walter turbine. Developed too late to be put into operational use, these boats were used purely as test beds. So great was the Allied interest in them that U-793 was commissioned into the Royal Navy after the war and used for extensive testing in 1947. (Artwork by Ian Palmer © Osprey Publishing)

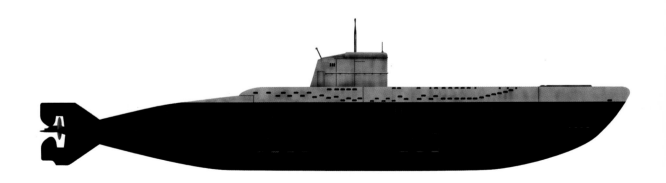

broken down using a catalyst to provide steam and oxygen, which were then mixed with water and diesel fuel, and the mixture combusted. The resultant products were very high temperature steam and pressurised carbon dioxide, which drove a turbine. The waste products were expelled and remaining water recirculated. The system worked superbly. An earlier experimental boat, although having poor handling characteristics when on the surface, achieved underwater speeds of up to 26 knots.

The Wa201 (the Wa prefix identifying the designer, Walter) was produced by the Blohm & Voss yard in direct association with Dr Walter, whilst Germaniawerft produced a second variant, the WK202. Four boats were completed, and were taken into service as U-792 and U-793 (Blohm & Voss), and U-794 and U-795 (Germaniawerft), respectively. All were used solely as test boats, and the build quality and efficiency of the Blohm & Voss boats were found to be superior. All four had numerous teething problems, always associated with revolutionary new designs, and were eventually laid up and finally scuttled in 1945.

THE TYPE XVIIB

The Type XVIIB was a direct successor to the Wa201, but larger and outfitted with two bow torpedo tubes as well as a *Schnorchel* system. Only three (U-1405, U-1406 and U-1407) were eventually commissioned, all being built by Blohm & Voss. The three were scuttled in 1945, but U-1407 was raised, repaired and taken into service in the Royal Navy as HMS *Meteorite*.

FOREIGN SUBMARINES

It is worth making brief mention of the small number of foreign submarines taken over and used by the Kriegsmarine during World War II. Most were used simply as training vessels, though some did see combat action, and indeed combat successes.

Probably the most significant of these was UA. This boat had in fact been constructed in a German shipyard on contract for the Turkish Navy as the *Batiray*. It had been completed and was at the point of being delivered to the Turks when war broke out and was taken over instead by the Kriegsmarine. Having been built in Germany to German standards, she was an easy enough vessel for the German crew to adapt to. In appearance, she was very similar to a German Type VII boat but with the deck gun mounted on a platform built on to the forward part of the conning tower. UA carried out seven war patrols, in the course of which she sank seven enemy ships totalling almost 41,000 tons, and damaged one other. She did, in fact, survive all her war cruises, only to be scuttled in May 1945 in Kiel as the war drew to a close.

One of the more interesting submarines to serve with the U-Bootwaffe was HMS *Seal*. This boat, a minelayer, had been damaged in action and, unable to submerge, was captured by the Germans. Repaired, she was taken into the Kriegsmarine as UB. She was, however, only ever used for training duties and saw no combat action. The reverse, of course, also happened: U-570 was captured and taken into service with the Royal Navy as HMS *Graph*.

Norway, too, contributed a number of submarines to the U-Bootwaffe. The bulk of the Norwegian submarine fleet was scuttled when the Germans invaded (one escaped to Britain). The Germans raised three, however, two of which did see service as UC1 and UC2, their duties purely with the training flotillas. UC1 was broken up in 1942 and UC2 was scuttled in 1945.

From the Dutch Navy's fleet of 12 submarines, seven escaped to Britain. The five that remained were taken into the U-Bootwaffe as UD1 to UD5. UD1, UD2 and UD4 were used purely as training boats. UD3, however, did carry out one war cruise, sinking a 5,000-ton freighter. She eventually returned to training duties before being scuttled in 1945. UD5 also undertook a single war cruise, sinking a 7,600-ton freighter before she too returned to training duties for the remainder of the war.

The invasion of France saw three partially completed submarines fall into German hands. They were taken over as UF1, UF2 and UF3. The construction of UF1 was never completed. UF2 was completed and used as a training boat. UF3 was also completed but for some reason never became operational.

The greatest number of foreign boats taken into the Kriegsmarine was from Italy, following the Italian surrender to the Allies. These were all designated with UIT numbers. UIT1 to UIT6 were in different stages of construction when taken over by the Germans. Most were destroyed in bombing raids either before or just after launching. None ever entered operational service.

A second batch, all submarines that were already in operational service before being taken over, were allocated numbers UIT21 to UIT25. UIT21 and UIT22 were in port in Bordeaux when the Italians surrendered. UIT21 was never used operationally and UIT22 was sunk in an RAF bombing raid on the port. UIT23, UIT24 and UIT25 were all operating in Far Eastern waters. All were seized by the Japanese in Singapore harbour and handed over to German crews. UIT23 was sunk by Allied aircraft whilst making her way back to Europe. UIT24 and UIT25 remained in German hands in the Far East until they too surrendered, at which point they were seized back by the Japanese. It is not believed that any saw operational use.

MIDGET SUBMARINES

These weapons were the preserve of the Kleinkampfmittelverbände, usually referred to in its abbreviated form as the K-Verbände. This department, formed in late 1943 and commanded by Konteradmiral Hellmuth Heye, specialised in the use of relatively crude and simple, mass-produced 'last gasp' weapons in the closing stages of the war. These included a number of midget submarine types, some of which were actually successful in sinking enemy ships but which, in reality, had little or no effect on the course of the war. These vessels were almost as dangerous to their crews as to the enemy, and the attrition rate amongst crews

The Neger one-man torpedo was a daunting weapon to use. It was incapable of diving, running on the surface where it was vulnerable to enemy fire. It was also susceptible to heavy seas, its operator protected by a flimsy plexiglass dome. Its small size, however, meant that it was not too easy for the enemy to spot.

was frightful. There were many projected designs, some of which never progressed beyond the drawing board. In order of size and complexity, those which were actually constructed included the following types of vessels.

THE NEGER

This was basically a manned torpedo, without warhead, with the pilot sitting at the forward end in a small cockpit with a plexiglass bubble canopy. Neger was in fact incapable of diving and many were spotted and shot on the surface by enemy warships. As a measure of improvement, a small diving cell was fitted, the new version being known as the Marder. This gave the pilot some chance of avoiding the enemy on his way to the target area, but even the Marder had to surface before firing its payload. Beneath the manned section was slung a standard live torpedo. The Neger/Marder simply lined itself up on the target and fired. Around 200 of these were produced, but the type was not particularly successful and losses were very heavy, so much so that operations were ceased in autumn 1944.

THE BIBER

The Biber measured just 7m in length and weighed three tons. It had a cylindrical hull with a small observation tower just forward of midships, and was propelled by a petrol-driven Opel Blitz truck motor for surface travel and a battery-powered electric motor for submerged travel. Its top speed on the surface was seven knots and submerged six knots. Radius of action was around 90 nautical miles. Maximum depth of 25m was attainable. The Biber carried two torpedoes

The Biber could also carry two torpedoes which, like those on the Molch, sat in recesses along the hull side. It had only a limited diving capability, up to 25m. As well as an electric motor for underwater propulsion, it carried a petrol motor from the Opel Blitz truck.

RIGHT
This shot shows an example of the Molch. It was broadly similar in appearance to the Hecht but carried two torpedoes, one to each side sitting in a curved recess running along its hull side. It was controlled by a single crewman.

OPPOSITE TOP
An example of the Hecht (officially the Type XXVIIA) mini-submarine with its single torpedo payload slung below. It had a two-man crew and was capable of diving to up to 50m. Just over 50 examples were built.

OPPOSITE BOTTOM
A Seehund, the largest and most successful of the mini-subs, being lowered into the water with its payload of two torpedoes in place. Further examples can just be seen sitting on their cradles on the dockside. Over 90,000 tons of enemy shipping was sunk by these vessels.

slung externally in concave indentations in the lower hull. Around 320 Biber were produced. Although they scored no sinkings in their first action on the Normandy invasion front in August 1944, all the vessels that took part returned to base safely, itself quite an achievement. Subsequent operations, however, saw heavy losses incurred.

THE MOLCH

The Molch was a one-man submarine with a 12m-long cylindrical hull, the forward three-quarters of whose length was packed with batteries. In the rear was the pilot's compartment, with hatch and periscope. This vessel was capable of diving to 30m and had a range of 100 nautical miles. One torpedo was slung on each side of the lower hull. Almost 400 of these craft were built, and were used at Anzio and along the Dutch and Belgian coasts. They had very poor handling characteristics, however, and were far from successful, suffering losses disproportionate to their rare successes.

THE HECHT

The Hecht, officially known as the Type XXVIIA, was a two-man submarine 10.4m in length and displacing some 12 tons. Electrically powered, it could achieve a top speed of some six knots and could dive to 50m. A single torpedo was carried, slung beneath the hull. A total of 53 Hecht were built, though the type does not seem to have been particularly successful, mostly being used for training purposes. The Hecht could also carry a mine in place of the torpedo or alternatively a 'passenger' in the form of a diver.

THE SEEHUND

The largest of the midget submarines, Seehund was a direct descendant of the Hecht, but longer, at 12m, and heavier, at 15 tons. The Seehund was equipped

with a 60 bhp diesel engine for surface travel, where it could make over seven knots with a range of around 300 nautical miles. Driven by its electric motor, it could achieve six knots submerged. Two torpedoes were carried externally, slung against the lower hull, one to each side. With excellent handling characteristics, and capable of diving to 50m, this was by far the best of the German midget submarines. It has been estimated that up to 90,000 tons of enemy shipping were sunk in operations using the Seehund.

U-BOAT ARMAMENT

For the first half of the war, the principal armament on most U-boats was the 8.8cm or 10.5cm naval gun, and/or the 2cm flak gun. As the war progressed and Allied anti-submarine measures became far more effective, U-boats tended to remain submerged wherever possible, surfacing only when safe to do so in order to run the main diesel engines to recharge their batteries. Effectively, the deck gun was becoming redundant. Being little used, around April 1943 it was removed from the Type VII in order to save some weight and achieve a modest reduction in drag.

At the same time, the danger from air attack having increased so much, U-boat flak defences were significantly enhanced. Despite the fact that several incidents are known where U-boats successfully fought off Allied air attacks, few U-boat commanders would willingly remain on the surface to engage an aircraft in combat unless diving was impossible or unsafe.

The main deck armament therefore was only effectively used in the early part of the war, usually against lone ships or convoy stragglers in waters where there was relatively little chance of encountering enemy warships. The deck gun would have been used most often to 'finish off' a merchantman that had been damaged by torpedo, but had failed to sink. Expenditure of additional torpedoes would be considered wasteful when much cheaper and plentiful artillery shells could be used.

THE 8.8CM DECK GUN

The 8.8cm gun used on U-boats was not directly related to the famous 8.8 or *Acht-Acht* flak gun which ultimately gained fame as an anti-tank weapon. More correctly entitled the 8.8cm *Schiffskanone* C/35, it was a purely naval weapon, developed from earlier weapons of this type used by the Imperial German Navy in World War I.

The gun was mounted on a low pedestal forward of the conning tower and was traversable through 360 degrees. It could be depressed to -4 degrees and elevated up to 30 degrees. The gun fired a 13.7kg high explosive shell with a muzzle velocity of 700m/sec for a distance of up to 12,350m. It could also fire a 13.9kg armour-piercing shell or an 11.2kg star shell. When submerged, the barrel bore was protected by a waterproof tompion inserted into the muzzle.

It was crewed by three men, the *Kanonier* (gunner), *Ladeschütze* (loader) and *Richtschütze* (gun-layer) supported by numerous other crewmen who would bring the ammunition up on deck from its storage under the floor plates of the *Zentrale*. On the deck, just forward and to port of the gun, was a small watertight ammunition locker giving the gun crew sufficient shells to allow the gun to be brought into action immediately whilst the bulk of the ammunition was retrieved from inside the boat. Two folding, padded, U-shaped supports were provided on both left and right sides of the gun for the gunner and gun-layer to steady themselves against rolling or pitching of the boat. In effect, the gun would be difficult to aim successfully in anything other than calm seas. In rough seas, the crew could strap themselves into position. Quite apart from being a poor gun platform, the narrow slippery deck of a U-boat was not a safe place to be in rough seas and gun crews would always be in danger of being washed overboard. The gun was controlled and directed, usually by the Second Officer (II Wach Offizier or IIWO), from the conning tower.

THE 10.5CM DECK GUN

The standard deck gun fitted to the Type IX in the early part of the war was the 10.5cm *Schiffskanone* C/32 mounted in the identical pedestal fitting as used for the smaller 8.8cm weapon on the Type VII. Able to traverse through 360 degrees, it fired a 23kg projectile up to 15,300m. Alternatively, it could fire a 23.3kg

RIGHT

A crewman operating a 2cm *Zwillinge*. This shot shows clearly how the gunner braced himself against two large curved, padded shoulder mounts. This weapon had a considerable recoil. The 'spider-web' sight for the gun can also be seen here.

BELOW

A side view of the aft deck gun shows the relatively large size of the 3.7cm weapon, not significantly smaller than the 8.8cm forward deck gun on the Type VII. This gun was not specifically intended as a flak weapon, but was also for use against surface targets.

armour-piercing shell or 14.7kg star shell. A crew of three was required to operate the gun, with additional crew members being engaged in keeping the gun supplied with ammunition from the magazine in the boat's interior. As the war

progressed, it became clear that any benefits derived from the presence of the deck gun were offset by the increase in the drag imposed on the boat when moving under water. By 1943, most deck guns had been removed from Type VIIs, but for some reason most Type IX boats retained their 10.5cm guns. The principal exception to this was the Type IXD2, particularly those boats of this type operating in the Atlantic.

THE 2CM FLAK GUN

Two basic designs of 2cm flak gun (*Flugabwehrkanone*) were used. The earlier version, the 2cm Flak 30, was a single-barrelled weapon, with 360 degree traverse and capable of 2 degree depression and 90 degree elevation. It fired a 0.32kg shell with a range up to 12,350m. Maximum cyclic rate of fire was 480 rounds per minute, but effective use was around half this rate.

A second, improved model, the 2cm Flak 38, was a very similar model but had an increased rate of fire at 960 rounds per minute. The second version was also produced in twin-barrelled (*Zwilling*) and four-barrelled (*Vierling*) versions. It was a direct development of a weapon designed for the army, and simply fitted to a naval pedestal mount (the Lafette C/35).

THE 3.7CM FLAK GUN

In the second half of the war, many U-boats received the 3.7cm Flak M/42. Also an army weapon adapted for naval use, it fired a 0.73kg round up to 15,350m at a maximum rate of fire of 50 rounds per minute.

OTHER WEAPONS

As well as the main deck armament and flak defence weapons, a limited amount of small arms were kept on board the U-boat for use by boarding parties, guards when the boat was in dock, etc. These would include the 9mm or smaller 7.62mm pistol, 9mm sub-machine gun, 9mm machine gun and 7.92mm rifle. A small number of 7.92mm machine guns could also be carried to supplement the boat's anti-aircraft armament. These could be fitted to mounts along the edge of the conning tower.

THE TORPEDO

German torpedo nomenclature can be extremely confusing. There were, however, only two principal types of torpedo used on U-boats, but with several variants in detonating devices (the pistol) and in directional control. These two principal types were in fact developments of torpedoes used in World War I, the G7a and the G7e. By World War II, torpedo sizes had been standardised at 54cm (21in.) so that all torpedoes, whether launched from surface ships or U-boats, were of the same diameter. The standard length was 7.16m and some 280kg of explosive was contained in the warhead.

TORPEDO TYPES

G7a(TI)

The G7a(TI) was a relatively simple weapon, propelled by steam from the burning of alcohol in air, supplied by a small on-board reservoir. The torpedo was driven by a single propeller. The G7a(TI) had a top speed of some 44 knots and a range of up to 6km. Its biggest drawback was its visible 'bubble' wake, meaning that it was best suited to night attacks. It featured an impact pistol type detonator which would be set off by the torpedo hitting the ship's side. Like many weapons from the early part of the war, it was manufactured to very high standards, and was thus expensive to produce.

G7e(TII)

Broadly similar to the G7a model, the G7e was electrically powered, being driven by a small 100 bhp electric motor. In this case two contra-rotating propellers were fitted. The G7e series left no visible wake, and the G7e(TII) had a range of some 5km at 30 knots. The electrically powered drive system meant that the G7e was easier and far cheaper to produce than the G7a.

G7e(TIIIa)

This was a development of the G7e(TII) with greater battery capacity, allowing its effective range to increase to 7.5km. It was used in conjunction with the FaT directional control.

G7Es(TIV) Falke

Introduced in July 1943, this torpedo was a little-used (only around 100 being manufactured) forerunner of the Zaunkönig acoustic torpedo. It carried a 274kg warhead and had a long range capacity of up to 7.5km, but a low speed of just of just 20 knots.

DETONATORS

The pistols used to detonate the torpedo were a source of great trouble to the U-Bootwaffe, with numerous failures to detonate being recorded in the early part of the war. The basic pistol was a dual-function component that could be activated by contact (*Aufschlagzündung*) or by the detection of the magnetic field generated by the hull of the ship (*Magnetischerzündung*).

DIRECTIONAL CONTROL

Three principal types of directional control were developed in World War II, all of which were used with some success after teething problems were eliminated.

The FaT (Federapparat Torpedo)

The original FaT design was first used on the G7a(TI). It was an excellent anti-convoy concept in that the torpedo ran in a straight line until reaching the target area and then changed to an 'S' configuration through the convoy until finding a target. The required launch position was alongside the convoy. A further development, the FaTII, was based on the G7e(TII).

The LuT (Lagenunabhängiger Torpedo)

This torpedo, similar in concept to the FaT, allowed the U-boat to attack the convoy from any angle rather than having to attain the ideal launch position alongside the convoy.

Zaunkönig (TVb)

This torpedo, based on the G7e, had acoustic detectors, which homed in on the sounds of the cavitation in the water caused by the propellers of the target. It was, however, prone to premature detonation when passing through turbulent waters, such as the wake of a ship. In addition it appears that it was only capable of detecting cavitation caused by ships moving at between 10 knots and 18 knots. This torpedo had a range of 5.75km at 24.5 knots.

Zaunkönig II (TXI)

This was a development of the basic Zaunkönig, which had the acoustic detectors tuned to specific frequencies of ships' propellers to avoid premature detonation, and was to be used with some success as an anti-escort weapon, fired from the stern torpedo tube against pursuing escort vessels.

Loading torpedoes into the cramped interior of a Type II was an awkward and laborious business, requiring the use of special winches and pulleys, and much sweat and effort.

THE MINE

There were a number of developments in submarine-launched mines during World War II, of which the four most significant were the TMA, TMB, TMC and SMA.

TM(TORPEDOMINE)A
This mine was for use in depths of up to 270m and carried an explosive charge of some 215kg. Launched through the torpedo tube, it was of the same diameter as the standard torpedo, but shorter at 3.4m, so that two could be launched from each tube at the same time. This was effectively a 'moored' mine, being attached to a heavy baseplate by a long cable.

TMB
Designed for use in shallow waters of up to just 20m, the TMB was shorter again, at just 2.3m, but carried a 580kg charge. Three could be carried in and launched from each tube. Rather than being 'moored', it was designed to lie on the sea-bed in shallower waters and be detonated either by magnetic or acoustic sensors.

TMC
This was a development of the TMB, larger at 3.3m in length, but with a 1,000kg charge. Two could be carried in and launched from each tube.

SM(SCHACHTMINE)A
This mine was designed for dropping from a vertical mine shaft in specially designed minelaying boats rather than launching from the torpedo tubes. It was 2.15m in length and carried a 350kg charge. It could be used in waters up to 250m in depth.

EMS (EINHEITSMINE SEHROHR TRIEBMINE)
This was a small free-floating mine, designed to float on the surface, untethered, drifting in the currents. It carried a small charge of just 14kg. Obviously, free-floating mines could not be tracked and could thus endanger all ships, not just the enemy vessels for which they were intended. They were therefore designed to be laid in enemy waters and become active a few minutes after laying, but then to sink after 72 hours, effectively making them safe before they could drift out of enemy waters and endanger other shipping.

MTA (MINENTORPEDO A)
This device was basically a torpedo with a mine in place of the regular warhead. It was for use in relatively shallow waters and, being attached to a torpedo body, could be fired into the waters in which it was to be active, from a range of up to 7km away. At the end of its pre-programmed run, the motor would switch off

and the torpedo-mine would sink to the sea-bed, thereafter to be detonated by acoustic or magnetic sensors in the same way as the TMB.

OTHER WEAPONS

Germany carried out a number of tests on the use of rockets fired from submarines. U-511 was used as a test bed for the employment of Wurfkörper 42 rockets fired from a wooden frame on her deck. Test firings both on the surface and from a submerged depth of 12m were successful but the project was never developed further.

A project was also planned for the use by U-boats of a towed missile container. This large towed vessel would contain a V2 ballistic missile. On reaching its launch point, the container, towed horizontally, would have ballast chambers flooded to turn it to a vertical position ready for remotely controlled launching from the U-boat. Development was under way and one container vessel completed and ready for testing before the war ended but the system was never used in anger.

THE POWERPLANT

All of the U-boat types covered in this volume were diesel powered, with additional electric motors coupled onto the same propeller shafts as the diesels. Diesels were used for surface running, and electric motors for running submerged.

Not until the advent of the *Schnorchel* was it possible for a U-boat to charge its electric motors by running its diesels whilst still at periscope depth. The *Schnorchel* was a simple 'breathing' tube that allowed air to be drawn into the boat whilst submerged. Its head contained a simple flap mechanism with a flotation ball. The rise of a wave against the head would lift the ball, sealing the tube and preventing the ingress of water. The main problem with the *Schnorchel* arose when the boat's depth was not correctly monitored and it slipped below periscope depth, or in heavy seas when the flap remained closed more often than open. When no air was being taken into the boat, the engines would draw their air from the boat's interior, creating a partial vacuum and debilitating the crew.

The diesel engines driving each propeller shaft were mounted on extremely robust foundations. Almost completely filling the engine room space, only a narrow access passage between the two allowed movement through the compartment. Serving in the confines of the engine room was hot, smelly and unpleasant. Many mechanical breakdowns were extremely difficult to work on because of the cramped space.

This photograph shows the *Schnorchel* raised on a Type IX boat. The recessed channel on the decking into which the *Schnorchel* tube was lowered can be clearly seen. Position of the *Schnorchel* varied. On some boats it was to port and on others to starboard.

The Type II was typically powered by 350 bhp diesels and 180 bhp electric motors. The larger Type VIIs featured first 1,160 bhp diesels, later increased to 1,400 bhp, backed by 375 bhp electric motors. In the Type IX and Type XXI, larger 2,200 bhp diesels were used. Type IXs generally featured 500 bhp electric motors but in the Type XXI the electric motors, which played such an important part in their underwater performance, developed a massive 2,500 bhp. The electric motors were coupled onto the same shafts as the diesels so that when they were out of use they would rotate freely, whilst the diesels drove the boat, and thus act as generators to recharge the batteries. Principal suppliers of electric motors for U-boats were Siemens, AEG and Brown-Boveri.

OTHER STANDARD EQUIPMENT

RADIOS

The standard method of communication between a U-boat and its shore-based command was the short-wave radio, operating on the 3–30 MHz range. Most U-boats were fitted with a combination of a Telefunken receiver and a 200-watt Telefunken transmitter, with a smaller 40-watt Lorenz transmitter as back-up. Once at sea, communication between U-boats utilised medium-wave radio on the 1.5–3 MHz range. Once again, the equipment was manufactured predominantly by Telefunken. Finally, signals sent to U-boats whilst submerged required the use of very long wave signals on the 15–20 MHz range. These required an enormously powerful transmitter on land, but were the only sure way of making contact with a submerged boat. These signals were also received on the same Telefunken equipment as the medium-wave signals.

RADAR

Basic radar equipment began to be installed on U-boats in 1940. The earliest operational type was the FuMO29 (Funkmessortungsgerät). This was predominantly used on the Type IX, but a few Type VIIs were also fitted with this equipment, easily detected on photographs because of the twin horizontal rows of eight dipoles on the upper front part of the conning tower. The top row were transmitters and the lower row receivers. An improved version, FuMO30, was introduced in 1942 in which the tower-mounted dipoles were replaced by a retractable so-called 'mattress' antenna, which was housed in a slot in the tower wall. This equipment was only partially successful in detecting other ships owing to the very low position of its mounting in respect to the ocean surface (on

The basic FuMB1 radar, known as 'Metox', used a crude wooden cross on which an antenna wire was fitted. This was known as the Biscay Cross, as shown here in the centre of the photograph. It was crude and flimsy, often being damaged as it had to be passed up through the hatch each time the U-boat surfaced.

The more elaborate mattress-style antenna for the FuMB is shown here. This was retractable, being withdrawn into a housing at the side of the tower casing.

surface ships, the radar is usually mounted high up on the mainmast or bridge top). Interference with the radar signal by the ocean surface in heavy weather meant that enemy ships might be detected visually before being picked up on radar. An improved version, the FuMO61, was little better in this respect but did provide good aircraft detection results.

A new type of radar-detector, the FuMB1 (Funkmessbeobachtung), also known as 'Metox', was introduced in July 1942. This equipment was used in conjunction with an extremely crude wooden cross-shaped antenna strung with wire and known as the 'Biscay Cross'. This antenna had to be rotated by hand. Unfortunately, the Metox's own emissions were detectable by Allied radar detection equipment, leading them straight to the U-boat. A later, improved version, the FuMB9 Zypern, was also found to be detectable by the British H2S radar detection system. Not until the FuMB10 Borkum set did the U-boat have a radar detection system that was not itself easily detectable.

This still left the problem of the existing equipment not covering the full radar spectrum, a problem eventually solved in November 1943 by the FuMB7 Naxos. Naxos and Metox used together finally gave the U-boats excellent all-round radar detection capabilities. The range of capabilities of Naxos and Metox were finally combined in a single system with the introduction of the FuMB24 Fliege and FuMB25 Mücke systems in April 1944.

SOUND DETECTION

The earliest form of sound detection equipment used on U-boats was the Gruppenhorchgerät (GHG) installed in early vessels. The sound detectors were installed in the hull on either side of the bow, so that sound detection was only truly

FuMB antennas, as shown here, were fitted directly to the face of the conning tower casing. The major problem with this type of antenna is that it could only cover the area in front of the boat, so that the boat would have to cruise round in a circle to obtain 360-degree cover

accurate when the boat was abeam of the vessel being detected. Improved sound detection came with the Kristalldrehbasisgerät (KDB) in which the sound detection array was contained in a rotating, retractable mount set into the foredeck. This was the system carried on most Type VII vessels. A number of Type VIIs were also equipped with the so-called Balcongerät (Balcony Apparatus) set into a 'balcony'-shaped fairing in the lower part of the bow. This gave a far better effective field than either the GHG or KDB systems.

OTHER EQUIPMENT

THE FOCKE-ACHGELIS

One particularly interesting, if not particularly effective, piece of equipment carried on most Type IXD boats after the summer of 1942 was the Focke-Achgelis rotary glider. Basically an unpowered helicopter with a triple-bladed rotor, it could be quickly disassembled and packed in a storage cylinder on the afterdeck. Once assembled, it was easily launched and remained connected to the U-boat by an 'umbilical' cord. From his vantage point high above the submarine, the pilot could spot any targets, or approaching enemy ships, well before the bridge watch. Unfortunately, if the U-boat came under threat and there was no time to reel in the

A clear view of the Bachstelze helicopter on its platform on the tower of a Type IX. This aircraft was intended to 'spot' for targets too far off to be seen by lookouts on the conning tower. In the event, it was only ever successfully used once to locate enemy shipping.

spotter, the umbilical cord would be cut as the U-boat dived and the unfortunate pilot left to be picked up later if possible. Only one enemy merchantman is recorded as ever having been detected through the use of this apparatus.

ALBERICH

An ingenious defensive measure for U-boats was the creation of Alberich. This was a synthetic rubber sheeting that was to be glued to the hull of the U-boat and which would absorb sound, thus making Allied sonar equipment much less efficient at detecting submerged vessels. Initially, considerable problems were encountered in producing an effective adhesive, with the result that the rubber sheeting would loosen and create turbulence in the water as the submarine moved along, making it easier rather than more difficult to detect. The theory was sound, however, and once an effective adhesive had been produced further tests were made that showed the system to be extremely effective. Only a very few U-boats were coated in Alberich, though it had been the intention that it would be widely used on the new Type XXI and Type XXIII boats. However, the war ended before it could be put into large-scale use.

BOLD

Bold was a fairly effective countermeasure against enemy escort ships. It was a simple device consisting of a metal canister packed with calcium hydride, with an inlet valve to admit water. When a Bold was launched, sea-water would enter the canister and react with the calcium hydride, releasing a dense volume of hydrogen bubbles. The canister was designed to hover at a depth of around 30m. The result would give a sonar 'signature' very similar to the U-boat itself. Its purpose was to attract the attention of the escorts whilst the U-boat itself quietly slipped away unnoticed.

APHRODITE

This simple device was merely a large (one metre diameter) hydrogen-filled balloon from which dangled strips of metal foil. It was attached to a cable with an anchor weight. Its purpose was to create a radar image similar to that of the U-boat. A U-boat travelling on the surface at night could release a number of such devices in the hope that Allied aircraft in the vicinity would home in on their stronger radar returns, giving the U-boat itself time to escape.

PART II

U-BOAT BASES & BUNKERS

The German U-boat fleet, under the command of Konteradmiral (later Gross-admiral and Commander-in-Chief Navy) Karl Dönitz, had shown its potential almost from the very outbreak of war. In September 1939, an early Type VIIB vessel under the command of Kapitänleutnant Günther Prien succeeded in penetrating the Royal Navy's Home Fleet anchorage at Scapa Flow, believed to be virtually impregnable, and sank the battleship *Royal Oak*. To compound Britain's agony, U-47 then escaped with relative ease.

At this time, however, U-boats still faced a tricky and lengthy voyage through German waters into the North Sea, or through the English Channel and on to the Atlantic, which served to reduce their operational service period and increase their vulnerability to enemy attack. Despite their deadly effectiveness, U-boats were of course much more susceptible to damage than surface craft. If caught on the surface their pressure hulls could easily be damaged, rendering them incapable of diving. They would then be virtually helpless.

Prior to the outbreak of war, U-boats were often to be seen moored alongside their designated flotilla tender or 'mother ship'. The clear danger posed by enemy

The first purpose-built U-boat base was the Salzwedel Kaserne in Wilhelmshaven. State of the art in its day, it survived the war intact and was used for some time as a boarding school for the children of British service personnel. It is still in good condition today.

air attack against them (even though Royal Air Force raids against German targets were initially rather ineffective) saw plans drawn up for protective concrete bunkers in German naval bases such as Helgoland, Hamburg and Kiel.

Following the fall of first Norway and then France and the Low Countries in the summer of 1940, a large number of additional operational bases became available to the U-Bootwaffe, and these were put to use almost immediately. In some cases, the Germans were simply re-occupying bases they had already made use of during World War I. The first such bases had been established in the Belgian port of Bruges in August 1917. These had proved highly successful, with the U-boat pens remaining largely undamaged despite numerous British bombing raids.

With the Norwegian and Channel ports under their control, the German Navy now had easy access to the North Sea and the Atlantic. This allowed them a faster turnaround time on operations and thus increased the number of boats at sea at any one time. Dönitz worked on a simple three-way split of his available submarines, with one third in transit to or from operations, one third on combat patrol, and the remaining third in port being fitted out, resupplied or overhauled.

U-boat bases were quickly established at Bergen and Trondheim in Norway, and at Brest, Lorient, St Nazaire, La Pallice and Bordeaux in France. Although these new bases had considerable advantages for Dönitz, they also brought his U-boats within much easier reach of the RAF.

Concrete bunkers had proven their effectiveness at Bruges during World War I; in the spring of 1941 the Germans capitalised on their previous experience in this area and built new bunkers along very similar lines at all of the main U-boat bases in France and Norway. These huge concrete edifices were erected in Germany too, at Helgoland, Kiel and Hamburg. Operational bases were not the only ones to be provided with these gigantic shelters: near Bremen, an entire U-boat construction plant for the advanced Type XXI boats was built within a massive concrete bunker on the banks of the River Weser.

Initially, these bunkers were considered virtually bombproof. As the war progressed, however, the RAF developed heavier and heavier bombs, and in 1943 many of the bunkers were provided with extensive strengthening to their roofs, as well as heavy anti-aircraft defences. Some of the roofs of these bunkers were now over 7m thick. Additional roofing was added to some bunkers, spaced some way above the main roof. Even the much vaunted bunker-busting 'Tallboy' bombs, weighing over five tons each and carrying over two tons of high explosive, usually failed to have much effect on the reinforced bunkers – though these vain attempts to put them out of action totally devastated the cities in which these bases were established.

One of the massive air-raid bunkers at the Salzwedel Kaserne. These structures were incredibly strong and the cost and effort of demolishing them being so great, many were simply left where they stood. The base was virtually untouched by Allied bombing.

In fact, these constructions were so strong that several of them survived the war almost unscathed. In some cases, attempts were made to demolish parts of them, but the effort required was so huge that most were left as they were. Almost all of the bunkers described in this work still exist, and many are still used as naval establishments. Both the Norwegian and French navies use some of the bunker facilities in their respective ports and the German Bundesmarine still uses part of the gigantic Valentin factory bunker at Bremen as a storage facility. Many of the bunkers still show clear traces of the original disruptive-pattern camouflage paint schemes, patriotic slogans and warning notices painted on their walls. A good number of them are now in private hands, generally used as storage facilities, and

Early stages in the construction of the U-boat base in Brest, as the concrete foundations are laid. Up on the hill in the background is the French naval academy, the École Navale, which was also taken over by the Germans.

many may still be visited. In some cases, such as the Fink II bunker in Hamburg, the entrances were simply dynamited to prevent members of the public gaining access and the bunkers abandoned, still with U-boats inside. In 1987, the past was brought back to life when a German Type VIIC U-boat sailed once again from the bunker at La Pallice. The boat was a replica specially made for the successful submarine movie *Das Boot*.

Given the difficulty of dismantling or destroying these massive structures, it seems likely that those that have survived thus far will be with us for some time to come.

DESIGN AND DEVELOPMENT

The U-boat bunkers were but one aspect of Germany's programme of defensive construction. Similar protective housing was planned to shelter *S-Boote* (E-boats) and *Räum-Boote* (R-boats) and to provide protected locks: damage to these could effectively seal off a port. In addition storage bunkers for munitions and matériel, general defensive pillboxes and artillery bunkers were planned. It should also be remembered that the work on the U-boat bunkers effectively competed for materials and manpower with the construction of the Atlantic Wall coastal defences.

CONSTRUCTION

As far as the German Navy was concerned, the responsibility for providing these defensive structures belonged to the Naval Construction Department (Marinebauwesens) under the command of Ministerialdirektor Eckhardt. The experience of building similar large-scale defensive structures on the German naval base at Helgoland was put to good use when the U-boat bases began to appear in the various captured French ports in 1941, and the general designs themselves closely followed the basic principles established during the construction of the Imperial German Navy U-boat base at Bruges.

Actual construction of the U-boat bunkers fell to the Organisation Todt (OT), the state construction agency under the control of Dr Fritz Todt. Todt had been given the task of completing Germany's West Wall defences in 1938, and to do so had assembled a virtual army of construction workers. It is estimated that well over 300,000 men were drafted into the organisation, living in camps erected by the building firms which had been awarded the construction contracts. The Organisation Todt employed thousands of German technical specialists and tradesmen to oversee this army of labourers. After the outbreak of war, some of these workers were legitimately recruited from abroad, but others were little more than slave labour, expected to work in extremely dangerous conditions and

BUILDING A U-BOAT BUNKER

This illustration shows the construction of the massive Valentin factory bunker near Bremen, near to the village of Farge. The second largest bunker to be built, it covered just over 49,000m² of ground on the northern bank of the River Weser. Almost a quarter of a million tons of concrete were used in its construction, as well as 27,000 tons of steel. The structure was erected at a total cost of 120,000,000 Reichsmarks (RM). Construction came under the control of the Marineober-bauleitung Weser, which authorised the creation of two construction cooperatives (*Arbeitsgemeinschaften* – abbreviated to ARGE). ARGE Nord consisted of the firms Lenzbau, Wayss & Freytag, Hochtief and Tesch, whilst ARGE Süd consisted of the firms Hermann Möller, Kögel and August Reiners. As the names imply, each of the cooperatives was responsible for construction work in either the northern or southern parts of the site. Consultant to the project was Professor Dr Arnold Agatz, one of the foremost experts on harbour construction who also acted as a consultant to the bunker construction programme in France. Completion was scheduled for the early part of 1945, though Hitler insisted that this should be brought forward to the second half of

1944. However, by the end of hostilities in May 1945, the complex was still not in service, despite being 90 per cent complete.

Railway lines were laid to the very centre of the complex, carrying materials straight through the bunker as it grew. A cement-mixing plant was also erected next to the bunker, to feed the project's insatiable appetite for concrete. The site resisted attempts by the Allies to destroy it with Tallboy and Grand-slam bombs: parts of it are still in use today.

One thing that marked the Valentin project out for special attention was the sheer volume of slave labour used during its construction. Over 10,000 forced labourers, prisoners of war and concentration camp inmates were used on the project. (As with the construction projects in France, there were some volunteers within the workforce.) A scale of charges was levied on the construction firms for the use of this manpower, running from 0.30 RM per day for a camp inmate, 0.40 RM per day for Soviet prisoners of war, up to 0.70 RM per day for West European workers. Over 4,000 members of the workforce lost their lives during the construction of the Valentin bunker. (Artwork by Ian Palmer © Osprey Publishing) often treated appallingly. The OT even had its own armed security element in the form of various Schutzkommando, and even a Polizei Regiment Todt.

The Organisation Todt was closely linked with the DAF (Deutsche Arbeitsfront), the official Nazi state trade union which had forcibly absorbed all independent trade unions and labour associations. Initially at least, relations between the German construction workers and local French labour hired to work on the projects were good. French workers and those brought in from other European countries were well fed, well paid and accommodated in a reasonable standard of comfort. There were even Spanish communists among them who had fled to France during the Spanish Civil War and had been interned. When the Germans invaded, these communists fell into their hands. Although they were, effectively, forced labour they were good workers and earned the respect of the Germans for their skills. This brought them relatively good treatment from their captors. In Norway, however, Soviet prisoners of war were put to work and their treatment was far less satisfactory. Worst of all was the treatment of the concentration camp inmates put to work on projects such as the Valentin bunker near Bremen.

After the fall of France and the Low Countries, a separate Todt element was set up to control construction in these occupied territories. The Organisation Todt Einsatzgruppe West was based in Paris, under the command of Oberbaudirektor Karl Weis. The Einsatzgruppe was subdivided into a number of command areas (*Oberbauleitungen*) many of which took direct responsibility for the construction of U-boat bunkers in their areas. Following the death of Fritz Todt in 1942, control of the OT was handed to Albert Speer who severed the links with the DAF.

The German firms actually involved were many. Famous construction concerns such as Siemens-Bauunion and Holzmann AG were responsible for the concrete work, whilst electrical installations were provided principally by Siemens-Schuckert. Machine manufacturing giants MAN (Maschinenfabrik Augsburg-Nürnberg) provided the powerful pumping mechanisms required to fill and drain the concrete pens and dry docks. In addition, much work was subcontracted to local firms. In some cases over 15,000 workers might be employed at any one time on the construction of one of the major U-boat bunkers. Construction workers were employed in 12-hour shifts starting or ending at 7am and 7pm: work was thus kept going around the clock. Huge arc lights and even searchlights were used to illuminate the site at night and allow work to continue. Only when the air-raid warnings sounded did work cease, albeit temporarily.

It is not entirely surprising that when selecting sites on which to erect the bunkers, existing French naval dockyards were often chosen (for example, Brest and Lorient): such locations were tidal and emerged into the open sea. Others were non-tidal (among them St Nazaire, Bordeaux and La Pallice) and built in

The roof support beams of one of the pens at the Brest U-boat base are lowered into place. Immensely strong, the roofing on these bunkers withstood several direct hits from Allied bombs specifically designed as 'bunker busters', with only minimal damage caused.

existing civilian harbours. Access to the basins containing the bunkers was through lock gates.

Once the sites had been chosen, the preparatory work involved was enormous. The sites were cleared, and construction began by digging out the foundations and driving in the massive steel piles. Huge cofferdams were built to hold back the sea while the sites for the pens were excavated below water level. During the ongoing excavation work, the concrete floors would be laid on the site at the rear of the pens where the various workshop areas were to be positioned, and the steel reinforcements for the walls would be prepared, ready for the shuttering to be erected and the concrete for the walls to be poured in.

Enormous quantities of materials were needed for the construction of these bunkers, with thousands of cubic metres of concrete being poured every day once construction work was in full swing. The principal materials, steel and cement, were both (initially at least) transported all the way from Germany. The cement was packed in countless small 50kg paper sacks, and such vast quantities of paper were used for these that it was considered necessary to recycle the empty sacks. Later, loose cement was loaded into railway trucks and shipped by the wagonload. The cement was sprayed with water, dampening the top layer and thus forming a crust that would prevent the cement from being blown away. The quantities needed to feed the massive construction projects became so vast that materials began to be sourced locally, provided suppliers could meet the German quality standards. Huge quantities of gravel and other ballast materials were also transported to the construction sites. Railway tracks were laid to allow the hundreds of thousands of tons of steel, cement and, most importantly, sand to be carried right onto the site. The huge amounts of concrete required for one of these mammoth structures required equally huge quantities of sand, so much so that this in turn required even more miles of railway track to move the sand from the shore to the building site. Materials were also transported to the site by sea using barges and lighters, and by road in countless trucks.

BUNKER DESIGN

As well as providing shelter for the U-boats themselves, the bunkers contained repair workshops, power generating plants (general power was drawn from the local electricity supply but diesel generator plants were provided to produce power in emergencies should the local supply be knocked out), pumping stations, storage facilities, offices, accommodation, ventilation units, heating units, telephone and

The Brest bunker gradually takes shape. Powerful arc lights installed throughout the site enable work to continue virtually around the clock. Attempts to disrupt construction of the U-boat bunkers in France through Allied bombing raids were relatively ineffective.

communication rooms and first aid posts. Narrow-gauge rail tracks also ran into the bunkers themselves to allow heavy equipment to be brought inside and to the U-boats. For safety's sake, munitions such as torpedoes were generally stored away from the U-boat pens in their own well-protected bunkers and brought into the complex when needed, by means of the narrow-gauge tracks.

The pens themselves were constructed in two styles, 'wet' and 'dry'. Dry pens were those capable of being pumped out and effectively used as dry-dock facilities for submarines requiring repair and maintenance. The actual dimensions of the pens varied but, as a general rule, the distance from the base of the pen to the level of the quay allowed for approximately 10m water depth, with a similar distance from quay level to ceiling. The height of the ceiling had to allow the overhead cranes to remove the periscopes fully from their housing for repair or replacement. The quayside was normally around 1.5m wide.

Each pen had at least one overhead crane running down its length. These had capacities ranging from one ton up to 30 tons, the U-boat being directed into whichever pen had a crane or cranes of the requisite capacity for the work required. Each pen was served by main pumps with a 3,000m^3 capacity and smaller auxiliary drainage pumps with a 380m^3 capacity. These pumps were located at pumping stations between each pen, usually with two of each of these pumps per station. This was by no means a universal arrangement, but it was by far the most typical set-up: some bases had all the pumping equipment located in the service areas in the main block behind the pens themselves. These powerful pumps took anything from three hours upwards to empty a pen completely and create a dry-dock facility.

This view of Brest shows the extent of the construction site for the U-boat base. The individual pens can be clearly seen, still awaiting the roofing. Note the use of barrage balloons to prevent attack by low-flying fighter-bombers.

Protection for the pen interiors was provided by massive armoured steel plates, some up to a metre thick. These could be in the form of steel shutters, which were lowered vertically from above the entrance to the pen, or conventional hinged doors. These armoured plates would in some cases extend down to the level of the quay (for dry pens) whilst others only provided cover for some two-thirds of the opening, leaving just under 2m of the entrance open. Some of the protective doors to the bunker complexes were hollow boxes made from thick plate, which were then filled with concrete.

Given the Kriegsmarine's urgent need for protected repair facilities for their U-boats, the dry-dock-capable pens were generally the first to be constructed. It was common for the first pens to be put into use as soon as they were ready, whilst the remaining pens were still under construction.

With the greatest threat to these bunkers coming from enemy aircraft, it is no surprise that the most innovative development work was carried out on the design of the bunker roof. The result of this was the creation of roofs that were virtually impregnable.

PROTECTED LOCKS

As several of the U-boat bunkers were located in basins in the inner harbour of their port, access would normally be via a set of lock gates. Though the bunker complexes themselves were immensely strong, the unprotected locks were definite weak spots. If these were put out of action, boats would be unable to enter or leave their pens. In order to protect this Achilles heel, especially after the British attack on the lock at St Nazaire, it was decided to enclose these locks in their own protective bunkers: St Nazaire, La Pallice and Bordeaux were all to have these. Effectively, these looked like miniature U-boat bunkers. Though never completed at Bordeaux, the locks at St Nazaire and La Pallice still stand to this day. The partially completed lock at Bordeaux was demolished after the war.

At St Nazaire the lock was built a few yards along from the lock which gave access to the inner harbour via the Normandie dry dock, which was damaged when it was rammed during a commando raid by HMS *Campbeltown*. She was one of the old 'four-stacker' destroyers supplied by the USA under the Lend-Lease programme. After the destroyer was rammed into the lock gates, a huge cargo of explosives carried on board was detonated, destroying the gates.

The new protected lock was almost directly in front of Pens 8 and 9 of the bunker complex. This lock, begun in August 1942, was some 155m long, 25m wide and 14m high. A roadway ran through the lock, entering via doors in its side, and crossed the lock waters by means of a bridge, which could be raised when a vessel passed through. The lock was capable of being pumped dry, and

The U-boat pens at St Nazaire today, still in a remarkable state of preservation. The rounded tops of the *Fangrost* beams on the roof are clearly visible against the skyline. (Mark Wood)

in addition to the intrinsic protection offered by the reinforced concrete roof and walls, had its own flak defences on the roof, with four emplacements for 2cm flak guns on a special platform on the western side. At La Pallice, the massive sheltered lock was 167m long, 26m wide and 14m high. It was not used until August 1944.

A number of fascinating new projects were planned, the most interesting of which was the proposal to turn the eastern portion of the Rove Tunnel at Marseilles (which opened out in the north-west part of the harbour at Port de la Lave) into a U-boat bunker, suitable for handling the smaller Type XXIII coastal boats. It was also planned to build bunkers at Rügen, Gotenhafen and at Nikolajew in the Crimea, and to create additional bunker facilities at Kiel, Bremen and Hamburg.

TOUR OF A U-BOAT BASE

Each bunker complex was subtly different from its counterparts in its layout: however, there were a number of standard features. The example we will use here to tour the layout of a bunker site, namely the complex at Brest, will illustrate most of the common features found in all the operational sites.

When the Germany Army, in the form of 5. Panzer Division, occupied the port of Brest in June 1940, it was only to discover that the withdrawing British troops had destroyed most of the port facilities. The Germans began urgent repair works immediately and within two months the first of Dönitz's U-boats, U-65 under the command of Kapitänleutnant von Stockhausen, entered Brest for repairs. By the middle of the following month, the port of Brest was fully functional once more.

Almost immediately, preparations began for the establishment of an operational U-boat base. Construction of protective concrete pens began in January 1941 and lasted for approximately nine months. The layout actually consisted of two bunkers in one. The first contained five wet pens, 115m long and 17m wide, each capable of accommodating up to three boats; the second contained eight dry repair pens 99m long and 11m wide, and a further two 114m long and 13m wide, each capable of accommodating just one boat. Overall, the bunker measured 333m in length and 192m in width, and its height was 17m.

The first U-boats to arrive at Brest were from 1. Unterseebootsflotille *Weddigen*, transferring from Kiel in June 1941, followed four months later by 9. Unterseebootsflotille. The first recorded use of the U-boat pens was in September 1941, though the complex was not fully completed until the summer of 1942.

The harbour at Brest was bounded by a protective mole (a harbour wall), the bunker being tucked in the eastern corner of the harbour, with the mole emerging from the eastern side of the bunker. The forward part of the bunker, containing the individual pens, opened out into the harbour or basin. In the Brest complex, there were five pens lettered A to E, then a further ten pens numbered in sequence.

The construction of the U-boat pens at Bordeaux. In many ways this could be any construction site in the word with tower cranes and a mass of steel reinforcing rods. Only the sheer scale and monstrous size of the edifices under construction sets them apart.

Pens A and B were fractionally under 116m in length and 17m in width. Each could accommodate two U-boats side by side. The external wall was some 7m thick, and there was a 6.3m-wide quay separating the two pens, with a 1.3m-thick dividing wall between them running down its centre. Pen C was slightly shorter, at 114m, but wider at 17.5m. It too could accommodate two boats. A 7m-wide quay separated Pen C from Pen B, with a 2.7m-thick dividing wall running along its centre. Pens D and E were 96m in length, Pen D being 17.8m wide and Pen E 16.8m wide. Again, each could accommodate two boats. The internal dividing wall between Pens C and D was 2.5m thick, that between Pens D and E 1.3m thick and that between Pen E and the first of the numbered pens 2m thick. The dividing walls between each pen had five openings in the case of the longer pens and four in the case of the shorter to allow for movement between the pens, spaced approximately every 13m.

Moving westwards there were eight numbered pens, all around 11m wide, with each being slightly longer than its predecessor at 96.1m, 96.5m, 96.8m, 97.1m, 97.5m, 98m, 98.5m and 99.1m respectively. The dividing walls between these pens alternated between 2m and 1.3m thick. These were all dry-dock pens capable of handling only one boat each. Then followed an 11m-wide section running the entire length of the complex from front to back, containing various offices. Finally, at the east end of the complex were two larger dry-dock repair pens, both 12m wide: Pen 9 was just under and Pen 10 just over 114m in length. The fact that virtually no two pens were identical, each differing by a metre or so in length and width, was by no means unusual.

All pens were provided with overhead travelling cranes that differed in their handling capacity. These cranes were located as follows: Pens A, C and D – 4-ton capacity; Pen B – 12-ton capacity; Pen 1 – 10-ton capacity; Pens 2, 3, 5 and 8 – 3-ton capacity; Pens 4, 6 and 7 – 2.5-ton capacity; Pen 9 – 5-ton capacity; and Pen 10 – 30-ton capacity.

Running parallel with the rear of Pens 1 to 8 was a corridor separating the front part of the complex from the rear. The front faces of Pens A to E were set much further forward than the numbered pens, so that there was a space between the rear of these pens and the corridor. Immediately behind Pen A was a ship repair workshop, behind Pen B a mechanical workshop and behind Pen C a torpedo storage room. Behind Pen D was a torpedo workshop and behind Pen E lay the complex Orderly Room. On the northern side of the corridor were, moving from east to west, a weapons repair shop, mechanical workshop, ship repair workshop, diesel room, electrical repair workshop, three further mechanical workshops and three ship repair workshops, the pump room and the firefighters' room. Powerful electric lighting allowed skilled machinists to work to fine tolerances on lathes and milling machines in the workshops deep within the bunker's gloomy interior. The standard format of having the rear of the complex provide all forms of repair workshops was highly typical. The east end of the corridor ran through to the entrance: on the northern side of this was the main boiler house which provided heating for the complex, and to the south of the entrance opening was a pillbox with firing slits to protect the entrance.

Moving to the roof, above Pens A, E and 4 were concrete flak gun emplacements providing an element of protection against low-flying aircraft. These were relatively small-calibre weapons, rarely larger than 4cm calibre and incapable of reaching the four-engined RAF and USAAF bombers which flew at very high altitude, but they could put up enough fire to force smaller aircraft to abandon a bombing/torpedo run. Above Pen 10 was a small tower containing the radio and signals equipment for the bunker.

Although certain bunkers, such as that at Brest, stored some torpedoes within the bunker, in general the bulk of torpedo storage was remote from the bunker site for safety reasons, usually in equally strong though much smaller bunkers connected to the main complex by narrow-gauge railway tracks.

PRINCIPLES OF DEFENCE

In common with most fortresses throughout history, the appraisal of a bunker's design shows that considerable thought was given to how the structure would be defended in the event of an attack. Though clear comparisons may be drawn between the fortresses of old and the massive U-boat bunkers, there were also significant differences. The principal defensive factor in the design of U-boat bunkers was the inherent strength of the structure itself. Their steel-reinforced concrete structures were (initially at least) impervious to any bomb likely to be dropped on them. As the power of enemy bombs increased, so did the level of protection on the roof of the bunker, first by simply adding additional layers of concrete, and later by means of the *Fangrost* concept. The latter ensured that bombs were detonated by a series of spaced beams set some way above the actual roof surface, thus ensuring that much of the blast was dissipated, leaving the structure unharmed. The concept continued to be developed and is not dissimilar to that which may be seen in spaced and reactive armour on fighting vehicles.

Given that the physical structure of the U-boat bunker was in itself virtually impregnable, consideration had to be given to what were considered the weak points of the complex. The most obvious danger zone was the seaward entrance to the bunker and the threat to it from low-flying aircraft. Such aircraft could not carry the massive bombs that (it was hoped) would penetrate the bunker itself; rather this was the task of the high-altitude four-engined bombers. However, they might hope to lob a bomb through the open entrance or drop a torpedo into the waters of the harbour aimed towards the pen.

In order to prevent such attacks, older ships were occasionally moored in the harbour in line with the entrance to the pens, and thus along the potential approach path of enemy aircraft. Extra-tall masts could be fitted to these ships to provide further obstacles. Barrage balloons would also be anchored around the bunkers to obstruct aircraft, and a small number of flak guns were often sited in concrete emplacements on the bunker roof. Though the latter might not seem like much of a defensive effort, it should be borne in mind that their primary duty was not to shoot down lots of enemy aircraft, but to put up enough fire so that, in conjunction with having to avoid barrage balloons, ships' masts and other obstacles, the enemy pilot would be unable to hold a steady enough course to make a successful run.

The flak guns used were generally of the 2cm type. These were used by the German Navy in three particular forms; single-barrelled, twin-barrelled (*Zwilling*) or four-barrelled (*Vierling*) configuration. This weapon could fire a 0.32kg shell, with a muzzle velocity of 899m/s, to a range of 12,350m, and could fire between 120 and 240 rounds per minute, depending on the exact model. A larger-calibre 3.7cm single-barrelled flak gun was also used. It fired a 0.73kg shell with a muzzle velocity of 820m/s to a range of 15,350m, and its rate of fire was around 50 rounds per minute. Occasionally 4cm Bofors-type anti-aircraft

The massive thickness of the roof of the Lorient bunker is apparent in this shot. The ultimate plan was for all bunker roofing to be covered with the special *Fangrost* concrete spaced beams intended to detonate bombs before they impacted against the roof itself.

la base sous-marine

Landward side of the St Nazaire pens today, now the home of a submarine museum. The massive thickness of the roof covering is apparent here, as is the intact state of the ingenuous *Fangrost* 'bomb-catching' beams. (Mark Wood)

guns were used. These fired a larger 0.95kg shell with a muzzle velocity of 854m/s, to a maximum range of 4,500m. These were all standard weapons widely used by the navy (and the army) both on land and aboard ship.

In addition to the anti-aircraft armament, several bunkers had defensive pillbox-like positions built into the structure near the landward entrances which could provide suppressive machine-gun fire. Although this level of firepower might seem rather inadequate, it should be remembered that penetrating the walls, even though they were considerably thinner than the roof, would be almost impossible: access to the interior could only be gained via a small number of these often narrow and easily defended entrances. Heavy machine-gun fire around these points would probably be sufficient to prevent anyone from gaining access. As well as being defended by such machine-gun positions, the entrances, like the seaward entrances to the pens, were usually protected by heavy steel doors.

LONG-RANGE DEFENCES OF THE FRENCH BASES

Faced with the threat of intensive Allied bombing raids, the first significant bunker defensive measure was the Luftwaffe's system of early-warning radar and spotter posts. At various sites along the French coast were establishments equipped with the Freya and Würzburg radar systems (**1** and **2**). These would detect formations of Allied bombers approaching the coast. Depending on the time of day, single-engined day fighters, such as the Fw 190 (**3**), or twin-engined Me 110 or Ju 88 night-fighters would be scrambled to intercept the enemy. Allied bombers could boast fairly powerful defensive weaponry, particularly when flying in close formation, but despite this many fell victim to the determined attacks of the Luftwaffe fighters. Those who survived would face a concentrated barrage of heavy anti-aircraft fire from large-calibre weapons, such as the 12.8cm flak gun (**4**), which

protected important installations such as the ports in occupied France. In many cases poor visibility, bad weather or heavy cloud over the target prevented planes from reaching their objective, as shown by events at Brest. On 3 September 1941, from a total of 140 RAF bombers which set out to attack the base only 53 actually made it to their target, the remainder having to return home. In another fairly typical raid, on 18 December 1941, 47 bombers left bases in England to attack the bunker. Six of these were shot down. Although two bombs landed in the water near the bunker (causing a pressure wave which killed five people inside because the pen doors were open), only five bombs landed on or near the bunker: these caused no significant damage to the structure. At the end of the day, the single greatest factor in the successful defence of the bunker was its inherent, massive strength (**5**). (Artwork by Ian Palmer © Osprey Publishing)

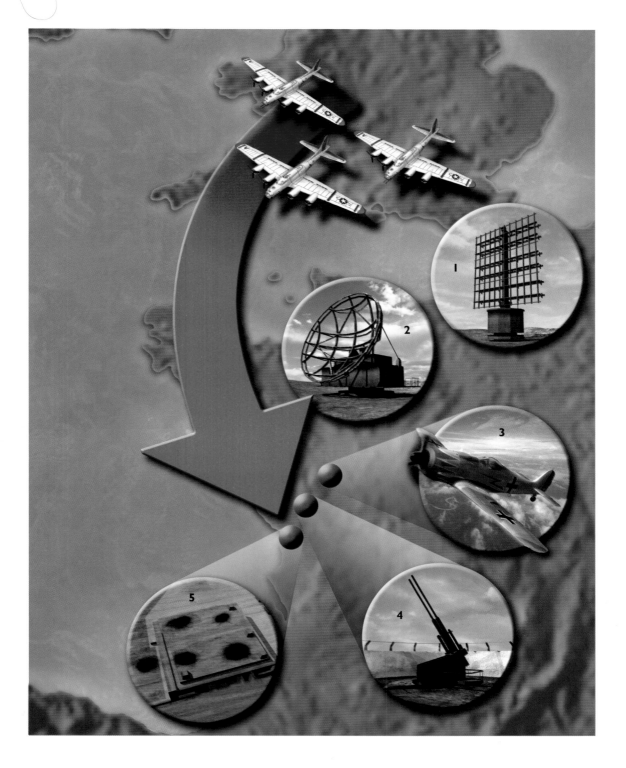

It is worth considering also that if the area to the landward side of the bunker fell into enemy hands, the complex itself would have been made all but unusable, as no submarine would be able to enter or leave without coming under heavy fire – and, because of the delicate nature of the submarine's pressure hull, this would almost certainly be fatal. If the areas around the bunker complex were to fall into enemy hands, the bunker itself would still remain virtually impregnable, with any attempts to storm it certain to cause heavy losses. Almost certainly the only solution would be to cordon off the area and hope to starve out the garrison inside, not unlike the situation with medieval fortresses under siege. Fortunately for both attackers and defenders this situation never arose. In some cases, Allied advances expediently and wisely chose to bypass towns declared by Hitler to be 'fortresses' and avoided wasting resources, incurring heavy losses, and losing the vital initiative by attempting to storm them.

The thick steel 'doors' that protected the seaward side of the bunker often took the form of overlapping steel shutters, either horizontal or vertical, or in some cases were huge steel plates mounted on barges which could be towed across the entrances. If the doors reached down only as far as quay level, the opening would be so small that any fast-moving, low-flying enemy aircraft, busy dodging flak and other obstacles, would have little or no chance of accurately aiming a bomb or torpedo into the gap. Other pens had doors that reached down to water level, but in all cases the area under water was open. Anti-torpedo nets were also strung out in front of the pen entrances.

The Bordeaux pens at an advanced stage in their construction. The pen walls are taking shape. The form of the landward end of the building is also apparent, the first and second floors over the ground floor clearly visible.

It should be noted of course that these were only the defences of the bunker itself. As a strategic installation, a harbour area would also have its own defences, with anti-aircraft weapons of larger calibre. In addition, Luftwaffe listening posts and radar would detect incoming enemy bomber waves and alert fighter or night-fighter squadrons which would intercept them. Given that these facilities were all on the coast, and within easy reach of air bases in Britain, daytime bombing raids could be provided with fairly powerful fighter escorts, even before the advent of long-range escort aircraft such as the Mustang and Thunderbolt.

Bombers, however, having survived enemy fighter attacks, and the heavy anti-aircraft fire around the port areas, would in almost every case find that the bombs they dropped had a negligible effect on the bunkers themselves, though collateral damage to the harbour areas and even the towns themselves was often severe. The bombers would then have to run the gauntlet of further fighter attacks as they made for home. In most cases, expending huge resources in terms of fuel and munitions and losing both aircraft and aircrew would have resulted in little or no damage to the U-boat bunker. Low-flying aircraft would have a better chance of evading enemy fighters and avoiding anti-aircraft fire but would be lucky to inflict any major damage unless they intercepted a U-boat on the surface either leaving or returning to the bunker.

In essence therefore, the U-boat bunker can be considered a defensive triumph, with most of them surviving the war virtually intact despite numerous enemy attacks. A few boats received damage from falling masonry inside the bunkers but this was nothing compared to the potential damage which might have been caused to boats moored in open, unprotected basins. The U-boat war was lost at sea, as Allied anti-submarine measures took an ever-increasing toll on German submarines and trained crews. The bunkers themselves, however, provided a safe haven for exhausted boats and their crews to the bitter end.

LIFE IN A U-BOAT BASE

Each of the French and Norwegian U-boat bunker complexes hosted at least one and in some cases two U-boat flotillas. These flotillas were basically fixed command structures to which individual boats were allocated. Boats could be, and indeed often were, re-allocated to other flotillas over a period of time. Each flotilla commander was himself an experienced U-boat commander, and indeed many of them were top aces who, having served their time in combat, were promoted and re-assigned to a shore posting, ensuring that their vast experience would survive to be handed on to those who followed.

The U-boat arm was initially commanded by Konteradmiral Karl Dönitz. On the fall of France, Dönitz made his headquarters in Paris, but in September 1940 he

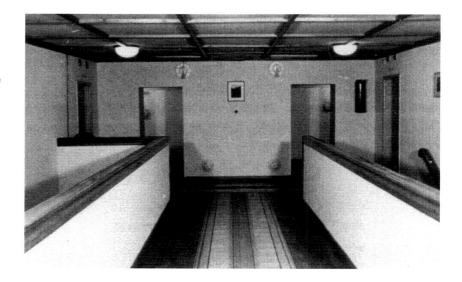

transferred to a luxurious mansion at Kerneval. The growing threat of enemy
attack, not only from the air but also in the form of commando raids (especially
after the events at St Nazaire) saw Hitler insist in March 1942 that he relocate
back to Paris. On being promoted to Grossadmiral and Commander-in-Chief
Navy, Dönitz retained his passionate interest in the welfare and performance of
his U-boats and was often on hand at the U-boat bases in France to welcome
home his Grey Wolves after a successful war cruise.

Chief of Operations under Dönitz was Kapitän zur See Eberhardt Godt, while the
post of Head of Organisation was held by Kapitän zur See Hans-Georg von
Friedeburg. The individual operational areas into which the U-boat force was
divided were each commanded by a flag officer. The post of Führer der U-Boote
West, based in Paris and covering the areas of operation in which most of the boats
from the French U-boat bunker complexes operated, was held by Kapitän zur See
Hans-Rudolf Rösing from its inception in July 1942 through to May 1945.

In general, U-boats operating from the Norwegian bunkers came under the control
of the Führer der U-Boote Norwegen, based in Narvik. This post was held by
Kapitän zur See Rudolf Peters from January 1943 to May 1944 and then by
Fregattenkapitän Reinhard Sühren from May 1944 until May 1945. It should be
stressed that it was the area in which the boats were to operate that determined
which flag officer would be responsible, rather than the area in which their home
port lay.

Efforts were made to rotate U-boat crews. On return from a gruelling war patrol,
the boat would tie up in the bunker and the majority of the crew would be

DEFENDING THE BASE FROM LOW-FLYING AIRCRAFT

This illustration shows a typical low-level attack by enemy aircraft on a bunker complex. Smaller single- or twin-engined aircraft, travelling at low altitude and at much greater speed than their heavier four-engined counterparts, had a much better chance of avoiding detection by enemy radar and aircraft spotters. The downside was that their payload was much smaller, though torpedo-carrying aircraft could inflict considerable damage if their payload entered one of the pen openings. Although the massive pen itself would suffer little damage, any U-boat inside would probably be destroyed.

A number of defensive measures were taken against such low-flying aircraft, several of which can be seen here. On the roof of the bunker are a number of concrete emplacements equipped with the four-barrel 2cm *Flakvierling* (**1**). With each barrel capable of firing up to 450 rounds per minute, each mount had a combined rate of fire of 1,800 rounds per minute. Multiply this by the number of mounts on the bunker roof, all firing at once, and it can be seen that if all three concentrated their fire on a single attacker, the pilot would face a daunting barrage. He would certainly have to manoeuvre sharply to avoid being hit, and would therefore reduce his chances of maintaining a course long enough to launch his weapon accurately.

In addition to the anti-aircraft weapons on the bunker itself, any important military base such as a harbour complex would be bristling with other anti-aircraft weapons of varying calibre, adding to the weight of fire being thrown against enemy aircraft. It is estimated, for example, that when the port at Lorient finally surrendered a total of 287 flak guns were seized. These ranged from light 2cm flak for use against low-flying aircraft, to massive twin 10.5cm and 12.8cm guns for use against high-altitude bombers.

In addition, the pilot would have to avoid the cables of barrage balloons anchored to vessels in the harbour near to the bunker (**2**), as well as extended masts fitted to such ships to provide further hazards for low-flying aircraft (**3**).

An anti-torpedo net drawn across the harbour in front of the pens (**4**) would provide yet another obstacle to a successful strike. Taking all these factors into account, it is understandable that light attack aircraft scored even fewer successes against the U-boat bunkers than the heavy bombers did. (Artwork by Ian Palmer © Osprey Publishing)

The *Soldatenheim* for sailors in Lorient, somewhat equivalent to the British 'Naafi'. Note the huge eagle and swastika mounted over the doors. Considerable care and attention were given to the welfare of U-boat sailors when in port.

granted home leave. A train was often laid on by order of Dönitz as BdU (Befehlshaber der U-Boote or C-in-C U-Boats) to ensure that the crews were transported home to Germany as quickly as possible and that as little of their precious leave as possible was lost in travelling. This train was known as the *BdU-Zug* or C-in-C's train.

Meanwhile a skeleton crew would stay with their boat, carrying out routine maintenance work. The crews were normally accommodated in barracks some way away from the bunker complex for safety's sake given the risk of (albeit ineffectual)

Land-based quarters away from the bunkers themselves were also provided at Lorient. Note the huge camouflage-painted concrete air-raid shelters at the rear of the U-boat *Unterkunft* or accommodation block.

Allied air raids. There was, however, a substantial amount of accommodation space within the bunker complex in which personnel could be housed if necessary. Very occasionally, crewmen engaged in maintenance work might actually sleep on board their boat in the bunker. In some cases, training facilities were even added to the bunker complex, an example of this being the 7m tank built onto the side of the Keroman I bunker and used for training U-boat crews in underwater escape drill.

During wartime, the U-boat bunker was a busy site. With one third of the fleet on operational duty, another third in transit to and from operational areas and the remaining third in port, it would be a rare occasion when the bunker was found to be totally empty. Boats in port would be undergoing repair and maintenance, refuelling, rearming, restocking food and other supplies, and generally airing the boat to remove the inevitable smell of several weeks at sea with 50 unwashed sailors. Water was far too precious a commodity to use for washing.

During the period of U-boat dominance early in the Battle of the Atlantic, bunkers would regularly witness the arrival of their resident U-boats after successful missions, bedecked with victory pennants representing numerous ships sunk as the U-boats ran amok amongst the poorly protected merchant ships. Bands would play on the dockside and female auxiliaries would wait with garlands of flowers ready to hang around the neck of the returning ace.

As the French ports that housed the U-boat bunkers were to find out, U-boat men lived hard and played hard. Those crew members who had to remain with their boat made the most of their off-duty time and lost no opportunity to paint the town red. The Military Police (*Feldgendarmerie*) had to work hard to keep them in check. Some very fine hotels, even small chateaux, were taken over as accommodation for U-boat crews in these French bases. Local cinemas showed German films and theatres put on German plays. U-boat crewmen were also provided with superior rations – small recompense for the dangers they faced. In general, the local French population was polite in its relations with the Germans though this deteriorated as the fortunes of war turned against Germany, especially after the Allied landings in Normandy.

U-boat bases were also home to a large number of administrative personnel, or *Marinebeamten*. These men, mostly officers but with a small number of senior NCOs, wore naval uniform but with silver rather than the traditional gold insignia, and were generally reviled by the sailors who referred to them contemptuously as Silberlings. These administrative personnel were directly attached to the U-boat flotillas, but generally had little or no sea-going experience (though photographic evidence shows a few individuals wearing the U-Boat War Badge, indicating that they at least had served at the front). Many of them took a dim view of what they saw as a lack of discipline on the part of the U-boat crews once they returned to port, and they were not beyond trying to throw their weight around, which of course did not go down well with the crews. These officials were responsible for handling pay, procuring supplies, and other such matters.

As the fortunes of war turned against the U-boats, successes became more rare, and mere survival became a considerable achievement – and the U-boat bunkers saw fewer and fewer celebrations. No longer were the quays packed with well-wishers: however the sight of these great concrete behemoths remained a welcome sight for the decreasing number of unscathed U-boats returning from ever more dangerous war cruises.

RESIDENT FLOTILLAS AND COMMANDERS IN EUROPE

BREST

Brest was home to 1. Unterseebootsflotille, commanded variously by Korvetten-kapitän Hans Eckermann (January–October 1940), Korvettenkapitän Hans Cohausz (November 1940–February 1942), Kapitänleutnant Heinz Buchholz (February 1942–July 1942) and Korvettenkapitän Werner Winter (July 1942–May 1945). By the time the flotilla moved from its home port of Kiel to France, it had already replaced its small Type II boats with the Type VII and also operated a number of Type IX boats from the bunker complex in Brest. The port also hosted 9. Unterseebootsflotille, a wartime-raised unit equipped with the ubiquitous Type

Work on the roof of the U-boat pens at La Pallice, positioning the steel reinforcing rods for the concrete structure. Huge numbers of foreign workers were employed on these projects. Some were forced labour but many were willing volunteers anxious for guaranteed, well paid work.

The pens at Lorient during construction. This shot, and the workers visible on the floor of the pen, give a good impression of the depth of water afforded by these pens when in use. Several of the pens were capable of being pumped out for use as dry-docking facilities.

VII. This flotilla was commanded by Kapitänleutnant Jurgen Oesten (November 1941–March 1942) and Korvettenkapitän Heinrich Lehmann-Willenbrock (March 1942–August 1944).

Brest was home to, amongst others, great aces like Kapitänleutnant Reinhard Sühren and Kapitänleutnant Adalbert Schnee. Sühren, who served his 'apprentice-ship' as a watch officer under Herbert Schultze in U-48, went on to command U-564 and sank 18 ships totalling 95,000 tons, whilst Schnee, in U-201, accounted for 24 ships totalling some 89,000 tons.

LORIENT

In the summer of 1940, 2. Unterseebootsflotille moved from its home port of Wilhelmshaven to the Lorient base in France. The two operational examples of the large Type IA U-boats served with this flotilla, though the bulk of its boats were Type VII and Type IX. Its commanders were Korvettenkapitän Werner Hartmann (January 1940–May 1940), Korvettenkapitän Heinz Fischer (June 1940–October 1940), Korvettenkapitän Viktor Schütze (October 1940–January 1943) and Fregattenkapitän Ernst Kals (January 1943–May 1945).

The U-boat bunkers at Lorient also housed 10. Unterseebootsflotille, operating a mixture of Type IX, XB and XIV boats. It was commanded by Korvettenkapitän Günter Kuhnke (January 1942–October 1944).

Aces such as Kapitänleutnant Fritz-Julius Lemp in U-30, Kapitänleutnant Günther Prien in U-47, Kapitänleutnant Otto Kretschmer in U-99 and Kapitänleutnant Joachim Schepke in U-100 all sailed from Lorient, between them racking up a total of over 720,000 tons of enemy shipping sunk. Lorient was also home base for Kapitänleutnant Reinhard Hardegen, commander of U-123, who sank 24 enemy ships totalling 138,000 tons. Lorient, as well as playing host to some of the highest-ranking aces, was also the home base to some of the most successful boats: U-48, U-99, U-103, U-124 and U-107, the five highest-scoring boats of the war.

LA PALLICE

This French base was home to 3. Unterseebootsflotille which moved from its original home in Kiel after the fall of France. Once its elderly Type II boats had been phased out, it operated exclusively with Type VIIs. The flotilla was commanded by Korvettenkapitän Hans-Rudolf Rösing (March 1941–July 1941), Korvettenkapitän Herbert Schultze (July 1941–March 1942), Korvettenkapitän Heinz von Reiche (March 1942–June 1942) and Korvettenkapitän Richard Zapp (June 1942–October 1944).

La Pallice was also home to many spectacularly successful aces, amongst them Kapitänleutnant Peter 'Ali' Cremer of U-333, Kapitänleutnant Heinz-Otto Schultze of U-432 and Kapitänleutnant Siegfried von Forstner of U-402 to name but three. These experts between them sank over 174,000 tons of enemy shipping.

ST NAZAIRE

This was the home of 6. Unterseebootsflotille, another flotilla which operated exclusively with the Type VII. Its original home had been the Baltic port of Danzig. The commanders of this flotilla were Korvettenkapitän Wilhelm Schulz (September 1941–October 1943) and Korvettenkapitän Carl Emmermann (October 1943–August 1944).

St Nazaire hosted two of the war's most famous boats: U-96 with its distinctive 'laughing swordfish' emblem, under Kapitänleutnant Heinrich Lehmann Willenbrock, with 25 ships totalling 183,250 tons to his credit; and the 'Red Devil Boat', U-552 under the command of Kapitänleutnant Erich Topp, destroyer of 35 ships totalling some 192,600 tons.

BORDEAUX

Bordeaux was home to 12. Unterseebootsflotille as well as a number of Italian U-boats. The German boats operating from this port were a mixture of Type IXs and Type XIVs under the command of Korvettenkapitän Klaus Scholz (October 1942–August 1944).

Although Bordeaux was better known initially as a base for Italian submarines and the so-called *Milchkuh* supply submarines, it also boasted its own ace, the phenomenally successful Korvettenkapitän Wolfgang Lüth. Lüth, in command of U-181, sank a grand total of 47 ships totalling over 221,000 tons, making him the most successful U-boat commander of World War II and earning him the Knight's Cross with Oakleaves, Swords and Diamonds.

TRONDHEIM

The bunkers at this Norwegian port were home to 13. Unterseebootsflotille under the command of Fregattenkapitän Rolf Rüggeberg (June 1943–May 1945). It was equipped with Type VIIC boats. Amongst the aces who operated from Trondheim were Kapitänleutnant Max-Martin Teichert, commander of U-456, who sank the cruiser HMS *Edinburgh*; Kapitänleutnant Hans-Günther Lange of U-711, an Oakleaves winner who sank the British destroyer HMS *Ashanti*; Oberleutnant Otto Westphalen, commander of U-968, who included three enemy warships in his total score; and Kapitänleutnant Paul Brasak, commander of U-737.

BERGEN

The U-boat bunkers at Bergen housed the boats of 11. Unterseebootsflotille, equipped with the Type VIIC. This flotilla was commanded by Fregattenkapitän

The interior of the U-boat bunker at Trondheim. Note the corrugated metal shuttering on the ceiling. As shown here, the wet pens were capable of accommodating two boats at the same time.

Hans Cohausz (May 1942–January 1945) and Fregattenkapitän Heinrich Lehmann-Willenbrock (January 1945–May 1945).

Aces sailing from Bergen included Kapitänleutnant Heinrich Schroeteler, Kapitänleutnant Rolf Thomsen, commander of U-1202, and also highly experienced ace commanders such as Kapitänleutnant Karl-Heinz Franke, Kapitänleutnant Horst von Schroeter, Korvettenkapitän Adalbert Schnee and Korvettenkapitän Peter 'Ali' Cremer, who had all been given commands with the new Type XXI U-boat.

KIEL
Kiel was home to 1., 3., 5. and 7. Unterseebootsflotillen. All of these moved into bases in occupied Europe after the outbreak of war. No bunkers were erected for these flotillas. Pre-war photographs tend to show the U-boats simply tied up alongside their depot ship. 1., 3. and 7. came under the command of Führer der U-Boote West whilst 5. Unterseebootsflotille came under command of Führer der U-Boote Ost.

WILHELMSHAVEN
This port was home to 2., 6., 22. and 31. Unterseebootsflotillen, though 22. and 31. used Wilhelmshaven only in the latter part of the war. 2., 6. and 31. came under the command of Führer der U-Boote Ost. 22. Unterseebootsflotille came under the command of 2. Unterseebootslehrdivision.

PILLAU
This port, on the Bay of Danzig, was one of the bases from which several of the U-boat training flotillas operated. For most of the war, the Baltic was firmly under German control and its waters were relatively safe for inexperienced crews undergoing training. At various times, Pillau was home to 19., 20., 21. and 26. Unterseebootsflotillen.

The air-raid bunker of 5. U-Flotille. Note the insignia over the entrance, a representation of the U-Boat War Badge.

GOTENHAFEN

On the western side of the Bay of Danzig, Gotenhafen was variously home to 22., 24., 25. and 27. Unterseebootsflotillen: all were training flotillas. It was also the base port of 2. Unterseebootslehrdivision.

HELA

On the Baltic, near Gotenhafen, Hela was a training base for U-boats but had no permanently assigned flotillas.

DANZIG

23., 24. and 25. Unterseebootsflotillen operated from this port. It was the final home of 23. Unterseebootsflotille, from August 1943 until the end of the war, specialising in training crews in underwater torpedo firing. All three flotillas were training units. Danzig was also the base of the Führer der Unterseeboote Ost.

In addition to the bases already listed, U-boat bases were established at the following locations:

Memel: in the eastern Baltic, this bases was but one of the temporary homes of 25. Unterseebootsflotille, and was also home base for 4. U-Bootlehrdivision.

Libau: north of Memel, Libau was another of the temporary homes for 25. Unterseebootsflotille.

Neustadt: this port, in Schleswig-Holstein, was not an operational base, but was home to 1. and 3. U-Bootlehrdivision.

Travemünde: to the north-east of Hamburg, this Baltic port was also home to 25. Unterseebootsflotille.

Eckernförde: This important naval base just north of the eastern end of the Kiel Canal was the final home of 24. Unterseebootsflotille. The waters off this port were used for ship speed trials.

Warnemünde: just north of Rostock, this base was the final home of 26. Unterseebootsflotille.

Königsberg: the East Prussian city was home to 32. Unterseebootsflotille before it moved to Hamburg when the city was threatened by the Soviet advance. The flotilla came under the command of Führer der U-Boote Ost.

Flensburg: adjacent to the Naval Academy at Mürwik, Flensburg was home to 33. Unterseebootsflotille, though boats spent much time in the Far East. This flotilla came under the command of Führer der U-Boote West.

Horten: on the southern coast of Norway, this base was dedicated to training and repair facilities. It was not home to any specific flotilla.

Narvik: this sea port in the far north of Norway, though not a U-boat base as such, was the command base of the Führer der Unterseeboote Norwegen.

La Spezia, Pola, and Salamis: La Spezia in north-west Italy, Pola, on the Adriatic near Italy's border with Yugoslavia, and the Greek port of Salamis all played host to 29. Unterseebootsflotille, a large operational unit with up to 54 boats under its control. This flotilla also used the French ports of Toulon and Marseilles. Boats operating from these bases came under the command of Führer der Unterseeboote Mittelmeer.

Constanza and Feodosia: Constanza on the Black Sea and the Crimean port of Feodosia were the main operational bases of 30. Unterseebootsflotille.

BASES IN THE PACIFIC AND THE FAR EAST

Once Japan entered the war, the Germans received several requests to send boats into the Indian Ocean, but these requests were politely ignored, the Kriegsmarine's U-boats being fully occupied in the Atlantic. However, as the tide of war began to turn against the U-boats, and pickings in the Atlantic became harder to find, the possibilities of success in the Far East became more attractive. With Allied countermeasures believed to be weak in these waters, Dönitz dispatched a group of Type IX boats, known as the *Monsun* boats, to seek fresh success in these far-off waters. U-boats operating in the Far East came under the command of Fregattenkapitän Wilhelm Dommes as Chef der U-Boote im Südraum.

A small number of bases were provided by the Imperial Japanese Navy, the most important of these being at Penang on the western side of the Malay Peninsula. Dommes was based in Penang, and German boats began to operate from this port in July 1943. Additional facilities, specifically for repair and maintenance work, were established at Singapore in the summer of 1944. These remained in use until Germany's surrender in May 1945. The Indonesian port of Batavia was the site of a further small repair and maintenance base for U-boats operating in the Far East, and Kobe, a Japanese port, played host to a small facility that was established specifically for repairing U-boat batteries plus general repair work.

The Elbe II bunker at Hamburg with a Type VII moored alongside. On top of the typical massive concrete roof of the bunker are situated various offices and workshops. This facility was primarily used for the fitting out of new boats.

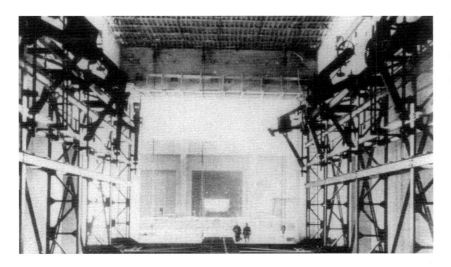

An interior shot of one of the special repair bunkers at Lorient. U-boats were rolled into these bunkers on a special cradle, effectively allowing these land-based bunkers to be used as 'dry docks'.

BUNKERS, BOMBS AND RAIDS –
THE BASES AT WAR

HAMBURG
Elbe II

Plans for a new U-boat bunker at the Howaldtswerke yards on the River Elbe at Hamburg were approved in 1940, with construction commencing at the end of that year. Erected by the firm of Dyckerhoff & Widmann AG at the east end of the Vulkan basin, the bunker was completed in March 1941 and consisted of two pens. Each pen was 112m in length and 22.5m in width and could accommodate three boats moored side by side.

To the rear of the bunker at ground level were a storage area on the west side and offices and electrical switch-gear on the eastern side. The entire upper floor of this rear area was fitted out with workbenches and various equipment such as drills, vertical and horizontal boring machines, and lathes. Landward access was via small, well-protected steel doors on each side of the bunker.

The Elbe II bunker was used primarily to provide cover for new Type XXI U-boats being fitted out, and for existing boats returning to the yard for refit or repair. Despite numerous Allied bombing raids, the boats in the interior of the bunker remained safe, though some damage to the roof of the structure was achieved. On the night of 8 March 1945 a force of over 300 RAF bombers attacked the Hamburg dock area, dropping almost 1,000 tons of bombs. This was only the start of a concentrated bombing campaign against the dock installations in Hamburg. At the end of March, the RAF returned with a force of over 450 bombers and dropped over 2,200 tons of bombs on the area, laying waste to the Howaldtswerke yards but doing little or no damage to the bunker. The massive hanging steel doors covering the entrance were blown off during an air raid on 8 April 1945, when once again over 400 bombers attacked the area.

Six submarines, U-2505, U-3004, U-2501 and U-3506 (all Type XXIs) plus U-684 and U-685 (Type VIICs), were sheltering in the Elbe II bunker when the war ended. The Type XXIs were all awaiting repair and the Type VIICs were not fully completed. All six boats were crammed into the westernmost pen.

Following the German agreement to surrender the city of Hamburg to British forces on 3 May, the crews of the Type XXIs made immediate preparations to scuttle their boats using explosive charges. U-3506, U-3004 and U-2505 were scuttled inside the pen, the others being moved out into the harbour waters before being sunk.

Fink II

The Fink II bunker, the largest to be built on German soil, was also constructed at Hamburg. Erected at the Deutsche Werft yards at Hamburg-Finkenwerder, the main contractors involved were Wayss & Freytag and Beton & Monierbau AG. Although plans were approved in 1940, work did not commence until March 1941.

The bunker was actually built on dry land at the Deutsche Werft yards, then a large triangular area of ground between it and the inlet from the River Elbe was excavated and the resulting area flooded. The structure consisted initially of four pens, all at just over 111m in length. The first was 27.5m in width, and the three remaining pens each 22.5m in width. A fifth pen was approved in September 1942 with construction beginning in May 1943 and completion in April 1944. This fifth pen, like the first, was 27.5m in width. Overall dimensions of the bunker were 153m in width and 139m in length.

The fifth pen was built slightly higher than the original pens, so that its roof could be supported by the edge of the original fourth pen. To the rear of the first four pens was a work area stretching back a further 20m; this same area behind the final, fifth pen stretched back for 39.5m.

The bunker could accommodate up to 15 boats, with three side by side in each pen. Landward access was by a single door on the west side of the bunker and a double door on the east. To the rear, on the east side of the projecting fifth pen, was a further single entrance door.

As with Elbe II, the Fink II bunker was intended primarily to give shelter to U-boats constructed at the adjacent yards whilst fitting out or being repaired or

refitted. Protection against low-level bombing was provided by three 3.7cm flak positions on the bunker roof.

The bunker did not suffer any particularly serious bombing raids until April 1945 when it suffered two separate attacks. The first, on 4 April, was a daylight raid carried out by US bombers with special armour-piercing bombs, and caused little or no damage. The second, on 9 April, was carried out by 17 Lancaster bombers carrying the massive five-ton Tallboy bombs, as well as two of the Grand Slam 10-ton bombs. Of the 17 bombs dropped, six hit the bunker. The roof of the bunker was actually penetrated, but it was the pressure wave from the explosion that caused the greatest damage. A number of Type XXIII boats inside received minor damage, whilst the floating dry dock containing two boats in the new fifth pen sank: the boats inside, U-677 and U-982, although submerged, remained relatively undamaged. The massive structure survived, though, and ended the war virtually intact.

HELGOLAND
Nordsee III
Helgoland was a long-established German naval base and a logical spot for the construction of a U-boat bunker. Plans were drawn up as early as 1939 and by 1940 work was well under way; construction was completed in June 1941. The principal contractor for excavation work was Grün & Bilfinger and for actual construction the Hamburg firm of Dyckerhoff & Widmann AG was selected.

The bunker was a fairly modest one, lying in the east basin of the harbour on Helgoland. It comprised only three pens, all of which were wet pens; each could accommodate three submarines. A floating dry dock was also provided which could be towed into one of the pens should dry repair facilities be required. The dry dock could accommodate only a single submarine.

The bunker was 156m in length and 94m in width, each pen being approximately 108m long and 22m wide, with a 6m-wide quay separating each pen. The roof

The Nordsee III U-boat bunker at Helgoland saw only limited use as an operational base, serving more as a repair and maintenance facility. This complex was used as a base for the Seehund midget submarines from the summer of 1944. It was also used to house E-boats.

was some 3m thick and the walls 2m thick. To the rear of the easternmost pen lay a workshop for periscopes and optical equipment as well as torpedo storage, whilst to the rear of the westernmost pen was a workshop area with welding facilities and also an oxygen tank storage area and a carpenters' workshop.

Of less importance to the U-boat war than many other bunker complexes, Nordsee III did not come in for much attention from Allied bombers until late in the war. There were no resident flotillas, and once the French and Norwegian bases fell into German hands, Nordsee III saw only 'passing trade' with boats calling in for repair or resupply. In fact, the U-boat bunkers were used just as often, if not more often, to shelter small surface craft such as E-boats.

After the Allied landings in Normandy in June 1944, the Nordsee III bunker became a staging point for the Seehund-type midget submarines under Vizeadmiral Heye, on their way from Wilhelmshaven to the invasion front, and at one point even housed a number of so-called *Sprengboote*. These were small motor boats packed with explosives which were driven directly at their targets, the operator leaping overboard at the last possible moment and being picked up by a control boat.

Defences on the bunker itself were fairly light, comprising just two 3.7cm flak guns and one 2cm flak gun together with a 2m searchlight. From late 1944, however, both the USAAF and RAF began to mount raids against the Helgoland base. A total of six major raids were launched against the complex between 1941 and 1945, the RAF raid on 18 April 1945 involving over 960 bombers. A final raid on the following day saw just 36 bombers drop 22 Tallboy bombs. The U-boat bunker suffered no significant damage in any of these attacks and was still completely intact at the end of the war.

KIEL
Kilian
Sited on the east bank of Kiel harbour, the relatively small Kilian bunker was built during the winter of 1941/42 to provide protection for newly built U-boats

The Kilian bunker at Kiel just before its demolition. This was not an operational base as such but housed newly built boats before their allocation to a flotilla and was also used as a repair facility for front-line boats.

This photograph shows a Type VIIC boat on its special cradle moving along the special transverse rail to line it up with the repair bunker at extreme right in this shot, the rails leading into its interior being just visible.

before they were allocated to their operational flotillas, as well as for the repair of operational and training boats.

Two pens were provided, separated by an internal dividing wall, each 138m long and 23m wide, allowing two boats to be accommodated one behind the other with three side by side. The bunker could therefore accommodate a total of 12 boats at full capacity. On the north-west (front) corner of the bunker was a small concrete tower to accommodate a flak gun position. Only a relatively small area of the bunker was allocated to workshop space, though this was spread over three floors (ground and two upper floors).

The overall length of the bunker was 176m, with walls just over 3m thick and a 4.8m-thick roof. Protection for the interior was provided by seven thick, hanging, overlapping steel plates forming a door, which reached down to water level. There was no special protection below water level.

The bunker was finally completed on 13 November 1943, having taken around one year to construct. U-1101, a Type VIIC, became the first U-boat to enter the bunker. The labour force consisted of well over 1,000 men, working around the clock in two shifts, and comprising to a large degree forced labourers, camp inmates and prisoners of war. The death rate amongst the workers, for whom no provision for shelter was made during bombing raids, was extremely high.

The principal contractor for the construction of Kilian was the firm of Dyckerhoff & Widmann AG. Initially, the bunker escaped the attentions of the Allies, and general raids on Kiel harbour facilities saw Kilian remain unscathed. On 9 April 1945, however, a massive bombing raid, which sank the pocket battleship *Admiral Scheer*, saw the protective doors of the bunker blown off by a near miss. Inside the bunker at this time were two U-boats, U-170 (not a new boat, but being used as a test bed) and U-4708. So great was the pressure wave from the bomb blast that the small Type XXIII U-4708 was lifted into the air and smashed against the side of the pen, causing such damage that she sank almost immediately. The larger and more robust U-170 escaped destruction. The concrete structure of the bunker remained intact and survived the war. The last few U-boats resident within were scuttled or blown up at the end of the war.

Konrad

This bunker was in fact a conversion of an existing facility, namely the Dry Dock III of the Deutsche Werke construction yard. Work commenced in April 1943, the intention being to provide shelter for boats undergoing minor repair or fitting-out work. During construction, the decision was made to change this to a production facility. Bombing raids slowed construction, which was not completed until October 1944. Work on this bunker was shared by a number of contractors including Wayss & Freytag AG, Habermann & Guckes AG, Holzverartbeitung GmbH and G. Tesch of Berlin.

The bunker was just over 162m in length, 35m in width and 13m in height. It was used to facilitate the construction of Seehund mini-submarines and also modular sections of the Type XXI. Subsequent bombing raids after the completion of the facility did little damage and the bunker survived the war intact.

BREMEN

Built on the north bank of the River Weser at Bremen, this complex was commissioned in early 1944. It was basically a sheltered construction complex which would be used (together with the much bigger Valentin bunker) to build the revolutionary Type XXI U-boat. The Type XXI's design integrated modular

The landward end of the massive Valentin bunker under construction. One of the steel roof-supporting arches can be seen at left, still not encased in concrete. Below this is the topmost workshop level.

sections so that the construction work could be distributed to suitable sites throughout Germany, sometimes far inland, then transported to assembly points at various shipyards for completion, launch and fitting out. A Type XXI could be built in about 176 days, about half the time it took to put together a Type VII or Type IX. The bunker was to be erected on land belonging to the Deschimar firm in Bremen on which an assembly yard had already been established. The bunker would simply protect this facility with a reinforced-concrete shell. The construction contract was awarded to the Hamburg firm of Wayss & Freytag.

In the eastern end of the bunker, which lay on a virtual east–west axis, an assembly line for the production of sectional modules was planned, whilst the centre section of the complex was to consist of two dry-dock pens for repair work. These pens would be connected to the westernmost section that consisted of two wet pens (but capable of being pumped out for dry-dock work), each capable of housing two Type XXIs. The pen areas were connected to each other, and to the exterior, by lock gates.

A heavy bombing raid by the USAAF on 30 March 1945 destroyed much of the construction, which was never completed.

Valentin

Plans were first made in 1943 for the erection of a protected assembly facility on the banks of the River Weser at Farge near Bremen. This was to be a custom-built facility for the assembly of the Type XXI U-boat. One of the principal reasons why this excellent submarine could not be brought into service soon enough to influence the war at sea was the interruption to the building programme caused by Allied air raids – hence the decision to build this massive, reinforced-concrete protected facility. The facility was a virtual assembly line: the partially assembled boats moved through various stages until, finally finished, they were lowered into a wet pen and sailed out into the River Weser from the bunker.

The Type XXI consisted of eight hull sections, numbered from stern to bow, plus the conning tower. Main assembly points for this submarine were at the Blohm & Voss yard at Hamburg, Schichau in Danzig and at Deschimar AG Weser in Bremen, with Blohm & Voss producing the greatest number. As soon as the Allies became aware that this revolutionary new boat was being assembled at Blohm & Voss, the yard came under persistent attack by Allied bombers and suffered serious damage. Valentin, had it reached completion, would have been a valuable asset.

Over 12,000 workers were employed in the construction of this gigantic bunker, of which around one third were foreign, and although many were volunteers, it has been suggested that over 2,500 were either prisoner-of-war forced labourers

TYPE XXI U-BOATS UNDER CONSTRUCTION AT VALENTIN, BREMEN

The Type XXI was assembled from pre-fabricated sections, the manufacture of which was subcontracted to various firms throughout Germany. These sections could be brought into the complex overland or up river by barge, and into the bunker via the opening into the River Weser.

The 13-stage assembly process would have begun in the south-west corner of the complex (**A**), where stages one to three would see the keel being laid and the partially completed hull modules welded together. Moving on 30-ton trolleys, each unit would be shifted northwards right to the opposite end of the bunker, where it would then be traversed into the central section (**B**) and moved back along the bunker. Here, during stages four to eight, the welding work would be completed, machinery installed, the tanks tested and the conning tower added.

On reaching the far end of the bunker, the boat would undergo stages nine and ten where its batteries, periscopes and *Schnorchel* tube would be fitted: the periscopes were lowered into place using a five-ton overhead crane (**C**). The roof of the bunker was higher at this point to allow for the extreme length of the periscope. The boat then reversed direction again, and moved towards the bunker exit. Through stages 11 and 12 the final fitting out was done, the antennae installed. Then (stage 13) the boat moved sideways into the flooded end chamber and into water some 9m deep, where it was tested to ensure it was watertight and fuel and oil taken on. The completed boat would then be moved

out into the River Weser. The seaward entrance/exit was protected by lock gates. The rear area (**D**), as in most bunkers, was given over to workshops, stores and similar units.

There were four levels in the Valentin complex. At ground level were the boiler house, assembly and mechanical workshops, toolmakers' workshop, a smithy and heat-treating workshop, a first-aid room and toilets.

A mezzanine floor was intended to accommodate an administrative area with various offices for quality control, provisions, medical supplies, accounts, a tool store, a despatch office and further toilet facilities. Among the facilities planned for the first floor were a battery storeroom, a plumbers' workshop, carpenters' shop, timber store, electrical workshop, metalworking shop and sheet metal store. At roof level more office accommodation was planned, including offices for the various managers of construction, personnel, business managers, accounts as well as radio operators and telegraphists. There were also stores for sheet metal, piping, wire, screws and other standard components plus oil storage.

The first orders for Valentin-produced Type XXI U-boats were placed in May 1944, with the first boats scheduled to be completed in October of that year. Delays in construction of the complex saw the first estimated launch put back until April 1945 – but the war ended before any boats could be produced at this facility. The current German Navy still uses the various storage and office areas at the rear of the bunker. (Artwork by Ian Palmer © Osprey Publishing) or concentration camp inmates. It is estimated that at least 4,000 died during the construction work on this bunker. Work ceased on 7 April 1945, at which point the bunker was around 90 per cent complete.

Allied bombing raids in late March 1945 succeeded in penetrating the partially completed structure with Tallboy bombs, but little damage was caused to the interior. There were only two major air raids, one on 27 March 1945 by the USAAF and one on 30 March by the RAF. The latter saw 15 Tallboys dropped, of which six were direct hits.

BERGEN
Bruno

Shortly after the invasion of Norway in 1940, the Germans established naval bases at several ports, Bergen being one of the most important. In May 1942 work commenced on the construction of a U-boat bunker at the Norwegian port. The bunker was built on a rocky outcrop in a small bay to the west of the town.

The bunker was planned to consist of ten pens, three of which would be wet and six dry. The tenth would be used for fuel storage. In the event, just seven pens were constructed: one of these was used for fuel storage, and of the remaining six, three were wet and three dry. The roof was up to 6m thick in places and

An operational boat is undergoing repair and maintenance in a dry-dock capable pen. The pen has been fully drained, so that the engineers can examine a damaged propeller. Just below the ceiling is the mobile gantry crane. The corrugated steel shuttering on the ceiling was to prevent any masonry dislodged by a heavy-bomb direct hit from becoming dislodged and crashing down onto any boat within the pen. On each side of the quay were fairly narrow walkways around 2.5m wide. (Artwork by Ian Palmer © Osprey Publishing)

The accommodation blocks for U-boat crewmen based in Bergen in Norway. After the Allied invasion of France resulted in the loss of all the Atlantic U-boat bases, the bases in Norway took on a much greater significance.

The accommodation blocks for U-boat crewmen based in Bergen in Norway. After the Allied invasion of France resulted in the loss of all the Atlantic U-boat bases, the bases in Norway took on a much greater significance.

the walls up to 4m thick. A further mezzanine level was built above the main bunker to provide additional storage space. This also had the beneficial effect of enhancing the level of protection against air attack for the bunker interior. The overall size of the Bruno bunker was 130m by 143m.

Unusually for such construction projects outside Germany, responsibility was not in the hands of the Organisation Todt. Instead a commercial construction firm, Wayss & Freytag AG, which had also worked on similar projects within Germany, was the main contractor. Each of the three wet pens, on the north side of the bunker, was 11m wide, and the dry pens 17m wide. Their entrances were protected by 3cm-thick steel doors formed by hanging, overlapping plates.

The base was to be the home of 11. Unterseebootsflotille for most of the war and following the Allied invasion of Normandy took on an even greater strategic importance as the French bases were, one by one, closed down and abandoned.

Work to enlarge and improve the bunker continued throughout the war. As the importance of the Bergen U-boat base grew, so did the Allied determination to destroy it. The first major bombing raid, comprising over 130 RAF bombers, took place on 4 October 1944. Although the RAF raid caused widespread destruction to the surrounding area and serious civilian casualties, its effect on the bunkers was minimal. Direct hits were achieved, but none succeeded in penetrating the thick, reinforced-concrete shell.

A further attack on 29 October saw almost 250 RAF aircraft involved, though fewer than 50 eventually found and bombed the target. Not one German casualty was inflicted, though once again there was considerable loss of civilian life. No damage was suffered by the bunker interior, all of the blast effect being dissipated in the space between the outer and inner roof levels. A third and final

The Dora II bunker under construction. The construction of these bunkers required huge resources in men and materials, both of which were in short supply towards the end of the war, and hostilities ended before Dora II was completed.

raid on 12 January 1945 was launched by 32 RAF bombers carrying Tallboy bombs. The bunkers at Bergen survived the war intact.

TRONDHEIM

Dora I

The U-boat bunker at Trondheim was the first to be constructed in Norway. It was a relatively small structure, measuring some 153m in length and 111m in width, with just five pens. Of these, three were 15m in width, had dry-dock capabilities and could accommodate just one boat each; two were 21m-wide wet pens, each of which could accommodate two boats. The main purpose of the bunker was to provide repair facilities for 13. Unterseebootsflotille. Air-raid protection was provided by three 2cm flak installations on the bunker roof.

As with most bunkers outside Germany, construction was overseen by the Organisation Todt, and specifically by the OT-Einsatzgruppe Wiking. The principal contractor was the Munich firm of Sager & Wörner. Orders for construction of the bunker were issued at the start of 1941 and it took fully 27 months to complete the work. Several thousand workers were involved, including around 800 Soviet prisoners of war used as forced labour.

Only one major air raid, on 24 July 1943, was suffered by the Dora I bunker: a subsequent raid launched on 22 November 1944, comprising over 170 RAF bombers, was abandoned because of poor visibility over the target area. Dora I survived the war intact.

Dora II

Almost as soon as work on Dora I had commenced, it was realised that a greater capacity would be required and planning began for a new bunker (Dora II) in the same harbour and just 140m away. Dora II was to have four additional pens, two

13.5m-wide wet and two 20m-wide dry, thus allowing for the accommodation of a further six boats.

Immediately behind the dry pens was the boiler room, and behind the wet pens a storage space. Running the full width of the bunker behind these would be all of the electrical gear for the bunker and, further to the rear, workshops for repairing the boats' battery cells, as well as torpedo storage areas.

Unfortunately, the demand for skilled workers by the huge bunkers being constructed in France meant that the small workforce available for the second bunker at Trondheim made slow progress and the structure was only 60 per cent complete when the war ended. A third bunker, Dora III, was also planned at Leangen, just to the east of Trondheim, but the project was cancelled before any serious construction work had been done.

BREST

Almost as soon as construction work on the pens began in January 1941 (see 'Tour of a U-Boat Base', p.96, for details), the site was subjected to Allied air raids. In the spring of 1943, work began on strengthening the roof of the bunker. Ultimately the roof had a thickness in excess of 6m, and a layer of concrete beams was laid across the roof some 3.8m above its surface (the *Fangrost* concept): these beams were around 1.5m high and spaced about the same distance apart.

Continued air raids caused very little damage to the bunkers and cost the Allies dearly in lost aircraft. Air defence for the bunker itself was provided by three 4cm flak guns in concrete emplacements and controlled by their own radar equipment.

Eventually, however, a series of Tallboy raids in early August 1944 was launched against the Brest U-boat bunkers. A total of nine direct hits were scored from 26 bombs dropped. Of these five actually penetrated the roof, but caused little or no damage to the interior and none whatsoever to the U-boats inside.

Throughout the war the U-boat bunker at Brest suffered more enemy air raids than any other base. Over 80 large-scale raids were launched between 1941 and 1945, and of these 11 were the so-called 'hundred-bomber raids' with up to 154 aircraft taking part. Around 50 aircraft were either shot down in these raids, or so badly damaged that they were destroyed on landing.

The rapid progress being made by Allied troops following the Normandy landings in June 1944 saw the U-boat bunker at Brest under serious threat. The last U-boat to depart from the bunker was U-256, under the command of

This shot shows a Type IX boat emerging from one of the repair bunkers at the Keroman complex at Lorient, the scale afforded by the crew members perched precariously on its bow showing just how large these boats were.

Korvettenkapitän Heinrich Lehmann-Willenbrock, which left on 4 September. Lehmann-Willenbrock was the real-life commander of U-96, upon which the fictional film *Das Boot* was based.

US forces finally captured the port on 21 September 1944 after four weeks of extremely bitter fighting. The US Army suffered over 10,000 casualties in this battle by the end of which the port itself had been almost totally destroyed – except for the U-boat bunker, which remained intact.

LORIENT

The port of Lorient fell to the German Army on 21 June 1940, and just 16 days later the first U-boat (U-30 under Kapitänleutnant Fritz-Julius Lemp) docked at the port for resupply. Lorient soon became one of the Kriegsmarine's most important U-boat bases. The base eventually housed two flotillas, 2. Unterseebootsflotille *Salzwedel* and 10. Unterseebootsflotille.

The first facility provided for U-boats was a winching system for pulling smaller vessels out of the water for inspection and repair. This was based around a smaller pre-existing facility for fishing boats on the Keroman peninsula, which was upgraded and enlarged. Here fishing boats were winched up a ramp onto a turntable, which could then direct them onto one of six sets of stocks. Because of both the limited capacity of the winching mechanisms and the size of the bunkers, these were used only for smaller U-boats.

The next major improvement was the building of the two so-called *Dom* bunkers or 'cathedral bunkers', also at Keroman: they acquired their name because of their high, arched roofs. These small bunkers were built at the fishing-boat repair facility, immediately to the east of the main complex, over the two southernmost

A Type II U-boat, disguised under tarpaulins, sits on its special cradle for transport into a *Dom* bunker after being winched ashore. Note the turntable in the background for directing the boat towards the appropriate bunker.

positions. Built by the firm of Carl Brand of Düren, each bunker was 81m long, 16m wide and 25m high and had walls some 1.5m thick. U-boats could be winched on trolleys directly from the water and along into these dry bunkers. They were nowhere near as well protected as the main bunker complex: they were intended to provide U-boats undergoing repair and maintenance with some measure of protection from shrapnel and the like. They were strong, but would not have been able to withstand a direct hit from a Tallboy as the main bunkers did on several occasions.

In April 1941, a more conventional-style U-boat bunker was also built further up the River Scorff, on the eastern bank across from the existing port dry-dock facilities. Known as the 'Scorff bunker' for obvious reasons, this structure consisted of two pens just over 100m long with workshop and repair facilities to the rear of the structure. The overall length of the bunker was 128m.

Surveyors meantime had been searching for a suitable location for the creation of a larger bunker complex. Once again the Keroman peninsula was chosen, and an area extending to around 50 acres was taken over by the Kriegsmarine. Work on the first bunker, subsequently known as Keroman I, began in 1941 with over 15,000 workers being employed in construction.

A rather ingenious design was created for this particular complex. The bunker consisted of a well-protected, enclosed wet bunker with five pens. On the east side of the bunker was an enclosed berth, the floor of which was sloped. Sitting on this ramp was a 45m-long cradle into which the boat sailed. The water in this berth would then be pumped out, effectively lowering the boat into the cradle which sat on a wheeled trolley, with the aid of an overhead crane. The trolley was then winched up a 160m sloped slipway: at the top, the cradle was moved from the trolley onto a similarly designed 48m-long traversing unit. This unit moved backwards and forwards along eight sets of rails, running between the two sets of five dry pens, allowing it to be brought perfectly in line with any of the individual pens. The trolley unit was then run off the traverser into the selected pen. The operation to move the submarine from Keroman I across exposed open space into the safe bunkers of Keroman II (see below) took between one and two hours from start to finish. The unique equipment was manufactured by the MAN (Maschinenfabrik Augsburg-Nürnberg) firm, and this amazing system was so well built that it is still fully functional today.

The pens in Keroman I were 120m long, 85m wide and 18.5m in height, with 2.4m-thick walls and a roof over 3m thick. Each pen was provided with a travelling crane. Keroman I was completed in September 1941. At the same time, work was under way on a further bunker complex, known as Keroman II, directly in line with the existing complex at the top of the slope. This contained a further seven dry pens, each 138m long, 120m wide and 18.5m in height. Each

One of the two *Dom* bunkers at Lorient. These smaller bunkers were used for repair and maintenance on the smaller Type II U-boats which were winched onto land and transported on a cradle along specially laid tracks.

KEROMAN I, II AND III, LORIENT

The largest and most impressive of all complexes was the one at Lorient. This illustration shows the entire complex.

At the former fishing-boat repair site (**1**) boats would be pulled up the ramp by winch onto the central turntable unit (**2**), which would then rotate to send the boat on its cradle towards one of the *Dom* bunkers shown around the central turntable (**3** and **4**).

At bottom right is the Keroman III bunker (**A**), a large unit with seven pens opening out into the River Le Ter. In the lower left of the illustration is the original Keroman I bunker (**B**): note the pen opening into the Le Ter (**5**). This entrance led to the ramp (**6**) that gave access to the upper-level Keroman II bunker (**C**), protected by a lock gate. The pen interior would be drained and the boat lowered by an overhead crane onto a special cradle on a wheeled trolley. It would then be winched up the 160m-long slope and onto the traversing unit (**7**) running between Keroman I and Keroman II. This unit was 48m long and 13m wide and ran along an eight-rail track. In addition to the entrance pen, Keroman I (**B**) had a total of five dry repair pens.

Directly opposite, in Keroman II (**C**), there were a further seven repair pens. The traversing unit allowed the boat to be lined up with any of the repair pens and winched along a four-rail track into the appropriate pen. It would normally take around two hours for a boat to be taken out of the water, winched up the slope and received into one of the repair pens. The traverser units themselves were stored in a separate pen alongside Keroman II (**8**).

An extension to Keroman II (Keroman IVb) and an extension to Keroman I (Keroman IVa) are shown under construction (**9**), though neither was ever completed: the resources were channelled into the construction of Keroman III instead.

(Artwork by Ian Palmer © Osprey Publishing)

The twin pens of the Scorff bunker at Lorient just prior to its completion, the left pen still being protected by a coffer dam. The concrete structure at the centre of the roof is a flak gun emplacement.

pen in Keroman II was provided with two travelling cranes. An eighth pen was also built but this contained the equipment for the traversing unit.

A third bunker, Keroman III, was begun in October 1941 and completed in January 1943. This provided a further seven pens, all opening out directly into deep water and capable of being used for both wet and dry docking. The pens were 170m long, 135m wide and 20m in height and each was provided with a travelling crane. The concrete roof was over 7m thick.

A further bunker complex, Keroman IV, was planned to provide facilities for the new Type XXI submarines, but owing to Germany's wartime reversals, this project was not carried through.

In addition to the bunker complex proper, the entire Lorient base was liberally peppered with smaller bunkers, including a complex of six torpedo storage bunkers to the north-west of the Keroman complex, linked to the base by a narrow-gauge track. The Lorient base was also heavily defended by a huge range of anti-aircraft artillery ranging from light 2cm flak guns, of which there were over 200, through medium 7.5cm and 8.8cm pieces, up to heavy 10.5cm and 12.8cm flak guns.

The bunker complexes at Lorient were bombed on numerous occasions but no serious damage was ever inflicted. A total of 33 significant air raids on the bunkers were recorded, though only one of these, on 17 May 1943, involved over 100 aircraft. At least 60 enemy aircraft were either shot down or seriously damaged during these raids. Additional protection against low-level attack by enemy aircraft was provided by mooring two elderly ships directly in front of the bunkers: they had particularly tall masts and barrage balloons tethered to their superstructure. Despite the Allied advances through France, the German garrison at Lorient held out right until the end of the war. The last U-boat to leave, U-155, departed on 5 September 1944, with two other boats, the severely damaged U-123 and U-129, left behind. The port finally surrendered to US Army troops on 10 May 1945, two days after VE-Day.

ST NAZAIRE

The port of St Nazaire fell to the Germans in the summer of 1940. Work on constructing the U-boat bunkers began in March 1941 in the southern basin of the harbour. The first four of an eventual total of 14 pens were ready for use by July 1941 whilst work continued on the remainder of the structure. The first five pens were some 130m long and 18m high. Each was 14m wide with a dividing wall between each pen 1.25m to 1.5m thick. Separating Pen 1 from the north-side exterior was a 22m-wide storage space area, running the full length of the

During the final stages of construction at Lorient, some of the wood shuttering still being in place around the concrete. The pens are already flooded ready to accept their first boats. The guard at the left is a member of the Organisation Todt, responsible for the construction.

pen. Between Pens 5 and 6 was a storage area running the length of the pen and some 8m wide. Pens 6 to 8 were identical to the first five. Then followed Pens 9 to 12, shorter than the previous pens at just 124m in length, but wider at 20m and separated by dividing walls 1.25m thick. A further space some 8m wide separated Pen 12 from Pens 13 and 14 which once again were 20m wide.

To the rear of the bunker complex, immediately behind each pen, were a number of workshop areas, each the same width as the pen. On the north and south side walls of the complex, in line with the rear of the pens, was a 5m-wide entrance door leading to a corridor running the full width of the complex. Overall the bunker complex was 295m wide. Six of the pens were wet whilst the others were capable of being pumped out and used for dry-docking. Its first resident U-boat flotilla, 7. Unterseebootsflotille *Wegener*, arrived in June 1941. In February 1942, the Wegener flotilla was joined at St Nazaire by 6. Untersee-bootsflotille *Hundius*.

In mid-1943 the Organisation Todt began work on reinforcing the bunker roof, adding almost 4m to its thickness. Originally, U-boats had first to enter the main (north) basin via the Normandie dock, and then to pass through a smaller lock into the southern basin. The British commando attack in March 1942, when the explosive-laden destroyer HMS *Campbeltown* was rammed into the gate of the dock and detonated, highlighted the vulnerability of the system. Accordingly, a new lock was built directly opposite the entrance to the bunkers, giving direct access to open water and protected by a concrete bunker.

The bunkers proved themselves during numerous Allied air raids, with no loss or damage suffered by any U-boat inside – despite the almost total destruction of the town. In all, 30 major raids were recorded on the St Nazaire bunkers, three in particular being extremely heavy. On 28 February 1943, over 430 RAF bombers pounded the port. This was followed on 22 March by another raid involving over 350 aircraft, and one on 28 March of over 320 aircraft. A total of 58 enemy aircraft are recorded as having been lost during these raids.

Following D-Day, the U-boats based at St Nazaire were withdrawn to Norway, the last of this batch (U-267) departing on 23 September 1944. The base, though, was rigorously defended, having been declared by Hitler to be a 'fortress'. Troops under the command of Generalleutnant Junck resisted all Allied attempts to take the port until the very last day of the war. During this period, however, numerous U-boats made the trip to St Nazaire carrying essential supplies: as late as February 1945, U-275 docked for repairs to its *Schnorchel* equipment. The very last boat to leave was U-255, which had been languishing at St Nazaire for some time awaiting repairs. Following the arrival in the autumn of 1944 of a seaplane carrying spare parts, repair work was carried out and U-255 eventually left St Nazaire on 8 May 1945, just in time to surrender to the Allies.

The interior of one of the St Nazaire pens today, used now for mooring small sailing boats. Note the gaps in the wall leading between the pens. (Mark Wood)

The last boat to put in to St Nazaire was U-510, which arrived at the end of a long voyage from the Far East on 23 April 1945. She was still there when the Allies finally took over the port, and was in such good order that she was taken into the French Navy where she served as the *Bouan*.

LA PALLICE

This base, often erroneously referred to as La Rochelle, fell to the Germans in 1940, but did not become a major U-boat operational base until the autumn of 1941. Initially, it was used by the submarines of the Italian Navy, but in the spring of 1941 it was decided that a new U-boat base would be built on the eastern side of the main basin of this port. Construction of the bunker began in April 1941 and on 27 October of that year, following the completion of the first two pens, it became home to 3. Unterseebootsflotille *Lohs*. The first U-boats arrived within three weeks.

Around 490 Organisation Todt personnel were involved in the construction of this bunker, overseeing 1,800 labourers. The bunker complex was to consist of ten pens. The first two to be completed were wet pens, 92.5m in length and 17m in width, allowing each to accommodate two boats. Pens 3 to 7 were dry-dock-capable, also 92.5m in length but just 11m wide, each capable of accommodating a single boat. Pens 8 and 9 were also dry-dock-capable but slightly longer at 100m. Pen 10, also intended to function as a dry dock, was never fully completed. It was to be 17m wide and capable of accommodating two boats.

The quays separating each pen were between 4.25m and 5m wide with a dividing wall running down the centre of each. The exception to this was the space between Pens 7 and 8, which consisted of a 15m-wide quay running all the way through the bunker complex and extending out into the basin as a 200m-long mole. This mole also carried twin railway lines.

Overall, the complex measured 195m by 165m and was 14m high. The roof thickness over Pens 1 to 5 was in excess of 7m. Work was still in progress to increase the existing 6.5m-thick roof over the remaining pens and to install bomb traps when the worsening war situation brought this to a halt. On the exterior, at the north-eastern corner of the rear of the bunker, was a 30m-wide and 50m-long concrete structure, some 25m high: this contained a generating station for the bunker. Against the southern side wall of the bunker by the side entrance door was an oil storage bunker.

The bunker suffered much less from the attentions of enemy bombers than some of its counterparts, only eight major raids being launched against it, none of which did any serious damage to the pens. Anti-aircraft defences on the bunker complex consisted of three concrete emplacements for 2cm light flak guns. In addition to the U-boat bunker complex, numerous other subsidiary bunkers were constructed, including three large torpedo storage bunkers around a kilometre to the north-east of the U-boat bunker complex. A command bunker and a small bunker housing the electricity transformer were located to the west of these storage bunkers. Also, a large bunker-type construction was built over the lock that allowed entrance into the basin where the U-boat bunker complex was located.

As with the other French bases, its usefulness decreased after 6 June 1944 and its boats were dispersed to other bases, primarily in Norway. This base, too, was declared a 'fortress' and its garrison held out until 8 May 1945. A Type VIIC U-boat (U-766) was still in residence when the base finally surrendered, and was taken into the French Navy as the *Laubie*.

BORDEAUX

The port at Bordeaux became an operational Axis naval base in the autumn of 1940 when it became home to the Italian Navy's submarine flotilla Betasom, whose operational success was, it must be said, somewhat limited. Admiral Dönitz decided in mid-1941 to erect a protective U-boat bunker in the port's Number 2 basin, entered first through a lock from the River Gironde into the Number 1 basin, then through a further lock between the two.

The U-boat bunker comprised 11 pens. Pens 1 to 4 were wet pens 105m long and 20m wide, capable of accommodating two boats each. Pens 5 to 8 were also 105m long, but just 14m wide, designed to accommodate one boat each. Pens 9 to 11 were dry-dock-capable, and were 95m long and 11m wide. Overall, the complex was 245m wide, 162m long and 19m high, with roofing just under 6m thick. At the north-east corner of the structure was a 58m-wide and 73m-long concrete blockhouse containing the bunker boiler room and electrical equipment.

The bunkers at Lorient near completion. Note the level of overhang of the roof, giving additional protection to the interior. The Lorient base survived virtually intact and was used by the French Navy after the war. It still survives today.

This base primarily served the larger Type IX boats used for long-distance cruises, as well as the Type XIV Milk Cows and the Type XB minelayers. Bordeaux became the home base for 12. Unterseebootsflotille, which also took over the remaining Italian submarines after Italy's surrender. All but one of these Italian submarines sailed from Bordeaux to the Far East on transport missions, some eventually being taken over by the Imperial Japanese Navy – thus having served three different masters.

Earlier in the war, Bordeaux was also visited by Japanese submarines, which successfully made the long journey from Japan to occupied Europe. As with all the French bases, Bordeaux came under attack by Allied bombers. However, the port suffered only seven major air raids from 1940 through to mid-1944: two larger bombing raids in August 1944 saw the bunkers suffer little or no serious damage. The base was finally abandoned in late August 1944 and was occupied by Free French Forces on the 26th of that month, the last few U-boats having put to sea just two days earlier.

AFTER THE WAR – THE FATE OF THE BASES

HAMBURG

At the end of the war, the Elbe II bunker fell into British hands intact. On 11 November 1945, British troops from the Royal Engineers blew up the bunker, using a stock of captured German Luftwaffe bombs: this caused the central dividing wall between the two bunkers to collapse and, without this support, the roof partially caved in. Three Type XXI boats, U-2505, U-3004 and U-3506, were still inside. The demolition work resulted in the roof totally crushing U-3506 when it came down, though the other two remained reasonably intact.

In 1949 the first salvage work on the U-boats inside the bunker began. The boats were pumped dry and internal components such as the precious accumulator cells, copper cabling and some diesel engines, were removed from the wrecks of the Type XXIs. U-2501, which had been sunk right at the entrance to the bunker in May 1945, was raised and scrapped during the 1950s; further operations saw the stern sections of U-2505 and U-3004 blown off to allow further materials to be salvaged. At this point work stopped owing to the unsafe nature of the bunker. The Type XXIs were left largely undisturbed for several decades – apart from the attention of souvenir hunters who discovered that access to the bunker was still possible, and would descend on the boats when they were briefly exposed at low tide.

In the early 1960s, some attempts were made to clear the site and a substantial quantity of reinforced concrete was removed before escalating costs forced a halt to the project. No further attempts were made to complete the demolition, a decision in which the sheer cost of such an operation played a major role.

A decision was finally made in 1995 to infill the pens, partly because they were still accessible and clearly in a dangerous state. It was feared that lives would be lost as it was proving impossible to keep souvenir hunters away. It was by now completely out of the question that the bunker might be demolished, as estimated costs had risen to a staggering DM 300,000,000. By 8 October 1995, the remains of the two Type XXIs had been buried under countless tons of sand. No further efforts to clear the partly demolished remains seem to have been made yet. Officially, there is no access to the area today but there is little or nothing to prevent a visit to the site. The bunker remains lie within the port of Hamburg, on the south bank of the River Elbe which runs through the city, just by the Vulkanhafen yard.

The Valentin bunker today. It is still used by the German military as a storage facility. The cost of demolition of such structures was astronomical so many were simply left standing and put to the most practical use possible.

In October 1945, the intact Fink II bunker was used by the Royal Engineers to effectively kill two birds with one stone. The bunker was filled with over 30 tons of unexploded German bombs from Luftwaffe stores that had fallen into British hands and needed to be safely disposed of. The detonation of this ordnance rid the British of this dangerous material and also caused the collapse of the bunker, bringing down the roof and shattering the walls. Further demolition work was carried out after the City of Hamburg authorised the clearance of the site in 1949. One of the firms contracted to remove the remains of the bunker was, ironically, Dyckerhoff & Widmann AG, one of the main contractors for erecting the bunkers during the war years.

By the 1970s, the famed Deutsche Werft firm, on whose land the bunker stood, had succumbed to the general world recession. The whole site, including the bunker area, was cleared, with only a few small buildings remaining, all traces of Fink II having been removed. The area was grassed over and is now a recreation facility open to the public.

KIEL

Demolition work on the Kilian bunker in Kiel began in September 1945 when troops from the Royal Engineers began preparations for dynamiting the structure. Several weeks were spent drilling hundreds of holes into the concrete structure and packing them with explosives. As with the Fink II bunker, a quantity of unused Luftwaffe bombs were also packed into the exterior. The resultant explosion collapsed the dividing wall between the two pens and brought down the roof, crushing the remains of the Type XXI boat U-4708 still inside. The ruins were left in this state until 1959 when further clearance work was carried out by a German civil contractor. There still remains, however, considerable visible evidence of the bunker's presence. Although the roof and walls are gone and most of the pen area has been infilled and generally used as a dumping ground, at low tide the remains of the lower parts of the walls can be seen and part of the rear workshop area has been left standing. The vertical pillars of the entrance to the southernmost pen are still visible, as is the pier that separated the two pens, though this is now heavily overgrown. Since the late 1990s the Kilian remains have been open to the public, with guided tours available by special arrangement.

The other bunker at Kiel, Konrad, was blown up by the Royal Engineers in 1946, with much of the remains left in situ until the 1960s. At that point the remains were cleared to make way for the expansion of the Howaldtswerke shipyard. No trace of the bunker structure remains, and the area where it was situated is now open land.

BREMEN

The massive Valentin complex at Bremen was used after the war for bombing practice by both the RAF and USAAF. Some bomb penetration of this incomplete bunker had been achieved in March 1945, though the structure remained mostly intact. For some reason, unlike the other German bunkers, the British made no attempt to demolish this structure. Perhaps its sheer size and the potential cost of such an operation were influential. In the autumn of 1964, the bunker was once again taken over by the German Armed Forces and is still in use as a storage depot for the Bundesmarine: access to the interior is therefore not possible.

The Valentin bunker still stands today relatively intact, and this massive edifice is well worth a visit. It can be accessed by public road via the village of Farge, some 25km downstream from Bremen on the banks of the River Weser. Near the front entrance is a memorial to the forced labourers who lost their lives during the construction of this colossus. A public footpath runs along the south face of the bunker beside the banks of the Weser, and visitors can look into the exit which was to have allowed the Type XXI U-boats to sail out of the bunker and into the river. Although this final launch pen is still filled with water, there is no longer any direct route from the pen to the river, the bank having been built up and the channel leading to the Weser filled in.

HELGOLAND

The U-boat bunkers on Helgoland were still relatively intact at the end of the war; many of the other defensive structures (gun emplacements and the like), however, were destroyed. Many were destroyed or seriously damaged, although a number of powerful weapons still remained operable. On the cessation of hostilities, over

The Dora I bunker at Trondheim at the end of the war. Tied up alongside are a Type VII, U-861, and a Type IX, U-995. The Dora bunker was used after the war by the Royal Norwegian Navy.

4,500 German personnel, including over 1,100 civilian workers, were still on the fortress island. Most military personnel were then evacuated to the mainland, leaving only a small handover party, which formally surrendered the Helgoland fortifications to Admiral Gould of the Royal Navy on 11 May 1945.

Following the decision of the occupying powers to demilitarise Germany, in August 1945 a special force of demolition workers, mostly German and under the command of a Royal Navy officer, began work on preparing for the demolition of all surviving structures, including the U-boat bunkers. Thousands of tons of explosives were shipped to the island and added to the vast amounts of unused ammunition already on site. The surviving bunkers were packed full of ammunition and explosives.

On 18 April 1947, preparations were completed and all personnel withdrawn from the island. From a British warship lying some nine miles offshore, the explosives were detonated. The resultant explosion went into the record books as the largest man-made non-atomic explosion in history. The U-boat bunkers were totally destroyed. Little remains, although one tower has been converted into a lighthouse.

BERGEN
Shortly after the end of the war, troops of the Royal Engineers demolished a large part of the Bergen U-boat bunker complex. In 1949, however, the Royal Norwegian Navy repaired and refitted the dry-dock facilities and at the same time infilled Pens 4, 5 and 6, forming a quay alongside the dry-dock facilities. These, along with the workshop part of the bunker, are still in use by the Royal Norwegian Navy today, so access to the interior is not possible.

TRONDHEIM
As with the complex at Bergen, a large part of the Trondheim bunker Dora II was demolished by the Royal Engineers at the end of the war. Only a small portion (the workshop area) remains and is used by a civilian boat-building and repair firm for storage. Dora I, however, survived intact and was taken over by the Royal Norwegian Navy, continuing its original function as a submarine bunker. In 1955 it was decommissioned and handed over for civilian use as a storage facility: a car park was built on the roof of the bunker in 1988. The pens can be photographed from various vantage points around the harbour.

THE FRENCH BASES
The U-boat bunkers at these bases fell into Allied hands in almost perfect condition with no significant damage from enemy attacks, with the exception of Brest. For details of the fate of the French bases following war's end, as well as information on how to get to the most accessible and best preserved sites in France, see Appendix 1.

PART III

U-BOAT CREWS

Few members of any elite formation in World War II sacrificed so many of their number in battle as the crews of the German U-Bootwaffe. Estimates of losses vary between 75 and 80 per cent but, in spite of this horrific rate of attrition, the U-Bootwaffe maintained an amazing esprit de corps to the end. Despite the appalling conditions under which they fought, and the low survival rate of the average U-boat in the second half of the war, the 'Grey Wolves' of Grossadmiral Karl Dönitz fought their war in a fashion which retained an admirable degree of chivalry towards their foes. Apart from the notorious *Peleus* incident, for which Kapitänleutnant Eck was executed in November 1945, their record in this respect is far better than that of their Allied opponents. So much so, in fact, that Allied war heroes such as Admiral Chester Nimitz came forward to speak in defence of Dönitz's tactics when he was tried at Nuremberg. The media, however, have made sure that the world knows what the Germans were supposed to have done to others, but not what was done to the Germans, and the numerous reports of German survivors being killed have barely been investigated.

Kurt Baberg once wrote, 'Those who did not share our hardships will never know the strength of the bonds which tie us together.' The nature of U-boat warfare meant that every man had to have complete confidence in his fellow crewmen, for the life of every man on board might at some point depend on any

One of the proudest of days for the U-boat crewman was the commissioning day of his new boat, mustered on the deck in his best blues as the *Reichskriegsflagge* was run up the small flagstaff at the rear of the flak platform. Here the crew of U-735 celebrate the *Indienststellung* of their boat. (Author's collection)

other individual member of the crew. An average of 48 men on a Type VII (55 on a Type IX) lived, ate, slept and socialised (in what little free time they had) in a tiny, dark, smelly steel tube sometimes for months at a time and often in the appalling weather conditions of the North Atlantic. The bonds that were formed between these men, as with most truly elite forces, were deeply felt and long lasting. Even today, half a century later, former U-boat men retain a well-deserved pride in their accomplishments against tremendous odds.

Despite more recent post-war works which have sought to play down the achievements of Dönitz's U-boats, those who served in the U-Bootwaffe can take great pride in the famous quotation from Winston Churchill: 'The only thing that ever really frightened me during the war was the U-boat peril.'

RECRUITMENT

Although the U-Bootwaffe was by no means the volunteer force it is sometimes portrayed as, for most of the war there was no shortage of German sailors willing to volunteer for the so-called 'Freikorps Dönitz'. The massive unemployment levels in Germany, which resulted from the slump of the late 1920s and early 1930s, allowed the German Navy to be particularly selective when choosing from the seemingly unlimited pool of available manpower. Generally speaking, the navy looked for men with a technical background, such as mechanics or metal workers.

Prior to the outbreak of war, applicants for the navy had to be between the ages of 17 and 23. A prospective sailor would apply in writing to the II Admiral der Nordsee (North Sea) or Ostsee (Baltic) with full personal details such as height, weight, age, religion, plus details of any qualifications including educational achievements (at least a satisfactory standard leaving certificate from *Volksschule*), technical skills, knowledge of foreign languages, sporting achievements and service with the Reichsarbeitsdienst and any political organisations such as the Marine-Hitlerjugend. This was to be accompanied by two passport photographs and a Volunteer Certificate, which was only available from the police and proved that the applicant had no criminal record and that the personal details he had supplied were accurate. A declaration of Aryan origin and German nationality was also required later. If considered suitable, the applicant would be required to fill in a questionnaire and undergo a medical with a local doctor. It was also considered important that the prospective sailor had good teeth, because they would not be able to access dental services for extended periods.

Assuming he was acceptable, the recruit would then attend the local military district (*Wehrkreis*) registration office where he would undergo a more stringent

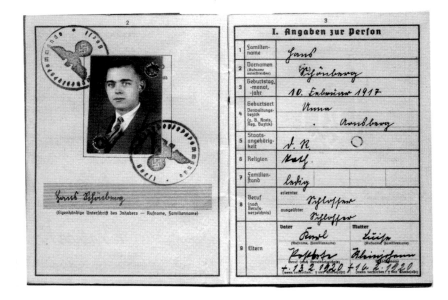

The *Wehrpass* of U-boat crewman Hans Schönberg. Issued when he first registered for military service, it was returned to his family as a keepsake after Schönberg was lost when his boat U-574 was sunk on 19 December 1941. Twenty members of the crew were rescued, but Schönberg was not one of the fortunate ones. (Author's collection)

medical and complete the paperwork required formally to enlist him. It would not be until 1941 that entry requirements would be relaxed somewhat to allow the general induction of unskilled manual workers. Having gone through the induction process, the sailor would be allocated to one of the Sailor Reserve Pools (*Schiffsstammdivision*) to begin training.

In Germany during the Third Reich period, on completing his education, the average young man would spend six months with the Reichsarbeitsdienst (Labour Service) to carry out construction projects, though it was effectively a paramilitary unit. On completion, he was liable for call-up. A telegram from the appropriate military district contained instructions to report for assessment and registration for military service. He would then be issued with a military pass (*Wehrpass*) as a form of personal ID, showing that he had either registered, or been assessed unfit for, military service: it proved that he had been officially 'processed'. On actual call-up this pass would be replaced with his official ID/paybook, the *Soldbuch,* which he would carry until killed in action or discharged at the end of his service, at which point the *Wehrpass* with details of his service and discharge would be returned to him or his next of kin.

In the period between registering and call-up, young men could volunteer for a particular branch of service rather than waiting to be allocated to one by the authorities. For many of those with technical skills, service as a volunteer in the navy would no doubt seem far preferable to service as a conscript in the army. Recruiting teams for the navy travelled throughout Germany and much of the statistical data relating to naval recruitment survived the war.

Germany made skilled use of propaganda. Successful U-boats and their commanders were heavily publicised, and postcard photographs of U-boat aces were avidly collected. Despite its massive superiority in sea power, Britain was being made to suffer, and the German people took the men of the U-Bootwaffe to their hearts. Magazines such as *Signal* and *Die Kriegsmarine* regularly featured photographic coverage of heroic U-boat crews, and the feature film, *U-Boote Westwärt*, released in May 1941, was a major hit. Small wonder then, that right through to the end of the war, many were still volunteering for service with the U-boats.

Although one might be forgiven for assuming that the bulk of naval recruits would have come from the coastal areas of north Germany or the great sea ports such as Hamburg or Kiel, statistics show that the typical U-boat crewman came from central Germany, principally Saxony. He was from a working-class background and had completed elementary schooling (*Volksschule*). He was probably Protestant and from a family background of skilled artisans. It is interesting to note that even among those U-boat men from a middle-class background, most came from a family where their fathers were master craftsmen. Only a tiny handful came from families with a military background. The typical recruit into the U-boat service of the navy was a skilled blue-collar worker.

Those who elected to serve as a seaman, where the highest attainable rank was that of Oberbootsmaat (senior bosun, a chief petty officer grade), had to sign on for a minimum of 12 years. For those who were slightly more ambitious and who

Known as 'Grey Wolves', the U-boat crewmen wore protective grey leather trousers and jackets. There were two distinctive types of jacket both shown here. The deck crew jacket is shown at left and the engine-room personnel jacket at right.

After being called to report for duty, the U-boat man handed in his *Wehrpass* and received his *Soldbuch* (pay book), which acted as his personal ID. This is the *Soldbuch* of Leutnant zur See Eberhard Marx, watch officer on U-437. Note the typical large ink stamped 'U' on the inside cover and page 1. (Author's collection)

elected for an NCO career, a minimum service term of 12 years was also required. In this case progression through the ranks to Oberfeldwebel, and later Stabsoberfeldwebel was possible. This was a warrant officer rank, more commonly expressed in terms of the serviceman's career grouping or trade – Stabsobersteuermann (senior coxswain), Stabsobermaschinist (machinist), etc. There was no option to choose a specific trade, which was decided by the navy on the basis of an assessment of the sailor's abilities.

Those who wished to become officers faced the most gruelling training. Officers had to sign up for a term of 25 years' service, and the requirements, physical, intellectual and psychological, were the most strenuous of all. After initial basic training, every U-boat officer served three-and-a-half months before the mast on a sailing bark, followed by a 14-month stint on a cruiser, one year at naval academy, six months' specialist training, and then one year on an active warship to gain experience and responsibility, before being voted to a commissioned rank by his peers if he had completed the training satisfactorily. Only then did he commence training as a U-boat officer. Officer training was physically arduous, with great emphasis placed on sporting activities. One test of strength and character was to hold up a heavy iron bar through which an electrical current, powerful enough to be very painful, was passed. The cadet was expected to withstand the pain without dropping the bar. In age terms, the average wartime U-boat crewman was in his mid-twenties, with the commander or 'Old Man' aged around 27. As the war progressed, the mean age dropped slightly and towards the latter part of the war, a U-boat commander was about 24 years of age.

ESCAPE TRAINING

One of the most important parts of a U-boat crewman's training was in escape techniques which were taught and practised at the U-boat school. In reality, escapes from sunken U-boats were rare. Most U-boats were either sunk with all hands in deep water with no chance of escape following a fatal hit by depth charges or bombs, or were fatally damaged on the surface so that some or all of the crew were able to abandon ship. The chances of survival in the cold waters of the Atlantic were minimal unless rescued very quickly.

The number of occasions in which a relatively intact U-boat was trapped on the bottom in waters shallow enough for escape attempts to be feasible was very small. In 12 recorded cases, U-boat crews or at least part of the crew escaped using the *Tauchretter*. Crewmen from U-767 in 1944 and U-2199 in 1945 escaped, in both cases from depths in excess of 200 feet.

Watched by a number of his comrades, a U-boat crewman has just reached the surface of the 8-metre training tank wearing his inflated *Tauchretter*. The training itself was not without risk, and numerous trainees suffered injuries such as perforated ear-drums having made numerous escape attempts both with and without the *Dräger* apparatus. (Artwork by Darko Pavlovic © Osprey Publishing)

In more recent times, much doubt has been cast on just how much truth there is to the image of the U-boat service as being filled purely with volunteers. Pre-war, the average annual intake into the navy was 13,000 men. Only 33 per cent of those who volunteered for the U-boat service would be considered suitable, and only 60 per cent of them were accepted. It is estimated that until mid-1941 all U-boat crewmen were 'genuine' volunteers. But as the war progressed, Kriegsmarine losses had to be replaced and, with competing demands for manpower from the army and Luftwaffe, conscripts began to appear in the U-Bootwaffe. In some cases they were already serving sailors from other branches of the navy, but others were fresh recruits sent straight to the U-boats after training. By the war's end, it is estimated that only 36 per cent of U-boat commanders were 'pure' U-boat men with no service in any other branch of the navy. In some cases, the transfers were simply expedient.

After the disastrous battle of Narvik where the German destroyer fleet was decimated (but the majority of crewmen survived), many destroyer crewmen, with their ships gone, volunteered for service in the U-boats and many junior officers were simply reassigned whether they approved or not.

By 1942, naval intakes had reached 42,000 per annum, with Dönitz seeking authority almost to double this figure. The demands for replacements for losses on the Eastern Front, however, meant that Dönitz's requirements were never fulfilled. So by the middle of the war, fewer and fewer U-boat crewmen were volunteers in the true sense. But it is not true that in some way the quality of U-boat crews had diminished, or that their status as a true elite had slipped, even if recruitment was no longer purely voluntary. Even at a stage in the war when U-boat losses were mounting and Allied anti-submarine measures were taking a terrible toll of U-boat men, there were sufficient volunteers to supply the U-Bootwaffe. As late as 1944, it is estimated that only 37 per cent of those volunteering for U-boat service were accepted. It was the selectivity of the U-Bootwaffe itself, in its determination to keep standards as high as possible, that resulted in so many being turned down, and not a shortage of volunteers. The navy then made up the shortage in suitably qualified personnel by transfers from other branches, or by allocating new draftees directly to the U-boats.

So, while the image of the U-Bootwaffe as a purely volunteer force is perhaps not completely accurate, neither is the alternative view of unhappy draftees being pressed into U-boat service to make up numbers. Although many were drafted into the U-Bootwaffe without option, one choice that was often given was whether the sailor wished to serve on a Type VII or a Type IX boat. The Type VII was much smaller and more uncomfortable, whilst the Type IX was in comparison quite roomy. However, in the case of an emergency crash dive, the Type VII could be under water some ten seconds faster and thus gave an increased chance of survival, so it was something of a 'Hobson's Choice'.

It is also worth pointing out that U-boat crews had to operate as an efficient, motivated team, with complete trust in their comrades. Just like a well-oiled machine where one faulty part can cause a disastrous breakdown, a reluctant recruit who resented his posting and did not fit in with the rest of the crew could spell disaster to a U-boat. In such a situation the commander would be as keen to replace him as the draftee was to leave. There is no strong evidence to suggest that U-boat crewmen were forced to serve in submarines against their will; on the other hand, there is no shortage of evidence of those who failed to meet the high standard expected of them being removed, for the good and safety of all. Clearly, once they had undergone the rigorous training, which saw them moulded into an efficient part of a well-motivated team, draftees were, in the main, content to remain.

TRAINING

U-boat training in the Kriegsmarine began in 1933 with the establishment of the Unterseebootsabwehrschule in Kiel. Ostensibly a school for anti-submarine defence, its name was intended to conceal the fact that it was actually training U-boat crews. Trainees received theoretical training in all aspects of submarine duties; the design and construction of submarines; weapon systems; the diesel and electrical propulsion systems; escape training etc.

In 1935, 1. Unterseebootsflotille *Weddigen* was formed, with U-7 through to U-12 (U-1 to U-6 were designated as training boats and attached to the U-boat school at Neustadt). These boats were small Type II coastal craft, known as 'canoes' to their crews.

U-boat men now had extensive practical exercises to back up the classroom theory. The U-Bootwaffe grew considerably in the intervening years and in 1937 a new training establishment was built for what was commonly called the Unterseebootsschule at Neustadt. By the outbreak of war in 1939, this establishment had doubled in size and had attained the status of a flotilla, the

BELOW LEFT
Many U-boats carried an officer candidate or *Fähnrich* on their strength. These personnel wore an officer-quality reefer jacket with rank indicated by shoulder straps. There are no sleeve rings, only the embroidered five-pointed star of a line officer.

BELOW RIGHT
Two officers relax on the flak platform of their U-boat. One wears blue service dress, the other a mix of grey leather trousers and grey green denim jacket. Such variety of mixed dress is typical. Note also the victory pennants indicating ships sunk.

Unterseebootsschulflotille. In April 1940, the school was redesignated as 1. Unterseebootslehrdivision (normally abbreviated as ULD) and moved to Pillau on the Baltic. Seven months later, 2 ULD was formed at Gotenhafen. By the end of the war four ULDs had been established. The training divisions had on their strengths a number of former liners, which had been converted to provide accommodation or act as depot ships for the U-Bootwaffe. At any one time up to 4,000 trainees might be attached to one of these training divisions. A full flotilla of U-boats was attached to each training division, 21. Unterseebootsflotille with 1 ULD and 22. Unterseebootsflotille with 2 ULD.

In the early part of the war at least, U-boat men received a full six months of U-boat training (over and above the normal navy basic training). Growing demands for rapid replacement of wartime losses saw the gradual reduction of this period to three, then as little as two, months. It should be noted that this was an average, however. There are examples of men being drafted into the U-boat arm and allocated to a boat with no special training at all, while even in the closing stages of the war there are further instances of men receiving extended training. The length of an individual's training depended on the assessment of his trainers.

NCO TRAINING

By the end of World War I, it became clear that naval NCOs required both specialist training and a more clearly defined system of recruitment and promotion. In future, the corps of naval NCOs would need to be trained professionals, and be willing to commit to a period of service of not less than 12 years. There was no facility for joining the Reichsmarine (and later the Kriegsmarine) as an NCO aspirant (in direct contrast to the situation with officers). Potential NCOs were selected for training after two or three years' satisfactory service in the ranks, having already exhibited such positive characteristics as self-discipline, loyalty and dedication. They first attended the appropriate trade school for enhanced training in their allocated career branch which could last anywhere between three and ten months. On satisfactory completion of this training they would report to Marineschule, Friedrichsort, the NCO training school. At this stage it would probably be fair to say that most NCO candidates, who had already served in the navy for several years, had much greater levels of experience and ability than aspirant officers.

At Friedrichsort, they would undergo extremely rigorous training, broken down into four main disciplines: theoretical classroom training, infantry training, nautical studies and sport. Although infantry training might seem somewhat anomalous, it was an essential part of the development of an NCO. It was here that he learned to give clear, concise and firm orders, especially on the parade ground in extensive drilling exercises, and developed the ability to command and earn the respect of his men. Sport was also considered of great importance (especially to the U-boat man who certainly needed to be fit and agile to move smoothly and at speed through the close confines and narrow hatches of a submarine in combat).

The NCO training branch of the navy was expanded in 1935 with the opening of a second NCO Marineschule in Wesermünde. At this time the *Marineschulen* specialising in NCO training were redesignated as *Marineunteroffizier-lehrabteilungen* 1 and 2. Finally, in 1938, a brand-new purpose-built NCO school was established at Plön.

OFFICER TRAINING

The standard training programme for a typical officer began with basic training which lasted around five months. On arrival at the officer selection camp at Dänholm, a two-day physical fitness selection test was held. This was extremely strenuous and around 25 per cent of the intake usually failed. Those who did not make the grade were invited to reapply once they had built up their physical stamina.

This was followed by sail training lasting for four months on a three-masted sailing bark. It was extremely arduous, and fatalities were not unknown. The worst recorded disaster was in 1932 when the bark *Niobe* capsized in a storm, with the loss of 70 trainee officers. The C-in-C Navy, Admiral Erich Raeder, subsequently invited the major commercial and merchant shipping lines to come to the aid of Germany and transfer their best men to the navy. Among those who found their way into the navy in this way were the future U-boat aces Günther Prien and Heinrich 'Ajax' Bleichrodt.

Officers who had successfully completed the first two stages were usually granted formal acceptance to the rank of Seekadet and progressed to cruiser training, an assignment aboard a warship, usually a cruiser. This took the form of a cruise into foreign waters, often virtually a 'round the world' trip with courtesy calls into many ports, lasting for up to nine months.

Having completed their sea cruise, potential officers transferred to the famous naval academy at Mürwick for seven months. On completion, they were promoted to the rank of Fähnrich zur See (midshipman). Up to this point, the training given was standardised, no matter what the eventual branch of the trainee. Most U-boat candidates were line or engineering officers. Later in the war, some of the larger submarines were also allocated a medical officer.

Line officers followed the training at Mürwick with a weapons training course, where they learned about naval armament. They were then attached to a warship for up to six months, at the end of which, assuming satisfactory reports, they were promoted to Oberfähnrich (senior midshipman). Senior midshipmen served at this rank for up to three years learning their trade, until, by a vote of their peers, they were promoted to the rank of Leutnant zur See.

Engineering officers took extra engineering examinations after their course at Mürwick. If successful, they carried out workshop training for up to five months. This was followed by six months' attachment to a warship, after which they were eligible for promotion to Leutnant (Ing.).

Officers destined for the U-Bootwaffe underwent a 12-week training course in which exercises at sea alternated with classroom theory. Fully equipped simulators were constructed in the training schools, enabling prospective officers to practise attack runs on model convoys. A total of 15 successful simulated attacks were required before the candidate could progress to the next stage of his training. The best and most promising candidates were often posted directly to an operational U-boat to hone their skills under the tutelage of an experienced commander. On completion of their training, others were posted to an operational training flotilla such as 23. Unterseebootsflotille in Danzig or 24. Unterseebootsflotille in Gotenhafen where they practised underwater attack procedures.

Other flotillas carrying out advanced training were:

19. Unterseebootsflotille	Pillau	Boat-handling techniques training
20. Unterseebootsflotille	Pillau	Basic tactical theory instruction
25. Unterseebootsflotille	Danzig	Shooting instruction
26. Unterseebootsflotille	Pillau	Shooting instruction
27. Unterseebootsflotille	Gotenhafen	Tactical training

Where a crew was assembled to take over a newly constructed boat, a typical training scenario might be as follows:

Baubelehrung (Familiarisation Training). A captain and senior crew members were sent to the shipyard where their new U-boat was being constructed, giving them the opportunity to learn just what made their boat 'tick', and to see it through its constructional stages so that they were totally familiar with every aspect of their vessel. This stage might last for up to three months leading up to the launch. In the last few weeks of this period, they might be joined by the remainder of the crew, normally a mixture of new personnel and seasoned veterans.

Unterseebootsabnahmekommando – UAK. The boat went through acceptance testing, with diving trials, silent running tests and the testing of all machinery and equipment. This would normally last two to three weeks.

Technische Ausbildungsgruppe für Frontunterseeboote – Agrufront (Technical Training Group for Front U-Boats). This was a much feared process where the boat, once formally accepted and commissioned into the navy with its new commander and crew, was put through the most rigorous training in realistic battle conditions. An experienced combat veteran, acting as 'umpire' and trainer, would accompany the boat, suddenly informing the commander that a certain piece of machinery or equipment was deemed inoperative, to see how the captain would react to the new emergency. Deep diving exercises were also held. Just how intensive and dangerous this training process was can be judged by the fact that, during World War II, 30 U-boats were actually lost in training, taking 856 men to their deaths. Once judged to have passed this stage and finally declared *frontreif*, or ready for front-line service, the boat would go back to the dockyard for a final overhaul. At this point, the crew would be given their final leave before returning to front-line combat service. Once reassembled, the crew would join the U-boat and move to Kiel for final fitting and the taking on board of supplies, torpedoes and ammunition.

As well as the various schools and training establishments already mentioned, of particular importance to the U-boat crews were the Marinenachrichtenschule (Naval Signals School); the Torpedoschule (Torpedo School); the Schiffsartillerieschule (Ships Artillery School); the Sperrschule (Naval Defences School dealing in blocking defences such as mines); and the Steuermannschule (Coxswain School).

APPEARANCE

In general terms, the basic service uniform of the U-boat sailor was identical in almost all respects to his counterparts in the remainder of the navy. There was, however, a range of specialist clothing, some of which was unique to U-boat crews, as well as other garments which were certainly worn more widely by that branch. The combinations of 'mixed dress' worn by U-boat men are almost legion in their numbers. Almost any of the garments described here could be found worn in conjunction with almost any of the others. In fact, just about the only thing that can be said with certainty about the appearance of typical U-boat men on operations was that there were probably no two in the crew who dressed the same. There are three forms of dress in particular, however, which will be seen with great regularity in photographs of U-boat men at sea.

The most common form of dress worn by the U-boat crewman was the protective leather clothing. This was no new development and had been around since the

BADGES AND CLOTHING

Shown here are a selection of the trade and rank badges worn by U-boat crewmen. The top row are shoulder straps for **1** Kapitänleutnant; **2** Oberleutnant; **3** Leutnant zur See; **4** Oberleutnant (Ing.); **5** Obersteuermann (helmsman); **6** Stabsbootsmann (senior bosun); and **7** Maschinist (engine room senior NCO).

Seamen wore a simple circular patch with devices appropriate to their trade: **8** Engine Room Personnel; **9** Torpedo Mechanic; **10** Radio Operator; and **11** Seaman.

Petty officers wore sleeve rank/trade combined patches: **12** Sanitatsobermaat (chief petty officer medic); **13** Mechanikerobermaat (engine room chief petty officer); **14** Torpedoobermaat (torpedo chief petty officer); **15** Oberbootsmann (bosun's mate); **16** Steuermannsmaat (helmsman's mate); **17** Funkmaat (PO Radio Operator); and specialist patches (worn on the left sleeve below the rank patch) for **18** Unterwasserhorcher (Underwater Sound Detector Operator) and **19** U-Bootstaucher (U-boat diver). There was a huge range of such trade and specialist patches, always embroidered in red thread, which could be worn in conjunction with the rank patch.

The Wehrpass or military pass (**20**) was carried by each German from the point at which he was registered for military service. It was a form of ID and also recorded his compulsory Labour Corps Service. On reporting for duty, it was replaced by a Soldbuch (**21**) but returned to him on his discharge on completion of military service or to his next of kin in case of death. The Soldbuch was a soldier's personal ID as well as a record of unit affiliation, medical history, decorations, kit issue, pay and leave.

Every member of the armed forces wore ID discs or 'dog tags' (**22**). Many variants in style are known, and large numbers of naval issue tags were in gold finish. The example shown records the sailor's blood group and Wehrstammrollnummer. The 'N' indicates Nordsee or North Sea

Fleet (as opposed to 'O' for Ostsee or Baltic). If the sailor was killed in such circumstances where the ID tag was recoverable, it was snapped in half. One half was buried with the sailor and the other half returned to the graves registration office.

One of the most popular common forms of dress worn by all ranks on U-boats was the denim blouse (**23**). It closely resembled the British battledress blouse in its design. Various combinations of insignia could be worn. Shown here are officer shoulder straps and a pin-back metal breast eagle. All insignia and buttons were removable to facilitate cleaning.

Lightweight denim working jackets (**24**) were also widely used by U-boat crews. Petty officers' rank was often shown by small metal 'corners' sewn to the lapels of their jackets to replicate the gold braid worn around the collar of their pea jackets. These jackets were widely worn both with a sleeve rank patch as shown here, or without.

Tropical issue kit was used in warmer South Atlantic waters or even further afield. Generally, shorts (**25**) would be worn on board rather than long trousers, together with the tropical shirt or tunic (**26**). These were all cut from golden tan-coloured cotton. Special shoulder straps were produced in tan with blue braid edging for the tropical tunic and shirt, but seem rarely to have been used. Most often, the standard insignia from the blue uniform was utilised as shown here on the tropical tunic (**27**). A field cap (**28**) in the same material was issued, very similar to the field cap used by the Afrikakorps. Alternatively, a lightweight white cotton version of the side cap (**29**) was often used.

In really warm temperatures, the white naval sports vest (**30**) also saw frequent use, especially by engine-room crews working in an extremely hot environment. The normal service navy buckle (**31**) was used on either a leather or webbing belt, and was steel with a dark blue-grey painted finish. (Artwork by Darko Pavlovic © Osprey Publishing)

Kaiser's day. Leather clothing was produced in black and dark brown, but the versions which the U-boat men made their own were those cut in pale grey leather. They also wore strong leather over-trousers lined with charcoal-black wool, which had no waist belt and were held up by braces. A matching leather jacket was supplied, also lined in black wool. 'Engine' personnel (*Maschinenpersonal*) wore a single breasted version, buttoned right up to the neck with a simple stand-up collar. It had two skirt pockets and one pocket on the left breast. Another 'reefer' style was produced from 1937 which was double-breasted, with a wider collar and normal lapels. Intended for deck or bridge personnel, it was particularly favoured by officers and warrant officers. These garments gave some protection against dirt,

ABOVE LEFT

The short *Affenjacke* or Monkey Jacket formed part of the parade dress uniform. Only used on formal occasions, it is seen here worn by Oberbootsmaat Springer, a crew member of U-995, a veteran, as shown by his High Seas Fleet badge, of service with the surface fleet.

ABOVE RIGHT

The blue reefer jacket was the most commonly worn attire of the U-boat crewman when away from the boat. It is shown here worn by Oberfunkmaat Zappe from U-467. His rank is indicated by the collar patches and gilt braid trim to the collar.

oil and burns in the close confines of an engine room, and also helped protect against the cold when on bridge watch in the chilly waters of the North Atlantic.

Another form of essential dress was the regulation foul weather clothing. These were not personal issue garments, but were on the ship's inventory and were only issued to individuals on watch. A rubberised cloth sou'wester (exactly like any other sou'wester worn by sailors and fishermen all over the world) was worn in conjunction with a large, rubberised, double-breasted, knee-length over-jacket with elasticated cuffs and a large collar which could be turned up to protect the side of the face and neck. Matching rubberised over-trousers were also worn.

One of the most unusual forms of dress worn by crewmen was the special U-boat uniform, which was almost an exact copy of British battledress in its styling. It consisted of a waist-length blouse with patch pockets cut from a grey-green denim cloth, with a button front and integral waist-belt. Matching trousers were also issued. The blouse was often worn without insignia, though senior ranks such as officers and warrant officers usually wore shoulder straps. The national emblem of the eagle and swastika in either cloth or metal form was usually, but not always, worn on the left breast. Occasionally, metal points, in brass, were worn on the collar by petty officers to replicate the braid worn on the pea jacket.

When France fell to the Germans in 1940, vast stocks of captured war matériel fell into their hands, including many uniforms, such as the British battledress. As these were very similar to the U-boat uniform, apart from being in brown denim rather than grey-green, they were issued to U-boat crews. In black-and-white photographs it is often impossible to tell whether crewmen are wearing German issue or captured British clothing. Of course at sea on an operational U-boat, there was no danger of crewmen wearing British captured clothing being mistaken for the enemy.

There were other forms of regulation naval issue clothing which, though not specifically intended for wear by submarine crews, were often utilised by them. The pre-war working dress was a single-breasted jacket with open collar and two patch pockets on the skirt. It came with matching straight-legged trousers and was cut from a brownish tan-coloured cloth. This form of dress was often used totally devoid of insignia though it may occasionally be seen with sleeve trade/rank patches on normal dark blue backing, stitched to the left sleeve.

Tropical service dress consisted of a single-breasted open-necked tunic with pleated patch pockets to the breast and skirt. It was cut from a golden tan denim twill material. Shoulder straps indicated rank, and in some cases a special blue rather than gilt braid was used on tan tropical NCO shoulder straps; the normal shoulder straps from the dark blue uniform were often worn by both NCOs and officers. A national emblem was worn on the left breast in either silk weave in gold on a tan backing, or in a gilt metal pin-on version. This tunic could be worn with either shorts or long trousers.

The issue sports vest was often worn in tropical climes, or by those working in particularly hot areas such as the engine room. It was simply a white sleeveless vest with a large woven national emblem stitched in blue thread on a white ground. It was often worn with standard naval issue sports shorts.

U-boat men often wore chequered shirts, a most un-nautical form of dress. They were actually issue items, but no doubt many men wore shirts they had provided themselves. These warm wool shirts were very popular among U-boat crews and are said to have originated from the vast stocks of French clothing which fell into German hands after the campaign of 1940.

A newly trained U-boat crewman wearing the light grey leather U-boat clothing for engine room personnel, and the *Bordmütze*.

The *Tauchretter* (**1** and **2**) could be fully inflated for use as a life preserver or escape apparatus, but was more commonly used uninflated for its carbon dioxide filter. The *Kalipatronen* (**4**) air filter consisted of a simple carbon dioxide filtering box with a breathing tube ending in a face-mask with elasticated straps. Several versions were in use and occasionally the *Tauchretter* filter box would be removed with its mouthpiece and used on its own.

Numerous types of life preserver were used by the navy. Some were simply bands of canvas packed with kapok filling and worn around the chest tied on with webbing straps (**3**). Others (**5**) were of traditional 'collar' type, fully inflatable, and fitted in the same way as the *Tauchretter*.

Oilskins (**6**) in black rubberised fabric were worn on top of the leather clothing, the large collar could be turned up to protect the back and sides of the head. Worn in conjunction with a woollen Balaclava-type toque and the sou'wester (**8**), very little actual flesh would be exposed.

The unmilitary-looking *Pudelmütze* (**7**) was a warm and popular form of headwear. Despite its appearance the *Pudelmütze* was very much an official issue item. (Artwork by Darko Pavlovic © Osprey Publishing)

Examination of wartime photographs of U-boats at sea will show that almost any form of headwear could be worn with any form of tunic or clothing. Probably the most popular and widely worn item of clothing was the *Bordmütze*, a side cap cut from navy blue woollen cloth, featuring a yellow thread national emblem on the front of the crown and a cockade in the national colours on the front of the flap. It was a smart and convenient form of headdress for wear in the close confines of a submarine. Officers could wear a version with gilt braided piping along the edge of the flap, but often elected to wear the standard Other Ranks version. U-boat men most often wore the elected emblem of their vessel on the side of their *Bordmütze*. A white version was also manufactured for wear in the tropics but was not widely used.

Officers and warrant officers usually wore their peaked service cap or *Schirmmütze*, which was made from dark blue wool with a black woven mohair band and black leather chinstrap. The peak was in black leather or fibre, bound in leather, for warrant officers. A hand-embroidered national emblem was worn on the front of the crown, with a national colours cockade wreathed in oakleaves on the band. For officers, the peak was covered in dark blue cloth bound in leather, with the edge embroidered in gilt wire or yellow cellulose thread to indicate rank. In most cases, the U-boat commander was a Kapitänleutnant zur See or Oberleutnant zur See, so the edge of the peak was embroidered in a scalloped design. Occasionally, higher ranks such as Korvettenkapitän commanded U-boats and in this case the edge of the peak was embroidered with a single wide band of oakleaves. The commander of the U-boat generally wore a white cover to his cap, making him instantly recognisable. This white cover was only to be worn on board; when on shore the commander reverted to wearing a standard blue topped cap.

The peaked field cap was occasionally worn in tropical regions. Similar to the famous Afrikakorps field cap, it was cut from tan denim with a long peak to shade the eyes from the sun. A national emblem woven in golden yellow on a tan base was worn at the front of the crown, over a cockade in the national colours.

Very occasionally, photographs show U-boat crewmen wearing the large and cumbersome tropical pith helmet, a cork helmet covered in tan or white canvas. Quite how the space was found to store these on an operational U-boat is difficult to imagine. A small number of steel helmets might also be carried, for wear by the gun crew or the anti-aircraft gunners should the boat go into action on the surface. Finally, mention should be made of the popular *Pudelmütze*, a knitted woollen cap with a pompon. Despite its non-military appearance, it was actually a piece of issue kit.

In the course of combat operations, when merchant ships were sunk, the sea was often littered with wreckage, which might include bales or crates of clothing. U-boat men were never slow to take advantage of such opportunities and a number of photographs show all sorts of bizarre forms of dress, particularly headdress. Straw boaters seemed a popular form of headwear, and one photograph shows a returning U-boat commander wearing a top hat, with the lapels of his reefer jacket covered in small cloth 'victory pennants'. An indication, perhaps, of just how far some U-boat commanders identified with their crew and were willing to join in the fun. On the other hand, a few more strict commanders insisted on their men being as smart as reasonably possible at all times, though, thankfully for the average U-boat crewman, they were very much in the minority.

The appearance of U-boat crewmen varied enormously; they wore an almost limitless combination of uniform and non-uniform items. Certain pieces of

ABOVE LEFT

A U-boat officer in dark blue service dress. The two sleeve rings indicate the rank of Oberleutnant zur See Dauter of U-448. As well as the U-Boat War Badge, Iron Cross First Class and German Cross in Gold, note that he wears the qualification badge of a Luftwaffe Observer, indicating prior service with the air arm before transferring to U-boats.

ABOVE RIGHT

When at sea, U-boat men typically wore a grey-green denim battledress-type jacket, as shown here worn by an Obermaschinist. Because of the restricted amount of water carried on board, most crewmen refrained from shaving and grew heavy beards, though some like this senior NCO, elected for neatly trimmed goatees.

equipment were not 'uniform' items, but were worn with great regularity. The most important was the so-called 'Dräger Lung' or *Tauchretter* life jacket. It consisted of an orange-brown inflatable waterproof 'collar' with a single strap at the back of the neck, which passed down the wearer's back, through his legs and buckled to the base of the collar at approximately waist height. An oxygen cylinder was contained inside the lower part of the apparatus, connected to a breathing hose and mouthpiece; there was also a canister containing carbon dioxide-absorbing material. Should air supplies on a submarine be run low, the *Tauchretter* was used in uninflated form as a simple breathing apparatus. With the collar inflated, and with its own oxygen supply, it could act as an escape apparatus for evacuating a sunken submarine, which was by far its most common application.

A standard life vest without the special *Dräger* apparatus was also used. Available in numerous patterns, it was often used by crews of the U-boat's deck gun. Most patterns were in a yellowish-orange rubberised canvas, with an internal oxygen bottle for inflation and a back-up mouthpiece should the oxygen fail; it consisted of the traditional collar and breast panels with canvas straps passing around the wearer's back and crotch to hold it in place.

An alternative version of the *Dräger* carbon dioxide filter, consisting of just the filter canister with hose and mouthpiece, was used to extend the air supply should the boat remain submerged for a lengthy period.

CONDITIONS OF SERVICE

When considering the conditions of service, two principal factors are important: the physical conditions in which the U-boat crew served, i.e. the U-boat itself, and the pay and benefits received for serving in this elite branch of the navy.

As it prepared to set out on a war cruise, which might last for around 12 weeks, a U-boat would carry up to 14 tons of supplies as well as a full load of fuel and ammunition. Every square inch of available space would be crammed full of fresh foods such as eggs, potatoes, fruit, vegetables, bread and meat, which would obviously be consumed first, preferably before they started to rot. Three meals a day would be served (combat conditions permitting), washed down with a variety of drinks such as coffee, tea, milk, fruit juice or cocoa. Once the fresh supplies had been exhausted, canned foods were used, backed up with vitamin supplements. On occasion, a merchant ship sunk by a U-boat would be carrying small livestock such as pigs or chickens, as in the case of the *Parnhyha*, sunk by U-162 in May 1942. If the livestock survived the sinking, the U-boat crew recovered them as a much-appreciated source of additional fresh meat.

What might sound like a very favourable rationing situation should be tempered by a number of considerations. U-boats travelled on the surface whenever safe to do so in order to preserve the boats' battery power and to increase speed. This often meant putting the boat at the mercy of atrocious surface weather conditions, which meant that the ship's stove could not be used and therefore hot food was not available.

Interiors of U-boats on active service were notoriously damp. When a boat was on the surface in rough seas, water would constantly cascade in through the open hatches to run into the bilges. When it was submerged in warmer climes, poor ventilation and the great heat being given off by the boat's machinery meant that temperatures of over 122° F (50° C) were not unknown. This heat, combined with high levels of humidity, meant that damp clothes rarely had a chance to dry and fresh foodstuffs rapidly rotted. Mouldy food was almost an occupational hazard for U-boat crews. Nevertheless, all things considered, the U-boat crewman had access to a much higher standard of provisioning than most other service personnel.

Space on an active service U-boat was at a premium. Although a typical Type VII or Type IX U-boat may seem quite large, it must be remembered that what the viewer

sees is the exterior hull, which encased the 'real' hull, known as the pressure hull. The gap between the two was open to the sea and was often used simply as storage space (for torpedoes, ammunition, life-rafts, etc.). At its widest, the pressure hull was just under 5m in diameter, and it of course tapered to a narrower section towards the bow and stern. Most of the interior was taken up by engines, electric motors, batteries, machinery and all sorts of essential equipment, leaving very little space to accommodate the crew. There were simply not enough sleeping spaces for all members of the crew. Most of the compartments dedicated to a specific element of the crew were barely longer than the bunks they occupied. Only the commander had the great luxury of quarters fitted with a curtain he could pull across to gain a modicum of privacy. But the commander's quarters were located as close as possible to the 'nerve centre' of the boat which was manned at all times and rarely totally quiet.

The officers' quarters doubled as the wardroom and had the luxury of a permanent rather than a fold-away table. Senior ranks slept in bunks and most junior ranks in hammocks, with a few of the less fortunate ratings being required to sleep on simple matting laid on the deck plates. Two men shared each sleeping place, with one in occupation while the other was on watch. Junior ranks tended to be quartered in the bow or stern torpedo room, which could be an active, noisy place with no privacy whatsoever.

Generally, formal discipline on board most submarines was relaxed. The strong esprit de corps and sense of kinship among U-boat men resulted in very high levels of self-discipline and trust. Although a few commanders were known as martinets, most took a relaxed view of discipline.

OFF-DUTY PASTIMES

One of the greatest problems on an operational U-boat was finding things to occupy the crew's minds when off duty. Boredom could be a serious problem. Many commanders would ensure that a good supply of records was taken on board so that music could be played over the boat's PA system. U-boat men were known for their love of 'inappropriate' music such as jazz and swing, which was regarded as 'degenerate' by the authorities. Radio broadcasts were also piped through the public address system and crews were occasionally given the chance to listen to foreign stations, which were strictly forbidden at home.

Reading was a widespread pastime with a good stock of novels being passed around. With more time spent underwater later in the war, and the consequent drain on the boat's batteries, lighting was kept to an absolute minimum to save power, so simple pleasures such as reading were very difficult. Card games such as 'Skat' were also a popular way of passing time, although, dependent on the feelings of the commander, actual gambling might be frowned upon.

Some officers might take the chance to give mini-lectures to off-duty crew, more often on moral than political issues. Dönitz ensured that Nazi 'political education' officer appointees were not permitted on board operational U-boats.

Off-duty crew members were often given simple tasks such as basic maintenance and repairs to machinery, as much to keep them occupied as for any other reason. Here one of the crew is reading in his bunk, while two of his comrades play cards. Another is busy peeling potatoes for the cook. (Artwork by Darko Pavlovic © Osprey Publishing)

The nature of life on a U-boat meant that the traditional navy blue service dress uniforms were not appropriate, so in most boats men wore pretty much anything that was comfortable. So long as a crew were efficient, effective, and could be depended on to do their duty, most commanders allowed their men considerable latitude in how they chose to dress.

ABOVE LEFT

One of the most important members of the U-boat crew was the chief engineer, typically with the rank of Oberleutnant (Ing.). He was responsible for ensuring the efficient running of the boat's diesel and electric motors, and indeed every mechanical and hydraulic component, and had to have an encyclopaedic knowledge of every technical aspect of the boat. Here, the LI snatches a few precious moments of sleep, still at his post.

ABOVE RIGHT

A U-boat on a long war cruise was not a pleasant place to be, stinking of diesel, rotting stale food, sweat and unwashed bodies. Then there was the WC, a tiny cubicle to serve fully 50 men. When opportunities permitted, crewmen would often take the opportunity to use the somewhat fresher-smelling 'outside toilet'.

The extreme shortage of fresh water on a submarine meant that little, if any, could be spared for such luxuries as washing or shaving. Most men returned from their war cruises heavily bearded. Although special soap was issued to allow a lather to be raised with sea-water, few U-boat men bothered. Although any beards grown were to be shaved off immediately on return to port, photographs exist of fully bearded U-boat men posing in their blue walking-out dress. However, it is assumed these were simply souvenir snapshots for the family album, as beards were definitely frowned upon once back in port.

The typical U-boat had two toilets or 'heads'. In the early part of the cruise one would be used as storage for fresh foodstuffs, which left just one small toilet to accommodate over 50 men. Not only would the smell be an unpleasant addition to the existing odours of the U-boat, but flushing the toilet was in itself a potentially unpleasant and dangerous task. Incorrect manipulation of the levers used in this complex operation could result in the contents being 'back-flushed' over the user. At least one U-boat (U-1206) was lost because of incorrect handling of the toilet-flushing apparatus. In this incident the U-boat had to surface immediately to ease water pressure and was attacked and fatally damaged by Allied aircraft on reaching the surface. The boat was fairly close inshore at the time, and the entire crew reached safety. There may well have been many other boats, which suffered a similar fate in the unforgiving waters of the Atlantic but with no one surviving to tell the tale. When on the surface in safe waters, crew members would often use the 'outside toilet'.

Probably the most unpleasant working conditions were those in the main diesel compartment. The main power source for most U-boats was two 6-metre-long turbo-charged diesel engines. When these were operating (which was wherever possible, to minimise the power drain on the boat's batteries), the noise in the diesel room was intense. Many engine-room crew members suffered hearing problems, sleeplessness, stress and even digestive problems after being subjected to this environment of constant intense noise.

The galley provided for the ship's cook was tiny. It had just enough room to accommodate a small, two-burner electric stove, with a sink/wash space. Here, the dietary needs of almost 50 men had to be catered for. As it was not always safe to surface simply to dump waste food material and leave possible clues of the boat's presence, rotting foodstuffs often had to be retained on board.

So, one can well imagine the odours prevalent in a U-boat after a few weeks at sea: an unpleasant cocktail of diesel fumes, rotting food, toilets and the smell of unwashed bodies. Not surprisingly the use of eau de cologne was widespread. One piece of equipment often used for purposes other than those for which it was intended was the Bold device, which launched a decoy consisting of a metal canister approximately 10cm in diameter. The crew, of course, found an alternative use for it, packing cans with rubbish and firing them from the Bold launcher in an effort to cut down on the amount of rubbish accumulating on board.

Pay, of course, plays an important part in motivating and maintaining the morale of any serviceman. In fact, the basic pay of a U-boat crewman was pretty much the same as his equivalent rank in any other service. What made all the difference were the special additional allowances. U-boat men could receive an allowance for serving in confined spaces (*Raumbeschränkungszulage*), diving pay (*Tauchzulage*) and numerous other allowances related to specialist training. The total additional allowances payable could almost double the U-boat crewman's salary and many were known to live off their allowances and bank their entire pay.

Another important factor was that the specialist training made many U-boat men eligible for faster promotion, especially in wartime when combat losses had to be made good. Promotion also brought higher pay, so U-boat men were generally well-off and would usually have plenty of cash to spend when off duty or home on leave.

The leave system for U-boat men was also highly advantageous. After a 12-week cruise the boat would be laid up in port for refit, repairs and cleaning.

No more than half, but sometimes only a small skeleton crew, would be left on board while the remainder were given 12 days' home leave. Guard duty would be rotated so that everyone took their fair share. A special express train (known as the *BdU Zug* or 'C-in-C U-boat train') would speed the U-boat men home to Germany from their ports so that as little leave time as possible was lost in travelling. It is estimated that most U-boat men would have had around two weeks' leave every six months. This should be compared with the unfortunate infantryman on the Eastern Front, for example, who might easily go for a year to 18 months, or even longer, with no leave at all. Considerable efforts were also put into providing sporting and leisure facilities for U-boat men on leave.

Relaxation on board the U-boat was another matter. The greater part of a U-boat's war cruise would often be spent in fruitlessly searching for a convoy to attack. When not at action stations, the crew's greatest enemy was probably boredom, with little to do other than read books or play cards. When travelling underwater, lighting was often cut to a minimum to save electrical power, so even reading was virtually impossible. A selection of records would be taken to sea for playing over the boat's PA system and, unlike civilians for whom listening to an enemy radio station was a serious offence, U-boat men would often be permitted to listen to music or news from British or American stations. Many commanders would invent simple competitions to keep the men occupied, the first prize in which might well be the commander taking over the winner's watch for him. Needless to say, in foul weather conditions in the North Atlantic, this would be a highly valued prize.

Wherever possible, if the boat found itself in safe waters (an increasingly rare situation as the war progressed), thoughtful commanders would allow crewmen on deck for fresh air or even to sunbathe or swim (with someone keeping a weather eye open for sharks). On occasions such as crossing the equator, great efforts would be put into arranging traditional ceremonies on deck, with one of the crew dressed as Neptune putting some poor unfortunate through an initiation ceremony, usually involving being dunked and drinking some disgusting concoction involving sea water and various foul liquids. The initiate might then be given a fancy hand-drawn scroll and perhaps be awarded a 'medal' cut from scrap tinplate.

A good U-boat commander valued his crew greatly. Many highly decorated U-boat aces insisted that their Knight's Cross or Oakleaves were worn on behalf of the crew. U-boat commanders were known to pull strings behind the scenes on behalf of their men when they got into scrapes, and even the C-in-C U-Boats, Karl Dönitz, interceded on behalf of his commanders if they in turn fell foul of the authorities.

BELIEF AND BELONGING

I was fascinated by the unique sense of comradeship, engendered by sharing the same fate and hardship in the community of a U-boat crew in which everyone depended on everyone else and in which every man was an indispensable part of the whole. Surely every submariner has sensed in his heart the glow of the open sea, and the task entrusted to him, and felt as rich as a king, and would have traded places with no one.

Grossadmiral Karl Dönitz

It is the duty of every captain to have faith in his men.

Kapitänleutnant Wolfgang Lüth

There are many factors which must be taken into account when considering the great sense of belonging and belief which pervaded the U-boat arm. The sense of belonging is easy to understand. The intense feeling of comradeship and generally high morale that persisted in the U-Bootwaffe throughout the war was similar to that in many elite military organisations.

The U-boats and their victories were widely publicised, and the most successful aces became household names throughout the Reich. It was recognised that, much as in the Great War, it was the U-boat that gave Germany a chance successfully to oppose the vastly superior strength of the Royal Navy. Spectacular successes such as the sinking of the *Royal Oak* at Scapa Flow by Günther Prien in U-47, the destruction of the aircraft carrier *Courageous* by Otto Schuhart in U-29, the sinking of the battleship *Barham* in the Mediterranean by Hans Diederich Freiherr von Tiesenhausen and the destruction of the pride of the Royal Navy, the carrier *Ark Royal*, by Friedrich Guggenberger in U-81 could only serve to enhance the already high standing of the U-Bootwaffe in the eyes of the German people. Many popular tunes were written to celebrate the U-boats and their exploits (the 'U-Boot-Lied', the 'Kretschmer Marsch', 'Torpedo Los' and 'Ritter der Nordsee', to name but a few). The tough conditions in which the U-boat men served were brought home to German audiences by realistic movies such as *U-Boote Westwärts*. U-boat men were truly the heroes of the hour.

The men of the U-Bootwaffe held their commander Admiral Karl Dönitz in high regard, referring to him as *Der Löwe* (the lion) and he in turn calling them his 'Grey Wolves', a name which could relate to both the grey-painted U-boats themselves and the crews in their special grey leather clothing. Dönitz took great pains to keep himself informed on personal facts about his men and their welfare, and when meeting a U-boat and its crew on return from a war cruise would chat on matters personal as well as military, a habit which greatly endeared him to them. If, for instance, a sailor at sea on a war cruise became a father, Dönitz would

Grossadmiral Dönitz made a point of welcoming as many returning U-boats as possible, knowing the value to morale of senior officers showing an interest in the welfare of crews serving in such a dangerous role.

ensure that a message reached the proud new parent. Although Dönitz expected his men to fight to the end even when the chances of surviving combat with the enemy were negligible, this seemed to do little to affect the esteem in which he was held. This esteem was not universal; Dönitz did have his detractors even within the U-Bootwaffe, but given the attrition rate in the U-boat service towards the end of the war, he did retain the admiration of his men to an amazing degree.

'I have a reactionary Army, a National Socialist Air Force, and a Christian Navy', said Hitler, and the navy was regarded as the least political of the three services. Nevertheless, there were undoubtedly many within the Kriegsmarine and in the U-Bootwaffe itself who wholeheartedly supported the National Socialists – at least in the early days of the Third Reich. At least one of the most highly respected and chivalrous U-boat aces was an early party member and even held rank in the SS but was obliged to give up his membership of both organisations when joining the navy in 1934. On the other side of the coin, one of the great early aces, Joachim Schepke, was not a party member, yet was known for his loyalty to the Nazi cause and is on record as having made several anti-Semitic remarks. The U-Bootwaffe contained all sorts of characters, from loyal Nazis to those who vehemently opposed the tenets of the regime they served. Interestingly, though himself an admirer of Hitler, Dönitz ensured that so-called 'National Socialist

Leadership Officers' (similar to Soviet 'political commissars') were never allowed to serve on U-boats, despite assertions to the contrary by some writers.

It seems that the U-Bootwaffe often went to great lengths to protect its own. Despite being half-Jewish, Kapitänleutnant Helmut Schmoeckel was permitted to serve in the Kriegsmarine throughout the war, firstly on the heavy cruiser *Admiral Hipper*, and then in command of his own U-boat, U-802. U-boat ace Werner Henke, commander of U-124, fell foul of the Gestapo after they tried to harass some of his friends. He stormed into the headquarters of the local Gauleiter, and then the Gestapo headquarters itself, branding them as thugs and gangsters. Despite an earlier incident when he struck an SS officer, Henke

It was common for female auxiliaries (nurses, signals personnel, etc.) to be on hand to welcome returning boats. Here a gaggle of *Blitzmädschen* or signals corps girls surrounds Wolfgang Lüth. Lüth was one of only two recipients of the Knight's Cross of the Iron Cross with Oakleaves, Swords and Diamonds. He sank a total of almost 230,000 tons of enemy shipping before being accidentally shot by one of his own guards, a few days after the end of the war.

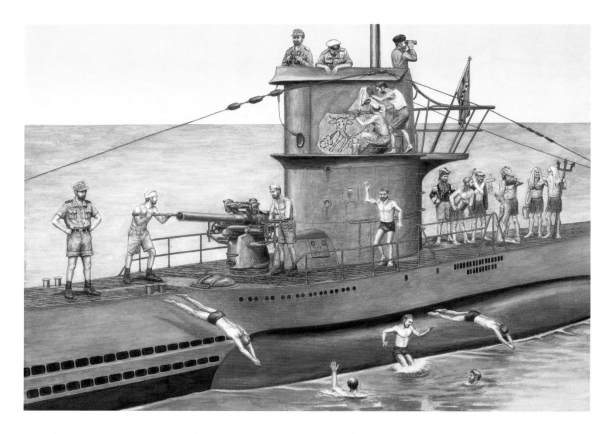

This illustration shows some of the activities in which U-boat crewmen might become involved when their boat reached fairly safe waters. One crewman is perched on the spray deflector on the outside of the conning tower painting on an emblem that has been decided on for the U-boat. On the quarterdeck, a group of crewmen are having an initiation ceremony for one of their number, who has crossed the equator for the first time. Further forward, two crewmen are servicing the 8.8cm deck gun; and just forward of the gun, one crewman keeps a vigilant watch for sharks while his crew mates take a swim. All the while, crewmen with binoculars on the bridge keep a wary eye open for any signs of enemy activity. (Artwork by Darko Pavlovic © Osprey Publishing)

received no more than a stern rebuke from Dönitz. It is hard to imagine any ordinary German citizen being quite so fortunate.

There are countless similar tales of U-boat men who were protected by their superiors after a run-in with the authorities. A punishment may have been ordered 'on paper', but the actual retribution meted out was derisory. When drawing up orders for the punishment of persistent 'grumblers' (in the Third Reich, pessimistic statements could often be declared 'defeatist' and bring the severest of punishments on those guilty of speaking their minds), even Dönitz himself made clear provision for front-line combatants 'harmlessly letting off steam'.

There were limits, however, to the amount of indiscipline that would be accepted. When the commander of a U-boat himself was the one who made seditious remarks, and did so in front of the crew, the risk to the morale and efficiency of the crew made punishment inevitable. Oberleutnant zur See Oskar-Heinz Kusch was reported for sedition by his own IWO (first watch officer) in just these circumstances. It was the very fact that his indiscretions were in front of his crew that led to his conviction and execution by firing squad. Even in captivity, those who broke the unwritten code of honour of the U-boat men would be harshly dealt with. One leading seaman who turned informer for his US captors at a POW camp in Arizona was discovered and killed by his fellow prisoners. His killers were promoted by Dönitz when news of the incident emerged, but were tried and hanged for murder by the US authorities in August 1945 once the war had ended and there was no danger of German execution of Allied prisoners in retaliation.

U-boat commanders, though proud and patriotic Germans, were quite notorious in their disrespect for the Nazi regime. On one famous occasion, U-boat ace Teddy Suhren of U-564 was approaching port to tie up alongside after a long war cruise when he leaned over the edge of the conning tower and yelled 'Are the Nazis still in charge?' When the reply 'Yes' came back, Suhren immediately put his engines into reverse and backed away from the quayside, much to the amusement of those watching. U-boat men were effectively a breed apart, with higher pay, better rations and more relaxed discipline; but equally, they endured a much greater risk of being killed in action.

Typically, U-boat men loved jazz (which was much frowned upon in the Third Reich), French women, and thoroughly good beer – in quantity. They hated the military police, ignored political issues and generally treated the enemy, whom Nazi propaganda sought to have them hate, with respect and chivalry. Like most elites, they worked very hard, and many of them liked to play hard, too.

Prior to the outbreak of war, U-boat men could show their unit affiliation by the wearing of a tally ribbon on their seamen's caps. This showed, in machine-woven gold wire gothic script, the name of their parent flotilla. Initially to be numbered, shortly after the introduction of the ribbon 'I. Unterseebootsflotille I', tradition names were given instead to the flotillas. All were named after U-boat aces of World War I, to foster unit pride and esprit de corps. The following ribbons were manufactured and worn until, just prior to the outbreak of war, they were withdrawn and for security reasons replaced by a simple ribbon with the legend 'Kriegsmarine':

Unterseebootsflotille *Weddigen*	1st U-Boat Flotilla
Unterseebootsflotille *Salzwedel*	2nd U-Boat Flotilla
Unterseebootsflotille *Lohs*	3rd U-Boat Flotilla
Unterseebootsflotille *Emsmann*	5th U-Boat Flotilla
Unterseebootsflotille *Hundius*	6th U-Boat Flotilla
Unterseebootsflotille *Wegener*	7th U-Boat Flotilla

The degree of pride with which these ribbons were worn can be seen in that fact that many donned their ribbons for special occasions, or to sit for portrait photographs, after their general use had been prohibited. In fact, during the special reception held for Prien and his crew in Berlin after the sinking of the *Royal Oak*, the ribbon 'Unterseebootsflotille *Weddigen*' can be seen being worn by the crewmen, though in most pictures the censor has carefully altered the photographs to cover the word '*Weddigen*'. Ribbons were also produced for the U-boat training schools and training flotilla and for the U-boat Support Ships and Escorts.

The sense of belonging to a small elite team was actively fostered by most good commanders in a variety of ways. Insignia were chosen by most boats and worn as a small badge on the left-hand side of the sailor's headgear. It could be the coat of arms of a city which had sponsored the building of the boat by fund-raising efforts, or perhaps a direct reference to the commander (Adalbert Schnee's boat bore the representation of a snowman – *Schneemann* – as a pun on his name) or any one of myriad cartoon-like animals or mythical figures – sharks and devils being very popular. The badges ranged from crude designs fashioned from scrap metal to die-struck, finely enamelled manufactured items. They all helped to foster team spirit and the all-important sense of belonging.

The wearing of combat decorations also played a major part in fostering morale in the German armed forces. Unlike the Anglo-American tradition of wearing just the medal ribbon rather than the award itself, Germans tended to wear the actual award (most of the combat awards being pin-back rather than suspended from a ribbon) in combat. These badges were outward signs of the fact that the soldier was a veteran of front-line combat and were worn with considerable pride. As far as U-boat men were concerned, however, the interior of a cramped submarine, with a million and one possibilities for snagging metal badges pinned to tunics as men squeezed through hatches and other confined spaces, was not a suitable place for wear of decorations and meant that, as often as not, such insignia were not worn when on combat patrol. On returning to land, however, and donning their 'blues' for going on leave, U-boat men wore their insignia and badges with every bit as much pride as any other soldier.

U-boat men were of course eligible for the same range of gallantry and service awards as any other serviceman and indeed the Iron Cross and other such decorations will be noted being worn in many of the photographs in this book.

On completion of his second operational war cruise, a U-boat crewman would qualify for the *U-Bootskriegsabzeichen* or U-Boat War Badge. This small gilt metal oval badge, showing a submarine lying across a wreath of laurel leaves with a national emblem at the top, was worn with great pride as the mark of a seasoned combat veteran. The badge was worn on the left breast of the uniform tunic and even on some of the special U-boat clothing, though not the leather garments. The award of this badge would be logged in the crewman's *Soldbuch* and his military records, and the badge itself was accompanied by an impressive

award document. Sailors who had lost their lives in action before completing their second war cruise could be posthumously decorated with the U-Boat War Badge. In such cases a special version of the award document, indicating the posthumous nature of the award, was sent to the sailor's next of kin along with an example of the badge; a letter of condolence from the flotilla commander would follow.

For those U-boat commanders who had been particularly successful, their achievements would inevitably be rewarded by a number of decorations. Initially, the successful commander would be presented with the Knight's Cross of the Iron Cross, usually after sinking a particular tonnage of enemy ships, though this general rule would often be waived for a particularly successful attack on a major enemy warship (e.g. Prien's sinking of the battleship *Royal Oak*, Tiesenhausen's sinking of the battleship *Barham* or Guggenberg's sinking of the aircraft carrier *Ark Royal*). Continued successes would then be rewarded by the Oakleaves to the Knight's Cross, the Oakleaves with Swords, and so on.

On a particularly successful commander's being decorated with the Oakleaves to the Knight's Cross, he would usually also receive the U-Boat War Badge with Diamonds. Based on the design of the regular badge, and made by the firm

ABOVE LEFT

The mark of a combat U-boat crewman was the U-Boat War Badge, earned after the completion of two war cruises. At top is a standard gilt metal version and below a machine-embroidered alternative, one which lack of photographic evidence suggests was rarely used. (Author's collection)

ABOVE RIGHT

The award document for the U-Boat War Badge, complete with facsimile signature of Karl Dönitz. This document is for the badge awarded to Maschinenmaat Siewert Bahnsen, a crew member of U-154. (Author's collection)

of Schwerin in Berlin, this version had a solid silver swastika, set with nine small diamonds, set over the original on the badge. This award was not a formal government award, but a token of gratitude and personal esteem presented by the Commander-in-Chief Navy. These awards were presented initially by Grossadmiral Erich Raeder, but the practice was continued by Dönitz. There was no formal award document for the badge, which was simply accompanied by a personal letter of congratulations from the C-in-C.

In the case of Dönitz, as C-in-C U-Boats, the tremendous success achieved by his men was rewarded by the presentation to him of a special unique version of the diamonds badge. In this pattern, not only the swastika, but also the laurel wreath which framed the badge, were set with diamonds. On his arrest in 1945, the badge was removed from Dönitz's possession and defaced by having the diamond-studded swastika snapped off.

In May 1944 a further award was introduced by Dönitz to recognise the bravery and commitment of U-boat crewmen, the *U-Boots-Frontspange* (U-Boat Front Clasp). This award was a clasp bearing a smaller version of the basic U-Boat War Badge, but had a pair of crossed swords at its base and a spray of six oakleaves emerging horizontally from either side of the central motif. The clasp was in bronzed metal and worn above the left breast pocket. There were no set award criteria, but a number of factors would be taken into account such as length of combat service, number of missions or war cruises undertaken, any conduct worthy of special merit and any specific acts of personal bravery. Recommendations for the award were made by individual U-boat commanders and each was approved by Dönitz. In November 1944, a further grade in silver was introduced to reward those who continued to distinguish themselves after the award of the bronze clasp.

One other rarely bestowed award which was held by a handful of U-boat men was the Honour Roll Clasp of the German Navy (*Ehrenblattspange der Kriegsmarine*). Instituted on 13 May 1944, this consisted of a small gilded metal wreath of oakleaves in the centre of which sat a fouled anchor with a swastika superimposed on its centre. The clasp had four prongs on the reverse by which it was affixed to the ribbon of the Iron Cross Second Class and worn from the tunic buttonhole. Only one U-boat commander received this rare decoration, Kapitänleutnant Ottokar Paulsen (U-557), and in his case the award was posthumous. Leutnant (Ing.) Waldemar Geschke (U-2) and Leutnant (Ing.) Albert Moors (U-416) were named in the Roll of Honour but as they did not at the time possess the Iron Cross First Class, a pre-requisite for the bestowal of the Honour Roll Clasp, they did not receive the actual award.

Given the very high rate of attrition in the U-Bootwaffe in the second part of the war, it will be appreciated that few U-boat men survived sufficiently long to earn

the U-Boat Front Clasp. In fact, an increasing number did not survive long enough to earn the basic U-Boat War Badge as the number of boats lost on their first mission grew alarmingly. The U-Boat War Badge and Front Clasp became a visible sign to others that its wearer had survived combat in the most difficult of conditions and had earned the right to consider himself truly part of this elite branch of the navy. Dönitz was well aware of the morale value of such decorations and made every effort to ensure that no red tape stood in the way of processing commanders' recommendations for awards to members of their crews.

Many successful commanders made courtesy visits to the shipyards which had built their submarines, to foster good relations and a sense of bonding between the men who built the U-boats and those who sailed in them. Special merit badges (*Werftleistungsabzeichen*) were awarded to shipyard workers for quality and proficiency in their work.

Particularly successful commanders generally considered the awards bestowed upon them as being worn on behalf of the entire crew, every good U-boat commander

Two proud U-boat crewmen pose with their freshly awarded Iron Crosses. The Iron Cross Second Class was normally only worn on the day of bestowal, or in full dress parade uniform, thereafter only the ribbon being used.

At the end of yet another war cruise, a grizzled warrant officer is on watch. He wears the double-breasted leather coat favoured by deck personnel, and like most officers and senior NCOs, he wears his peaked visor cap. On the side of his cap is the emblem of his boat, the prancing devil of U-732.

On a leather strap around his neck is a pair of top-quality powerful binoculars (**1**). Several weeks of life in the damp, oppressive interior of the U-boat has left him with red-rimmed eyes and a full beard. Soon, he will avail himself of the luxury of a hot bath and a shave, put on his best blues, pack his kitbag (**2**) and set off for a well-earned spell of home leave.

For a U-boat which had been tossed around for several days fighting strong currents and a North Atlantic gale, the chance to take an accurate fix on its location with a traditional old fashioned sextant (**3**) would be most welcome. The standard navy sextant had a black protective finish and was usually stored in a wooden box.

Most U-boat bridges were equipped with a pedestal mount for the *U-Bootzieloptik* or UZO (**4**), a large, heavy set of binoculars in an extremely thick, pressure-tested case. When a surface attack was about to be launched, the command, '*UZO zum Brücke*' ('UZO to the Bridge') would be given. The UZO would be fitted to the clamp in the centre of the pedestal to form an aiming device, data being transmitted to the attack computer. (Artwork by Darko Pavlovic © Osprey Publishing)

realising that the boat's crew had to operate as a team, with everyone deserving a share of the plaudits. Because of the 'teamwork' nature of service on a submarine, it would often be difficult to identify specific individuals for reward, and it was often the case that U-Boat Command would allocate a number of Iron Crosses to a particular boat and leave it to the commander to decide who would be decorated. In several cases, commanders demanded additional awards if they felt that the efforts of their men had not been sufficiently recognised.

Dönitz's own pride in his U-boat fleet can also be seen reflected in the magnificent baton or *Admiralstab*, presented to him on his elevation to the rank of Grossadmiral in 1943. These batons had been symbolic badges of rank of Grand Admirals and Field Marshals since Imperial times. Crafted by the prestigious Berlin jewellery firm of H. J. Wilm, the baton consisted of a 3.3cm diameter hollow shaft made from silver and covered in blue velvet. This shaft was then set with a pattern of Iron Cross, Gold Fouled Anchor, and Wehrmacht Eagle motifs. One finial, crafted from platinum and featuring a gold anchor border, showed on its end the German *Balkenkreuz*. Around the sides was the legend '*Zum Freiheitskampf des – Grossdeustchen Volkes. Januar / 1943*'. The top end, however, surrounded by gold lettering reading 'Der Führer – Dem Grossadmiral Dönitz' featured on the face of the finial, the U-Boat War Badge, crafted from 18-carat gold and with the submarine lying across its centre made from genuine platinum. This immensely valuable artefact was stolen from Dönitz when he was taken into custody and now resides in a museum in England.

By the final days of the war, most U-boat men must have long since realised that military defeat was inevitable. No one could have failed to notice the number of boats which failed to return, and many must have felt that each time they put to sea, it might well be their last. Yet the morale of the U-Bootwaffe remained remarkably stable even in these darkest days. The most important factors in maintaining this morale were pride in what they as U-boat men had achieved, an intense feeling of loyalty to their crew comrades, and the knowledge that they had fought their war as cleanly and as honourably as any. Even today, although the march of time means that fewer former submariners remain with us, the Verband Deutscher U-Bootfahrer e.V. thrives, producing a regular magazine for former U-boat crewmen.

COMBAT ACTION

Once the vessel was cleared for sea, a U-boat would set off on its war cruise from its home port, usually escorted out into the open sea by a surface vessel (the *U-Bootsbegleitschiff* or U-boat escort ship). A typical Type VII U-boat would have a crew make-up along the following lines:

Commander	Kapitänleutnant, usually referred to as 'Herr Kaleu'. There were a few Korvettenkapitän-ranked commanders and a number of commanders with the rank of Oberleutnant zur See, particularly later in the war.
First Officer	Typically, an Oberleutnant zur See (or Leutnant zur See on boats where the commander was an Oberleutnant). The First Watch Officer was usually referred to as the IWO.
Second Officer	Usually a Leutnant zur See and referred to as the 'Zweiter Wach Offizier'.

Engineering Officer	Generally a Leutnant or Oberleutnant zur See, his title was 'Leitender Ingenieur' or Leading Engineer and he was normally referred to as the 'LI'.
Third Watch Officer	This post was held by a warrant officer grade, typically the Obersteuermann or Navigator.
Fourth Watch Officer	This was a non-commissioned post often held by the Oberbootsmaat or bosun.

The remainder of the crew would be made up approximately as follows (total crew numbers could vary from boat to boat):

Stabsobermaschinist	Chief Warrant Officer	(1)	Engine Room
Obermaschinist	Senior Warrant Officer	(2)	Engine Room
Maschinenobermaat	Chief Petty Officer	(2)	Engine Room
Maschinenmaat	Petty Officer	(5)	Engine Room
Maschinenobergefreiter	Leading Seaman	(11)	Engine Room
Maschinengefreiter	Able Seaman	(5)	Engine Room
Funkobermaat	Chief Petty Officer	(3)	Radio Operator
Funkobergefreiter	Leading Seaman	(1)	Radio Operator
Funkgefreiter	Able Seaman	(2)	Radio Operator
Oberbootsmann	Senior Warrant Officer	(2)	
Bootsmann	Warrant Officer	(1)	
Matrosenobergefreiter	Leading Seaman	(7)	
Matrosengefreiter	Able Seaman	(3)	
Obermechaniker	Senior Warrant Officer	(1)	Torpedo Room
Mechanikermaat	Petty Officer	(2)	Torpedo Room
Mechanikerobergefreiter	Leading Seaman	(1)	Torpedo Room
Mechanikergefreiter	Able Seaman	(1)	Torpedo Room
Sanitätsmaat	Petty Officer	(1)	Medical Orderly

When at sea, most of the crew operated in a rotation of eight hours on duty, eight hours' sleep, and eight hours of miscellaneous tasks, which might include a spell on lookout duty, general maintenance tasks, eating, and some off-duty relaxation time. Bridge watch duty lasted four hours. On bridge watch, one of the watch officers would be present together with four lookouts. In heavy seas, special safety belts were worn which clipped onto mounts on the bridge, to prevent the lookouts being swept overboard. Engine-room personnel worked a different rota, with a simple six hours on and six hours off duty. This was a more exhausting schedule, but engine-room crewmen were excused the sometimes arduous bridge watch.

The cook (known as 'Smutje') was the only man on board not expected to serve a watch. His task was simply to ensure the crew was well fed. Because of the frequent changes of shifts, men needed some hot nourishment almost constantly,

and the cook's task was certainly not a 'cushy' number. Good cooks were highly valued by their comrades.

The boat would have orders to patrol a sector of ocean designated on a chart by an alpha-numeric grid reference. Reaching the area of operations might take several days and, wherever possible, the boat would travel on the surface in waters that were considered relatively 'safe'. A typical Type VII U-boat could attain a top speed of some 17 knots on the surface, with an average cruising speed of 10 knots. Underwater, however, using its battery-powered electro-motors, a maximum speed of around 7 knots is all that might be expected, with an average speed nearer to 4 knots. In particularly heavy seas the boat might be tossed around so much that it would make little, if any, headway and so might dive to take advantage of the calmer waters deep under the surface. This would gradually drain the batteries, so the boat would have to return to the surface within about 24 hours to run its diesel engines in order to recharge the batteries. Only after the advent of the *Schnorchel* breathing device could a U-boat charge its batteries by running its diesels without surfacing. Even this was not without danger, however. The *Schnorchel* tube

Life on a combat U-boat during an operational cruise. Here we see the crew of the bow compartment snatching a meal, their foldaway table resting on two spare torpedoes. Until some of their payload was fired off, space in this compartment was very limited.

featured a ball valve, which was raised by the swell of the sea, so that it would shut to prevent ingress of water, then lower and open again as the swell faded. If the valve shut whilst the diesels were running, the engines would then draw air from the vessel's interior causing a partial vacuum and intense pain and discomfort to the occupants. 'Snorkelling', therefore, was only really suitable in calm waters. There was also the added danger that the exposed head of the *Schnorchel* tube, or the wake it left in the sea, would be spotted by an enemy vessel or aircraft.

Assuming no enemy activity, the journey to the operational area could often be one of extreme boredom, with little to occupy the off-watch sailors. When the vessel was on the surface, a full watch was mounted, with a watch officer and between four and six lookouts, each scanning a sector of the horizon and sky with powerful binoculars for any sign of danger, and of course any possible victims. This was potentially a very dangerous duty. Quite apart from having to suffer the rigours of whatever foul weather the Atlantic threw at them, the lookouts could very easily become drowsy after long periods of staring at an empty sky or horizon. A lookout who dozed off might be overlooked as the bridge watch dashed back into the boat once an alarm was called, his absence only noticed when it was too late.

When preparing to attack the enemy, 'action stations' (*'auf Gefechtstationen!'*) would be called. The crew would vacate the bridge and close all vents and hatches. The diesels would be shut down and the electro-motors would take over. The bow planes would be angled down and speed increased so that water flowed over them in the same way in which air flows over the elevator flaps on an aircraft, thus forcing the boat underwater faster. At the same time the dive tanks would be flooded to make the boat heavier; any crewmen not occupied on essential duties would rush to the bow compartment to increase the weight in the forward part of the boat.

If the boat was in a position of extreme danger, the cry 'Alaaaarm!' would ring out, signifying a fast dive. In many cases the boat would start diving as the vents were being closed and even before the bridge was cleared. There was a real danger of flooding if the bridge crew were not quick enough in entering the boat and securing the main hatch. It has been estimated that the safety margin in time between a boat submerging and the arrival of the expected enemy aircraft could be as little as ten seconds, so it is no surprise that crews used every conceivable method of shaving a few seconds off the diving time.

Once at the required depth below the surface, the boat would level off and hydroplanes would be used to keep the boat stable and stop it from rising to the surface. U-boats normally had a slightly negative trim, so that if fully stopped they would slowly sink. In order to stay at the required depth, some forward

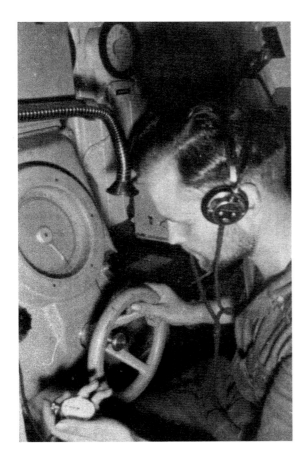

movement was therefore needed and this, in conjunction with skilled use of the hydroplanes, kept the boat level. Although compressed air could shift water fore and aft between bow and stern trim tanks to adjust the balance of the vessel, the simple expedient of moving unoccupied crew members from one end of the boat to the other was often used instead.

In the tiny radio room, underwater sound detection equipment listened for the noise made by the propellers of enemy ships. Sound carries a long distance under water, but various conditions such as the salinity of the water could affect the efficiency of the equipment. The Germans had very highly developed acoustic detectors, and an experienced *Unterwasserhorcher* (sound detector operator) could differentiate between the sound of a slow-moving merchantman and the faster-revolving propellers of escorting warships.

Having found a likely target, the commander would bring the boat to periscope depth and, using the navigation periscope, would check that the area was safe and

ABOVE LEFT

On operations, the sound detector operator played a highly important role, both in detecting propeller noises from the convoys they hunted, and in detecting the destroyers which hunted the U-boats in turn. (F. Saez)

ABOVE RIGHT

In order to help the crew relax from the tensions of service during operations, when no enemy was around, records of the captain's and crew's favourite tunes would be played over the intercom. Here the radio operator prepares to play the latest choice.

also that the sky above was clear. The boat would then surface, venting the diesel exhausts into the dive tanks to help the boat to surface quickly and also save precious compressed air. If no escorting enemy warships were in the vicinity, the boat would carry out its attack on the surface, preferably in darkness, as it was extremely difficult to spot a surfaced U-boat at night. If attacking on the surface, the IWO would supervise checking the torpedo gear and setting up the UZO, while the commander conned the ship into the best attack position.

The UZO, or *U-Bootzieloptik*, was a pair of sturdy and powerful binoculars which fitted to a special mount on the torpedo-aiming pedestal on the bridge, and was linked to the attack computer in the commander's control room. The computer would adjust the settings for any subsequent changes in the U-boat's course or speed. This data fed onto an indicator in the torpedo compartment so that the appropriate setting could be made for them. A panel with illuminated buttons indicated readiness to fire and the firing order. Although the fire order could be transmitted automatically, the order to fire was normally given verbally by the IWO, called down through the hatch into the central control room (*Zentrale*) and to the seaman operating the firing buttons in the torpedo compartment. In the central control room, the LI would be monitoring the trim and speed, whilst the *Obersteuermann* charted the boat's movement on the small map table.

A total of 14 torpedoes would be carried. Five were pre-loaded in the tubes (four bow and one stern), one was in between the two electro-motors, four on the decking of the torpedo compartment with two more under the decking, and finally two in the space between the pressure hull and the exterior skin, under the hull decking.

If a surface attack was considered too hazardous, the boat would be brought to periscope depth and a submerged attack planned. The commander would enter the so-called 'Commander's Control Room', which was simply the empty conning tower space through which everyone had to pass to reach the bridge. It housed the attack periscope, to which was affixed a small seat resembling a bicycle saddle. This space also contained the torpedo calculator, operated by the IWO who would feed in data given by the commander. Regulations required that the hatch down into the *Zentrale* should be closed, but it was generally left open so that orders could be called down into the boat, rather than transmitted by a voice tube. The helmsman would steer the boat on the direct orders of the commander.

Meanwhile, in the radio room, the signals personnel would keep a listening watch on the radio. To avoid detection, radio silence was generally observed until such point as the enemy had already become aware of the boat's presence. The sound detector operator would also be listening out for the sound of any approaching high-speed screws which might indicate the presence of an enemy escort vessel.

Once the order to shoot (in fact the term used was 'release' or '*los*', as in '*Torpedo Los!*') had been given and a spread of torpedoes fired, tanks in the forward part of the hull would be flooded, taking on extra water to compensate for the lost weight of several tons of torpedoes. As the torpedoes sped towards their target, their running time, which would have been calculated with regard to their speed and the distance to the target, would be counted off using a stop-watch. A detonation at the appropriate time would indicate a hit, whilst one several seconds late could indicate a harmless detonation at the end of the torpedo's run. No detonation at all would indicate a faulty torpedo, an all too familiar occurrence. At this point, if any escorting warships were in the area, retribution would follow swiftly.

Of all the anti-submarine weapons the U-boat man had to face, few were as dreaded as the depth charge or *Wasserbombe*. Crew members were well aware that if a depth charge exploded close enough to cause a rupture in the pressure

The depth charge was used as an anti-submarine weapon by all navies. Here, a German seaman tends to the depth charges on an E-boat. The cylindrical steel container was by far the most typical style used by most nations.

hull, they were effectively doomed to a horrifying death, the chances of being able to surface and abandon ship being slim indeed.

The depth charge itself was a simple canister-shaped charge. The canister was packed with a high explosive such as Torpex and had a pressure-sensitive detonator, which was adjustable from the exterior using a simple key. Once the estimated depth of the U-boat was established, this depth setting would be applied to the detonator using the key, and the depth charge dropped overboard. Charges could be launched either from a projector on the side of the vessel, or simply rolled off the stern of the ship where they were held in special racks. Once the pressure-sensitive detonator detected that it had reached the required depth, the charge would explode causing a massive pressure wave. A depth charge would normally have to explode within 30–50m from the submarine to cause serious damage. A direct hit was not necessary. Hollywood movie images of depth charges exploding within a few feet of a submarine and the boat surviving are purely fictional.

Should the U-boat's sound detector operator detect the noise of a warship's high-speed propellers, the boat would turn from its course and dive much deeper to avoid the inevitable salvo of depth charges. Depth charges were set to explode at a predetermined depth, so a cat-and-mouse game would follow as the enemy warship tried to second-guess the U-boat commander. 'Asdic' detection equipment bounced a 'ping' of sound through water and caused an echo to rebound from any object in its path, giving a fair indication of the object's approximate location, but not its depth.

Asdic was named for the Anti-Submarine Detection Investigation Committee. Its concept, now known as sonar, had been in existence since around 1918 and had been continued and developed by the Royal Navy in the years that followed. Asdic equipment sent a sound wave through the water from a transmitter, and any 'reflection' of this sound from an object underwater was picked up by a receiver. The time taken for the reflecting sound to hit the receiver gave an indication of the distance of the object. The system was far from perfect and false readings could be obtained from whales or large shoals of fish. Rough water conditions and differing salinity or thermal layers in the water could also affect readings, as could the propeller wash of other ships and the noise of the ship with the Asdic device itself passing through the water if going at any significant speed. Asdic contact would normally be lost when the search vessel was around 300m from the target object. The U-boat commander would try to judge this point and, just as the contact was lost, make a sharp turn to the left or right. Going to full speed at this moment also caused considerable disturbance in the water which caused Asdic to lose contact. The Kriegsmarine also developed the anti-Asdic device known as Bold, which gave a false reading on Asdic similar to the reading for the submarine itself. The effect lasted for up to 25 minutes, giving the U-boat time to make good its escape. For all its power, a depth charge dropped in the right spot, but too deep or too shallow in relation to the target, would merely shake the U-boat about, causing little real damage.

Psychologically, however, being trapped within a damp steel tube deep underwater with no means of escape, having to endure the eerie ping of the Asdic bouncing from the hull and the fast-approaching swish from the propellers of an enemy warship laden with high explosive, could strain the nerves of even the most resolute U-boat man. As the depth charges exploded, the boat would be shaken about, throwing anything that was not fastened down onto the deck. Glass or

plates would be smashed. Lights would fail. Any glass faces to gauges and dials would shatter and leaky valves would let in jets of water at high pressure. It was not unknown for up to 300 depth charges to be dropped over a 24-hour period.

From here on, the skill of one man, the U-boat commander, was what really mattered. The electro-motors would be run at greatly reduced speed, and even orders on the boat would be given in hushed voices, everything being done in as near total silence as possible in the hope that the enemy would lose track of its quarry. These cat-and-mouse games could go on for many hours, each hour that passed giving ever-greater cause for concern as the air began to go stale and the batteries which drove the electro-motors were slowly depleted. In order to recharge them, the boat had to surface. Warships would play the same game, and often hove to on the surface, stopping the engines so that the U-boat would think they had departed. They would wait for the unsuspecting U-boat to increase its speed and give away its position, or surface under the guns of the warship.

If a U-boat was fatally damaged by a depth charge, escape was well nigh impossible. Even if the water was shallow enough that the hull was not crushed by water pressure as the boat plummeted into the depths, very few successful escapes using the *Tauchretter* were ever recorded. In most cases, the crew would be trapped in their steel coffin facing an agonising wait as their air slowly gave out. Indeed, those whose boats were crushed by water pressure probably met a swifter, if not kinder, death.

If a U-boat was struck while on the surface, those on the bridge would have a good chance of escaping the submarine, assuming they were not fired upon by their attackers. Even here, however, the water temperature might mitigate against survival, depending on the season of the year and the latitude at which the boat was sunk. Unless the boat was sinking very slowly, the engine-room crew would have very little chance of survival. In contrast to the naval tradition of the captain going down with his ship, the U-boat captain was usually in his position on the bridge if the boat was caught on the surface, and would stand a good chance of escape along with the rest of the bridge watch and many of those in the *Zentrale* just below. Unless the boat was in imminent danger of sinking, efforts would be made to scuttle her before any enemy boarding crew could gain access. The famous 'Enigma' decoding machine would be disposed of, or at least its secret rotors dropped overboard, as well as any orders, charts or other information useful to the enemy. These attempts were not always successful and a small number of boats were captured intact (U-110, U-570, U-505, and U-1024) or at least did not sink until some or all of the priceless Enigma rotors were salvaged (U-559). If the enemy really had given up and left the scene, the U-boat would surface and open its hatches to vent the foul air in the boat and allow crewmen standing around the base of the ladder leading up into the conning tower to gasp a few breaths of fresh air.

In the early part of the war when Allied air cover was sparse and vessels could often be found travelling unescorted, attempts were often made to sink the target

Grossadmiral Dönitz occasionally presented signed, dedicated formal portrait photographs of himself to U-boat men who had distinguished themselves in some way. Here one crewman shows an example of such a photograph to his admiring crewmates.

U-377 shown post-refit with a 2cm *Flakvierling* on its extended, lower *Wintergarten*. This boat was commanded by Kapitänleutnant Gerhard Kluth, just visible on the conning tower to the left in the white-topped cap. U-377 is believed to have been struck by one of its own T5 acoustic torpedoes during an attack on an Allied convoy on 15 January 1944.

with gunfire. Indeed the U-Bootwaffe initially kept fairly strictly to the accepted 'prize rules', which dictated that merchant ships had to be stopped and searched. If the vessel was an enemy ship or a neutral ship carrying cargo into an enemy port, the crew had to be evacuated safely before the vessel could be sunk. The U-boat obviously had to surface to carry out the search, and as the boat was on the surface anyway, it made sense to sink the target with gunfire rather than waste precious torpedoes. It was also common at this time for a ship which had been torpedoed, but had failed to sink, to be finished off with gunfire. A few well-placed hits along the waterline usually precipitated the sinking of the quarry.

The Type VII, which formed the backbone of the U-Bootwaffe in the first part of the war, was fitted out with an 8.8cm quick-firing naval gun mounted on the foredeck ahead of the conning tower. This gun was served by a crew of three, a gun layer, a gun aimer and a loader, supported by at least three men acting as ammunition carriers. The ammunition was stored in thick card containers under the decking of the radio room. These heavy shells had to be manhandled through the narrow confines of the U-boat's interior, up through the conning tower, across the bridge, down on to the after deck and along the slippery deck to the gun mount on the foredeck. The gun sights were also stored within the boat's interior and had to be carried out and attached to the gun by the gun crew each time the gun was used. Clearly, the main gun would only be used when in relatively safe situations where interruption from enemy aircraft or warships was considered unlikely.

Later changes in the prize rules relaxing the requirement to stop and search, together with the increasing air threat, meant that, increasingly, U-boats would attack enemy vessels on sight. As a result, the deck gun became gradually less important and was eventually removed altogether from most U-boats. At the same time, the significance of the U-boat's defensive armament took greater priority. At the start of the war most Type VIIs were armed with a 2cm flak gun, on a platform at the rear of the conning tower, which was intended as an anti-shipping weapon but took on more of a defensive role against enemy aircraft. Larger platforms were fitted which could take twin 2cm flak guns, and eventually an entire second platform known as the *Wintergarten* was fitted just below the upper platform, which could carry a 3.7cm flak gun or a four-barrelled 2cm *Flakvierling*.

Although there are several recorded examples of U-boats successfully shooting down attacking enemy aircraft, it was a brave flak crew indeed which would take on an enemy bomber or fighter. The flak crews had very little protection and the odds were stacked heavily in favour of the aircraft. Although for a period in 1943 U-boats were ordered to fight it out on the surface, this order was soon rescinded and boats would dive to escape aircraft wherever possible.

If U-boat crewmen survived the sinking of their boat, their trials were not over. With a few notable exceptions, U-boat crewmen were usually rescued and treated reasonably well immediately after their capture. For some reason, however, the Allied perception seemed to be that U-boat crews were predominantly made up of hardened Nazis. This may have been because of their generally high morale and their belief that the losses that they were inflicting on the Allies, in the early part of the war at least, would bring ultimate German victory. Many U-boat crewmen were badly treated and there are even records of some committing suicide after capture to avoid further torment. Even when the war was over, the perception that they were dangerous Nazis meant that many were held captive long after their counterparts from the surface fleet were released. Mostly, however, they were content that they had survived, unlike 29,000 of their comrades. The attrition rate of somewhere between 70 and 80 per cent is the highest casualty rate of any of the armed services in any of the combatant nations of World War II.

PART IV

TACTICS AND OPERATIONS

COMMAND AND CONTROL

At the pinnacle of the German Navy hierarchy sat the C-in-C Navy, the Ober-befehlshaber der Kriegsmarine (Grossadmiral Raeder 1928–43 and Gross-admiral Dönitz 1943–45).

Answering to the commander-in-chief was the Commander U-Boats, the Befehlshaber der U-Boote, generally referred to by the initials BdU. This post was held by Dönitz from its creation in 1940 through to 1945. During that entire time, the Chief of U-Boat Operations was Konteradmiral Eberhardt Godt. Many of the senior staff posts at BdU were held by veteran U-boat commanders.

BdU was divided into two departments, BdU-Op (Operations) and BdU-Org (Organisation – i.e. Training and Development). BdU was originally based in Germany but moved to occupied France in 1940 and then back to Germany in March 1943.

Thereafter, between BdU and the individual flotillas, came the submarine commander, Führer der U-Boote, or FdU in various theatres, thus FdU West, FdU

A Type VIIC running on the surface. Her gun crew is closed up but although the turret lacks the typical white horizontal band of a training boat, this is obviously a front-line boat undergoing gunnery exercises.

U-735, a Type VIIC launched at Danzig in 1942. This boat was sunk during an Allied air attack in Oslo Fjord on 28 December 1944. There was only one survivor. (Author's collection)

Mittelmeer, FdU Norwegen, etc., each of these operational areas having control over a number of individual flotillas.

FdU and other senior command posts which existed were:

FdU West. Established 1942. Based first in Paris, then Angers, and finally moved in 1944 to Bergen.

FdU Norwegen. Based first in Narvik, then merged with FdU West post in Bergen in 1944.

FdU Italien. Based first in Rome, subsequently moved to Toulon.

FdU Mittelmeer. Based in La Spezia.

FdU Ost. Based in Danzig.

FdU Mitte. Established in 1943. Based in Kiel.

Chef der Unterseebootbasen in Ostasien. Controlled U-boats operating out of Singapore and Penang, the so-called 'Monsoon Boats'.

Admiral der Schwarzes Meer. Controlled U-boats operating in the Black Sea. Based in Constanza.

U-BOAT FLOTILLAS

The flotilla was effectively a fixed command structure, but one where the boats over which it had control could change fairly frequently.

1. Unterseebootsflotille *Weddigen*	Brest (originally Kiel)
2. Unterseebootsflotille *Salzwedel*	Lorient (originally Wilhelmshaven)
3. Unterseebootsflotille *Lohs*	La Rochelle (originally Kiel)
4. Unterseebootsflotille	Stettin (training flotilla)
5. Unterseebootsflotille *Emsmann*	Kiel (training flotilla)
6. Unterseebootsflotille *Hundius*	St Nazaire (originally Danzig)

7.Unterseebootsflotille *Wegener*	St Nazaire (originally Kiel)
8.Unterseebootsflotille	Danzig (training flotilla)
9.Unterseebootsflotille	Brest
10.Unterseebootsflotille	Lorient
11.Unterseebootsflotille	Bergen
12.Unterseebootsflotille	Bordeaux
13.Unterseebootsflotille	Trondheim
14.Unterseebootsflotille	Narvik
18.Unterseebootsflotille	Hela (training flotilla)
19.Unterseebootsflotille	Pillau (training flotilla)
20.Unterseebootsflotille	Pillau (training flotilla)
21.Unterseebootsflotille	Pillau (training flotilla)
22.Unterseebootsflotille	Gotenhafen (training flotilla)
23.Unterseebootsflotille	Salamis
23.Unterseebootsflotille	Danzig (training flotilla)
24.Unterseebootsflotille	Memel (training flotilla)
25.Unterseebootsflotille	Libau (training flotilla)
26.Unterseebootsflotille	Pillau (training flotilla)
27.Unterseebootsflotille	Gotenhafen (training flotilla)
29.Unterseebootsflotille	La Spezia
30.Unterseebootsflotille	Constanza
31.Unterseebootsflotille	Hamburg (training flotilla)
32.Unterseebootsflotille	Königsberg (training flotilla)
33.Unterseebootsflotille	Flensburg

The number of boats controlled by any one flotilla could vary and, as already mentioned, boats could be assigned to different flotillas throughout their service.

In addition to these units, within U-boat Command were a small number of other important functions:

U-505, a typical Type IXC with her distinctive axe-head tradition insignia, enters a U-boat pen in occupied France. Commanded by Oberleutnant zur See Harald Lange, she was forced to the surface and captured north-west of Dakar on 4 June 1944 after having undertaken a total of 18 war patrols and having sunk eight enemy ships.

Agrufront (Ausbildungsgruppe für Front-U-Boote). A specialist training unit which reported on the readiness of both the crew and the boat for front line action after concentrated training exercises.

Unterseebootsabnahmekommando. This was the group which took possession of the U-boat from the shipyard for its official acceptance into the Kriegsmarine.

STATISTICS

During World War II, some 1,171 U-boats were operational. Of these, only some 325 actually carried out attacks on enemy shipping, sinking or damaging the enemy. Over 800 U-boats, therefore, were used only on training duties, were never used operationally, or were used but failed to find or attack the enemy.

Allied shipping losses to U-boat attacks were in the order of 3,000 vessels, representing well over 14,000,000 tons. Over 4,000,000 tons of shipping was sunk by the top 3 per cent of the U-boat commanders. Of all Allied shipping lost, almost 70 per cent was lost to attacks by U-boats. Not surprisingly, the vast majority of losses, well over 2,600 vessels, were lost to torpedo attacks or a combination of torpedo attack then gunfire to finish the victim off where the target was so badly damaged as not to warrant wasting an additional torpedo. Around 160 enemy ships were sunk by the effects of gunfire and around 100 by mines, the remaining losses being by various other methods or combinations of the above.

THE U-BOAT CAMPAIGN

TACTICS

Before considering the actual U-boat campaigns, a brief examination of the tactics employed may be useful to understanding the operations.

At the onset of war, Hitler had insisted that U-boats, and indeed surface ships also, should operate within the terms of the Prize Ordinance. The German rules, or to give them their correct title, 'Article 74 of the German Prize Ordinance', was based on an agreement which became effective in 1936, the *Procès Verbal to the Rules of Submarine Warfare* set forth in Part IV of the Treaty of London of 22 April 1930. This stated:

Except in the case of persistent refusal to stop on being duly summoned, or of active resistance to visit or search, a warship, whether surface vessel or submarine, may not sink or render incapable of navigation a merchant vessel without having first placed passengers, crew and ship's papers in a place of safety. For this purpose the ship's boats are not regarded as a place of safety unless the safety of the passengers and crew is assured, in the existing sea and weather conditions, by the proximity of land, or the presence of another vessel which is in a position to take them on board.

This highly restrictive set of rules required that any suspect ship be stopped and searched, and then sunk only if it were found to be carrying contraband. Even then, the crew had to be evacuated and its safety assured before the sinking. Whilst the first part of this rule created problems which, while difficult, were not insurmountable, it was almost impossible for a U-boat to assure the safety of the crew of a ship it had sunk. Placing the crew into lifeboats was not sufficient to comply with these rules, as there was no guarantee that the survivors in the lifeboats would subsequently be picked up. Clearly the restricted space within a U-boat precluded taking the enemy crew on board, and this left the U-boat captain in an almost impossible situation. Unless the lifeboats were within easy rowing distance of land, or on a busy shipping lane where their rescue in a short period of time was almost certain, the U-boat captain would almost certainly

Prior to the construction of the massive concrete U-boat pens, boats were required to moor in the open. Loading large quantities of stores into a U-boat through narrow hatches was a laborious and time-consuming business during which the boat was extremely vulnerable to attack.

find himself in breach of Prize Ordinance rules. Moreover, some merchantmen would attempt to ram the U-boat if the chance arose, and would certainly send off a warning signal by radio which could bring swift attention from enemy ships or aircraft, so that a leisurely stop and search routine was hardly a viable option.

Although the liner *Athenia* was sunk in the opening days of the war by Kapitänleutnant Fritz-Julius Lemp of U-30, who had mistaken her for a troopship, German adherence to these rules continued for some time. Hitler was keen not to sink ships which might be carrying neutrals such as Americans, and thereby risk the USA being drawn into the war in a repeat of the *Lusitania* incident in World War I. Nevertheless, restrictions on attacking enemy ships were gradually eased, though adherence to the Prize Ordinance continued to a considerable degree until as late as August 1940. Ships travelling in convoy however, were soon considered fair game for the U-boat commander.

Restrictions were first eased on 23 September when U-boats were given permission to attack any ship using its wireless to summon aid. On the following day, restrictions against attacks on French vessels were lifted. On the last day of the month, the application of Prize Rules was lifted against vessels encountered in the North Sea. A further extension of the area in which the use of Prize Rules was to be lifted was declared on 2 October and on 17 October U-boats were permitted to attack all ships positively identified as 'hostile'. Attacks on liners, previously prohibited, were permitted from 17 November if the vessel was identified as 'hostile'.

In the early part of the war, U-boats tended for the most part to act alone, patrolling designated areas in search of the enemy. This was as much due to the sheer lack of available numbers as to any other factor. In the early months of the war it is estimated that there were rarely ever more than around half a dozen U-boats at sea at any one time. Notwithstanding the small numbers of boats available, a number of notable successes were scored within weeks of the outbreak of war. In mid-September, British attempts to beef up the strength of convoy escorts by adding small aircraft carriers were thwarted when the carrier *Courageous* was sunk by U-9, and barely one month later Kapitänleutnant Günther Prien in U-47 penetrated the fleet anchorage at Scapa Flow and sank the battleship *Royal Oak*.

Although the convoy system had already been introduced at the start of the war, lack of suitable numbers of escort vessels meant that the bulk of shipping was still sailing independently, many vessels depending on their relatively fast speed to keep them out of danger. The older, slower vessels, too, were left out of convoys lest they slow them down too much, the convoy only being able to proceed at the speed of the slowest ship if it was to stay together.

ATTACKING A NIGHT CONVOY

Night attacks on the surface were used very successfully during the first half of the war, as the low profile of the U-boat in darkness made it very difficult to spot. This U-boat has taken part in a night attack on a convoy in which an enemy merchant ship has been successfully torpedoed but has failed to sink.

Having survived the counter-attack by convoy escorts, the U-boat surfaces at first light to apply the coup de grâce. Such surface sinkings became less common as the war drew on, as the chances of the U-boat being detected on the surface by enemy aircraft or surface vessels dramatically increased. In fact, deck guns were eventually withdrawn altogether; they were virtually worthless as an offensive weapon and simply produced excess drag, slowing down the boat's underwater speed. In this scene, the dull cloud-laden sky camouflages the boat from any enemy aircraft that might be patrolling. The boat's commander has therefore decided to surface and use his deck gun now that the convoy and its escorting warships have passed, saving precious torpedoes for future targets and also giving his gun crew an opportunity for much-needed practice.

The gun was also only likely to be used in moderately calm waters, stormy seas making accurate shooting from a relatively unstable gun

platform even more difficult. The three-man gun crew are servicing the weapon while additional crew members bring up fresh 8.8 cm ammunition all the way through the boat from its storage space under the decking of the radio room. All are wearing steel helmets, a rarely used piece of headgear on a U-boat, and have taken the sensible precaution of donning life preservers over their protective leather clothing.

The attack is being directed by the second watch officer, gunnery control being one of his allocated duties. He is directing the gun from his position in the conning tower, observing the fall of shot through his binoculars and giving instructions to the gun layer to adjust his aim.

The first shot, into the enemy's radio room to prevent the broadcast of a distress call, was successful, and the bridge area is ablaze. The second shot, aimed at the waterline to hole the vessel and speed her sinking, has just fallen short and having made adjustments to the aim, a third shot is about to be fired.

This action may well take some time, as a ship's buoyancy depended partly on the cargo carried. In some recorded cases, over 100 shells were fired to sink an enemy vessel by gunfire. This would only be attempted in areas where the commander was confident of remaining undisturbed by the enemy. (Artwork by Darko Pavlovic © Osprey Publishing)

What has become universally known as the 'Wolf pack' originated in World War I, though during that conflict it was never fully developed. There is considerable argument over who was responsible for the introduction of the tactic, Dönitz himself claiming credit whilst others scorn his claim and suggest that Kommodore Bauer may have been the originator. Given that military units operate in groups (battalions, regiments, etc.), aircraft fly in groups (squadrons, wings, etc.) and even surface ships rarely operate solo but in concert with other craft from their flotilla, the concept of operating U-boats in groups must have been one which many U-boat commanders saw as having definite advantages. Dönitz, however, in his capacity as BdU was certainly the one who was in a position to implement and develop the tactic.

Initially, the early version of what has generally become known as wolf pack tactics consisted of attacks on Allied convoys by groups of U-boats. When one boat spotted a convoy, other boats within striking distance would be instructed to join in the attack. These boats before and after the attacks operated independently and so the 'pack' only existed for the duration of the attack. True wolf packs, where the boats operated as a group from the outset, only came into general use in 1941.

During the first part of the war, the 'group' tactic worked relatively well and some considerable successes were achieved. Many of the better commanders, however, developed their own tactics. The perceived wisdom at the time was that a U-boat would stand off from the convoy by a couple of kilometres or more, submerged, and fire a 'spread' of torpedoes at the convoy, anticipating at least some hits. Aces like Otto Kretschmer, however, found that at night, with the U-boat being such a small vessel, he could approach a convoy on the surface and even penetrate into the convoy without detection. From such a close range, he

U-47 returns to port after a mission. Note on the side of the conning tower Prien's famous 'snorting bull' emblem painted in white. The 'Bull of Scapa Flow' was adopted by the entire flotilla to celebrate Prien's achievement.

would be almost guaranteed a hit with each torpedo. Barring faulty torpedoes, Kretschmer's goal of 'one torpedo – one ship' was attainable.

OPERATIONS
1939

In August 1939, just prior to the outbreak of war, a grand total of just 18 U-boats were sent to sea. Of these, five were the small coastal Type II craft and 13 the ocean-going Type VII. Britain had declared a blockade of Germany on 26 September and, using the small force of U-boats now at sea, Germany intended to return the favour and carry out its own blockade of the British Isles.

The first recorded group attack (not allocated a code-name as in subsequent operations) took place in October 1939. Six U-boats were sent out to intercept British convoys. Originally the force was to have consisted of nine boats but two (U-34 and U-25) were undergoing repair in dry dock and one, U-47 under Prien, was detached for the mission to Scapa Flow. Three boats, U-40 (Barten), U-42 (Dau) and U-45 (Gelhaar), were lost to enemy action en route. For those boats that saw action, U-37 (Hartmann), U-25 (Schütze) and U-48 (Schultze), the operation was moderately successful. Three enemy merchantmen from Convoy HG3 were sunk: the *Baoule* by U-25, the *Yorkshire* by U-37 and the *Clan Chisholm* by U-48. A further group of four boats was sent out in November but without success. No Allied ships were sunk. Fortunately, this time, no U-boats were lost either. No further group attacks were made until the summer of 1940.

A typical early Type IX, U-66, pulls into port after a war cruise. Note the bouquets of flowers on the bridge and the crowds of well-wishers on the quayside. Such happy events were common in the early part of the war, but became less so as losses grew and fewer and fewer victories were scored.

U-331, a Type VIIC and one of Germany's most famous submarines after her sinking of the British battleship *Barham* in the Mediterranean on 25 November 1941. U-331 was herself sunk in a controversial attack by Allied aircraft on 17 November 1942.

From the outbreak of war until the end of 1939, 147 enemy ships were sunk. Of these, 100 were sailing independently and only 22 were in convoy. The remaining 25 were lost to mines laid by U-boats. No U-boats were lost to enemy action during this period.

1940

Between January and May of 1940, 126 Allied ships were sunk, totalling over 500,000 tons. Once again, the majority of these victims had been travelling independently.

Very few specific anti-shipping operations were carried out in March and April, with the bulk of the available U-boat number being allocated to Operation *Weserübung*, the invasion of Norway. U-boats were to patrol the entrances to Norway's fjords to prevent any Allied incursions. In the event, although many choice targets appeared before the waiting U-boats, torpedo problems meant that a substantial number of potential sinkings were lost.

The quality of the torpedoes available to the U-boats left much to be desired. Dönitz was almost beside himself with fury at the number of reports being received from his U-boat commanders of faulty 'eels'. Magnetic pistols were not functioning correctly, causing premature detonations, and the depth-regulating mechanisms on the torpedoes were faulty, meaning that many ran too deep and passed harmlessly under their intended targets to explode ineffectually at the end of their runs. Dönitz was extremely outspoken in his criticisms, so much so that the C-in-C Navy, Grossadmiral Raeder, had already fired off an extremely terse note to Dönitz over his aggressive tone. On the positive side, the restrictions on the circumstances under which U-boats were permitted to attack were being

A Type VIIC approaches the U-boat
bunkers at La Pallice. The availability
of ports with direct access to the
Atlantic, with bomb-proof pens in
which the returning boats could
shelter, made life, for a time at least,
much easier for the U-Bootwaffe.

eased, with the waters around Great Britain being declared an exclusion zone in which all ships were liable to attack.

With the successful conclusion of the campaign in the west, the Kriegsmarine now had at its disposal a number of captured French naval installations which provided ideal locations for U-boat bases, giving them direct access to the Atlantic without having to pass through waters heavily patrolled by the Royal Navy. The considerable saving in journey time also gave the U-boats a much greater operational range, allowing them to patrol much further out into the Atlantic. Bases were also established in Norway giving direct access to the North Sea and faster access to the North Atlantic and the North-West Approaches.

Two further group operations were launched in June 1940. The first, code-named *Prien*, included six U-boats, one of them U-47 under ace commander Günther Prien. Convoy HX48 avoided interception, although three merchant ships, stragglers from the convoy, were sunk. The other, code-named *Rösing*, was less successful. Comprising five U-boats, it failed to intercept the convoy it sought. A further un-named pack in mid-August failed to achieve any successes, though a group, also un-named, sent out at the end of that month and once again including in its number Günther Prien in U-47, intercepted Convoy SC2 and sank five ships. Four of them – some 18,500 tons in total – fell victim to U-47: the *Neptunian*, the *Jose de Larrinaga*, the *Gro* and the *Possidon*. U-28 accounted for the fifth, a smaller 2,400-ton freighter. Despite the modest successes scored by the wolf packs up to this point, the U-boat war in general was going well. The period between summer and the end of 1940 became known to the Germans as the first 'Happy Time'. Between June and December 1940, over 360 enemy ships were sunk, accounting for almost 2,000,000 tons. U-boats were ranging well out into the Atlantic, well beyond the areas in which air cover could be provided, and were wreaking havoc amongst poorly protected convoys.

On 21 September, Convoy HX72 came under attack from a group of nine U-boats in the Atlantic off the west coast of Ireland. The convoy was protected by seven escort warships, a mixture of destroyers, corvettes and sloops. A total of 11 ships totalling over 50,000 tons were sunk. The roll call of this pack is like a catalogue of aces – Prien, Schepke, Kretschmer, Bleichrodt and Jenisch. Schepke alone accounted for seven ships totalling over 50,000 tons.

In October, a further group of six boats – U-38 (Liebe), U-46 (Sohler), U-99 (Kretschmer), U-100 (Schepke), U-101 (Frauenheim) and U-123 (Moehle) – tore an Allied convoy, SC7, to shreds in four days of constant attacks that resulted in the sinking of 16 merchants: *Aenos* (U-38), *Beatus, Convallaria, Gunborg* (all three sunk by U-46), *Empire Miniver, Niritos, Fiscus, Empire Brigade, Snefjeld, Thalia* (all U-99), *Assyrian, Soesterberg* (U-101), and *Sedgepool, Boekolo, Shekatika* and *Clintonia* (U-123), totalling over 150,000 tons.

This was followed immediately by an attack on Convoy HX79, also off the Irish coast, which saw a further 12 ships, totalling over 75,000 tons, sunk by a pack comprising U-28 (Guggenberger), U-38, U-46, U-47, U-48 and U-100. A further 75,000 tons of shipping was sent to the bottom. Heinrich Liebe in U-38 sank two ships, the *Bilderdijk* and the *Matheran*, totalling between them 14,500 tons; Engelbert Endrass in U-46 sank two ships, the *Ruperra* and the *Janus*, representing a total of 14,500 tons; Prien in U-47 bagged four ships, the *Wandby*, the *Uganda*, the *Whitford Point* and the *La Estancia*, some 20,100 tons, and damaged two others, the *Shirak* and the *Athelmonarch*. In U-48, Heinrich Bleichrodt sank the *Shirak* that Prien had earlier damaged, for some 6,000 tons. Finally, in U-100, Schepke accounted for three ships, the *Loch Lomond*, the *Sitala* and the *Caprella*, totalling 20,900 tons.

The year ended with HX90 being intercepted in the North Atlantic by a small pack of three boats, U-47, U-52 and U-101, resulting in six ships, *Ville d'Arlon, Tasso, Goodleigh, Appalachee, Lady Glanely* and *Kavak*, being sunk.

An unidentified Type VIIC in an Atlantic swell. With her decks almost awash and only her conning tower clearly visible, it can be well seen how difficult such relatively small boats were to spot when making night attacks on Allied convoys on the surface.

1941

In order to compensate for the still relatively slow rate of new builds coming from Germany's shipyards, in August 1940 the Italian Navy was invited to base some of its submarines in German-occupied French ports for operations into the Atlantic. These Italian submarines were never particularly successful. In just under three years, the 30 or so Italian submarines which had operated out of Bordeaux sank just 105 Allied vessels and lost 16 of their own number. The Italians were allocated their own area of responsibility in which German U-boats thereafter did not operate, Dönitz having no interest in seeing these boats come under his command.

The year began well. On the night of 23 February, Convoy OB288 was attacked by a pack consisting of four U-boats, U-69 (Metzler), U-73 (Rosenbaum), U-95 (Schreiber) and U-96 (Lehmann-Willenbrock), supported by the Italian submarine *Bianchi*. Eight ships totalling nearly 44,000 tons were sunk and a 9,000-tonner seriously damaged. However, this first so called 'Happy Time' came to an abrupt

U-boat crews typically adopted an insignia for their boat. Some particularly popular emblems were used by more than one boat. Here we see the Olympic rings, which were adopted by at least 14 boats including U-344 and U-505.

end in March 1941 when, after a spell of remarkably low losses, three top aces, Prien, Schepke and Kretschmer, were lost in convoy attacks. Prien in U-47 was lost on 7/8 March when attacking OB293 and both Schepke and Kretschmer on 16/17 March during attacks on HX112. Kretschmer and most of his crew were picked up and six survivors from U-100 were saved but Prien's U-47 was lost with all hands.

In early 1941, Hitler arranged for a number of Focke-Wulf FW200 Kondor aircraft to be made available for a brief period for anti-shipping strikes in cooperation with the U-boats. These four-engined long-range aircraft were based on pre-war civilian airliners. Instead of patrolling U-boats calling in other submarines to form a wolf pack on locating a convoy, they were instead to call in an air strike. In an early success in February 1941, U-37 spotted a northbound convoy out of Gibraltar. A flight of Kondor bombers homed in on the convoy and succeeded in sinking nine ships.

The spring and summer of 1941 were fairly lean times for the U-boats, even though Dönitz was permitting them to travel further afield, ranging out into the mid-Atlantic and even the South Atlantic. An attempted attack on a convoy spotted by a Kondor in February also went wrong when the boats ordered to attack failed to find the convoy.

What was unknown to the Germans was that the British had begun to take advantage of the installation of radar on their escort ships, this being one of the reasons the lost aces had been detected by the British during their attacks in March. Until now, U-boats running on the surface had avoided detection by Asdic and, being so small, were difficult to detect by sight. Dönitz, though aware of the decline in successes, was unaware that the British were now making use of radar.

Some Germans believed that the problem lay with British interception of German radio traffic, the enemy intercepting signals directing the U-boats towards their targets. In fact this view was held by many of the U-boat aces who went to great lengths to avoid using their radios when at sea. As Dönitz was confident that the German codes were unbreakable, he remained confident that even if the enemy were detecting U-boat signals they would not be able to decipher the content. The use of land-based high-frequency signal-detecting equipment in various locations, however, allowed triangulation on the chatter of signals between U-boats and BdU as the 'wolves' prepared to attack. Even without breaking the codes, the Allies could detect the presence of U-boats in a particular area and route the convoy away from danger.

In the spring of 1941, U-boats which had been operating well out into the Atlantic were recalled to eastern waters when a number of tankers which broke out into the Atlantic with the battleship *Bismarck* and heavy cruiser *Prinz Eugen* were tracked down as a result of interception of German radio signals, and sunk. It was intended that, as well as servicing the warships, the tankers would also be used to refuel these U-boats.

Disaster struck for the U-boats in May, though they were unaware of it. Germany used an ingenious system known as 'Enigma' to encode its messages. This was a piece of equipment somewhat similar in appearance to a typewriter, with a basic keyboard. The message was typed out in clear and automatically converted to a series of electrical impulses which were scrambled via a series of rotors. The basic Enigma machine used by the army had three such rotors and one had been captured by the Allies at the outbreak of war. The naval version, however, was more secure, featuring a greater number of rotors from which the three to be used could be chosen. A huge number of combinations existed, making deciphering extremely difficult.

On 9 May 1941, however, U-110 (Lemp) had been mortally wounded by Allied warships and forced to the surface. As the British hurried the surviving U-boat crew members below decks out of sight of what was happening, volunteers boarded the rapidly sinking U-boat and retrieved the Enigma machine. Lemp, who had stayed on board in an attempt to ensure the destruction of his boat and its secret materials, was shot.

British intelligence now had an example of the naval Enigma. With material captured from U-110, together with documents captured from a number of German naval support vessels over a period of months, including the trawler

The U-boat base at Bordeaux was also home to a number of Italian Navy submarines. Here one of these Italian boats is in one of the dry-dock pens for repair. These Italian boats were not particularly successful and did not contribute greatly to the Battle of the Atlantic.

U-203, a Type VIIC, tied up at her moorings in this winter scene. Note her ship's crest, the town crest of Essen. This relatively successful boat carried out 22 war cruises during which she sank over 96,000 tons of enemy shipping. She finally met her fate on 25 April 1943, sunk by the British destroyer HMS *Pathfinder*.

Krebs, the weather ships *München* and *Lauenberg* and the tanker *Gedania*, the British were able to begin decrypting previously secure signals from BdU ordering U-boats to patrol certain sectors or to meet with tankers for refuelling. In a very short period of time, most of Germany's tankers were ambushed and sunk. At the same time, British intelligence at Bletchley Park were increasingly able to use electro-mechanical devices to help them to speed up what had previously been lengthy and laborious long-hand attempts to decipher encrypted messages. Only in February 1942, after the introduction of a new Enigma machine that used four rotors instead of three, together with a separate cipher for U-boats, known as 'Triton', did U-boats signals become, temporarily at least, secure once again.

Fortunes improved slightly in June when Convoy OG69 was located by a Kondor and a pack consisting of U-68 (Karl-Friedrich Merten), U-79 (Wolfgang Kaufmann), U-126 (Ernst Bauer), U-203 (Rolf Mützelburg), U-331 (Hans-Diederich von Tiesenhausen), U-561 (Robert Bartels), U-562 (Herwig Collmann) and U-564 (Reinhard Suhren) directed to attack. Seven ships were sunk (*Kellwyn, Hawkinge, Inga I, Erato, Lapland, Wrotham* and *Norita*). All, however, were relatively small freighters, between them totalling just over 11,000 tons.

By July 1941, high-frequency direction-finding equipment, known colloquially as 'Huff Duff', was now being installed aboard ship, allowing the direction from which signals from U-boats were emanating to be detected. Although it would be the following year before this equipment was used on a large scale, its effects were to be felt rather swiftly by the U-boats. The requirement for the U-boat which first detected the convoy to shadow it until the pack gathered, giving regular updates on the convoy speed and direction, allowed HF/DF-equipped escorts to detect the presence of the shadowing 'wolf' and attempt to drive it off or destroy it before the pack gathered. Alternatively, they could keep the U-boat occupied in trying to evade them whilst the convoy changed course and made good its escape. Even if the shadowing boat was able to keep track of the convoy and allow the others in the pack to gather, the troubles facing the U-boats were far from over. U-boats were ordered to send a brief signal to BdU indicating that they were about to attack a convoy. If more than one escort was equipped with HF/DF, the location of the signal source could be determined and the efforts of the escorts concentrated in the directions from which it was known the attack would come. It is small wonder then, that some of the more astute U-boat commanders decided, despite assurances that their radio codes were secure, to maintain radio silence at all times during offensive operations.

On the outbreak of war, Britain already possessed basic, but effective, aircraft-mounted radar which would allow the detection of small targets such as a surfaced U-boat at distances between three and six miles, dependent on the altitude of the aircraft. Improved long-range radar was beginning to be introduced by 1939 which increased this range to as much as 15 miles. By 1940, ASV II (Airborne-Surface Vessel) radar was entering service, giving an improved range of up to 36 miles. This equipment could lead an aircraft up to a range of just one mile from its target. Under one mile distant it was not effective, so there was still a need for eagle-sharp eyesight on the part of aircraft crews and, of course, this equipment would be of limited use in night attacks. However, backed up by radar, and with Asdic equipment allowing them to detect the U-boat when submerged, the Allies now possessed a growing array of effective defensive measures against U-boats.

During the period from the summer of 1940 until the end of that year, U-boats sank a total of around 280 enemy ships, accounting for nearly 1,500,000 tons. The provision to Britain of 50 decrepit old destroyers from the USA under the Lend-Lease programme in September of that year, although much needed in a time when escorts were in very short supply, had little or no effect as the U-boats continued to rampage across the Atlantic.

As the effectiveness of Allied anti-submarine measures grew, and along with this the numbers of well-organised and well-protected convoys increased, the concept of packs of submarines roaming around looking for victims began to look less valid. Moreover, the British cracking of the Enigma codes allowed them to avoid the waiting packs and to vector their own warships and aircraft to wait in ambush.

EMERGENCY DIVE!

This plate illustrates what happened when a U-boat dived to escape the enemy. The sound detector operator (**1**) sits in the tiny radio room, its door open so that he can communicate with the adjacent control room. He wears headphones and turns the handwheel which rotates the sound detector head on the boat's foredeck. The sound detection gear is extremely sensitive and will pick up the slightest noise. The operator will be ready to snatch off his headphones at the sound of depth charges splashing into the water, as the explosions heard through his headphones would be deafening. Two diving planes operators (**2**) sit in the control room guided by the engineering officer. The hand wheels they operate alter the angle of the diving planes causing the boat to dive deeper or rise in the water. The commander (**3**) sits at the periscope in the conning tower, hoping to take a shot at the escort vessel which is tormenting them. Finally, in *Zentrale*, the Obersteuermann (navigator) (**4**) plots each change in course ordered by the commander. With more time spent submerged as surface cruising became increasingly dangerous, opportunities to take a sextant reading were infrequent, and with the effect of underwater currents pulling the boat off course, accurate plotting was essential, and difficult. (Artwork by Darko Pavlovic © Osprey Publishing)

One of the early Type IXAs, U-37 was another 'lucky' boat. She survived 22 war cruises during which she sank a total of 55 enemy vessels and damaged a further two. In Eckernförde, on 8 May 1945, she was scuttled by her crew to prevent her capture. Her last commander was Kapitänleutnant Heinrich Schuch.

The later tactic, and that which has become generally accepted as the true wolf pack principle, was to have a patrol line of submarines laid out across the anticipated route of the convoy. Once an individual U-boat had spotted the convoy, it would signal this fact and then track the convoy whilst the remainder of the pack gathered. The individual members of the pack were not necessarily from the same flotilla as the lead boat, but would simply be other available boats within striking distance ordered to join the attack.

In the autumn of 1941, Dönitz sent his U-boats westwards once again. In early September a pack of 19 boats, U-38 (Schuch), U-43 (Lüth), U-81 (Guggenberger), U-82 (Rollmann), U-84 (Uphoff), U-85 (Greger), U-105 (Schewe), U-202 (Linder), U-207 (Meyer), U-372 (Neumann), U-373 (Loeser), U-432 (Schultze), U-433 (Ey), U-501 (Förster), U-552 (Topp), U-569 (Hinsch), U-572 (Hirsacker), U-575 (Heydemann) and U-652 (Fraatz), was dispatched westwards to patrol the waters between Iceland and Greenland. Operating between 28 August and 12 September 1941, this pack, code-named *Margrave*, intercepted Convoy SC42 to the south-west of Iceland and sank 22 ships. Two U-boats, U-207 and U-501, were sunk.

The east-bound return patrol, now code-named *Brandenburg*, and including U-74 (Kentrat), U-94 (Ites), U-373 (Loeser), U-552 (Topp) and U-562 (Hamm), intercepted Convoy SC44, also to the south-west of Iceland, sinking a further five merchant ships and one escort. A second pack, comprising U-73 (Rosenbaum), U-77 (Schonder), U-101 (Frauenheim), U-432 (Schultze), U-502 (Rosenstiel), U-553 (Förster), U-558 (Krech), U-568 (Preuss) and U-751 (Bigalk), intercepted Convoy

HG75 in the waters to the south-east of Iceland but succeeded in sinking just one ship. A third pack, code-named *Raubritter*, and comprising U-38 (Schuch), U-82 (Rollmann), U-84 (Uphoff), U-85 (Greger), U-93 (Elfe), U-106 (Rasch), U-123 (Hardegen), U-133 (Hesse), U-202 (Linder), U-203 (Mützelburg), U-569 (Hinsch), U-571 (Möhlmann) and U-577 (Schauenburg), intercepted Convoy SC52 and sank five merchants. It also attempted to locate Convoy ONS33 but failed to make contact. Despite these modest successes, the overall results were somewhat disappointing, considering the number of U-boats involved and the efforts invested. The Germans of course were still unaware that the British were monitoring their radio signals, or that British escorts were equipped with HF/DF and radar.

In September 1941 U-371 (Driver) became the first U-boat to enter the Mediterranean, the first of its three patrols in these waters. It was joined a few days later by U-559 (Heidtmann) and U-97 (Heilmann). U-331 (Tiesenhausen), the last of the first batch, arrived on 30 September. Two boats, U-75 (Ringelmann) and U-79 (Kaufmann), joined them in October and, during the course of November, nine more boats, U-205 (Reschke), U-81 (Guggenberger), U-433 (Ey), U-565 (Jebsen), U-431 (Dommes), U-557 (Paulsen), U-562 (Hamm), U-95 (Schreiber) and U-652 (Fraatz), were sent into these waters, bringing U-boat strength up to 15.

Initial results were far from impressive, only a couple of barges and two small coasters being sunk during the first month's operations. On 13 November, however, Guggenberger in U-81 made up for the previous lack of success by sinking the British aircraft carrier *Ark Royal*, a tremendous psychological victory for the Germans. Three days later, however, U-433 was sunk by a British corvette. The commander and most of his crew were picked up by the British. A second major victory for the Germans occurred on 25 November when U-331

Yet another victim of the Grey Wolves meets its end. Just visible at bottom right, a crew member of U-48 watches as the *Alice F Palmer* burns. It was rare for U-boat crews to have the opportunity to observe their victims sink; most often they were desperately trying to avoid retribution from convoy escorts.

intercepted a British task force and torpedoed and sank the battleship *Barham*. Once again this great victory was followed by a German loss when *U-95* was torpedoed and sunk by a Dutch submarine on 29 November. The commander and 11 of his crew were rescued. On 14 December *U-557* torpedoed and sank the British cruiser *Galatea*. Two days later however, an Italian patrol boat mistook *U-557* for an Allied warship and rammed her. All hands were lost.

Up to the end of November, some 15 boats had successfully penetrated into the Mediterranean. In December, much against Dönitz's will, he was ordered to send more, a political move intended to show support for Germany's Italian allies. On 1 December *U-96* was detected attempting to pass through the Straits of Gibraltar (the incident was recreated in the movie *Das Boot*) and so badly damaged that it was forced to return to base. *U-558* was caught the following day and suffered the same fate. A number of other boats, *U-202* (Poser), *U-432* (Schultze) and *U-569* (Hinsch), were also severely damaged trying to break through the Straits and forced to return to base. *U-372* (Neumann), *U-375* (Könenkamp), *U-453* (von Schlippenbach), *U-568* (Preuss), *U-74* (Kentrat), *U-77* (Schonder), *U-83* (Kraus), *U-573* (Heinsohn), *U-133* (Hesse), *U-577* (Schauenberg) and *U-374* (von Fischel), all successfully passed through. All in all, 26 boats succeeded in entering the Mediterranean during 1941, four of which were sunk within days of arrival. Operations against convoys in this area were also unsuccessful, a large convoy of over 30 ships, HG76, suffering only three losses during an attack by 11 U-boats, though in addition to the merchants, the escort carrier *Audacity* and the corvette *Stanley* were also sunk. Three U-boats, *U-127*, *U-131* and *U-434*, were lost.

The winter of 1941 also saw the launch of the first Type XIV U-tankers, *U-459* and *U-460*. Capable of carrying over 400 tons of extra fuel for replenishing other U-boats, these tankers were also capable of diving much deeper than conventional

U-375, a Type VIIC, was built at the Howaldtswerke yard in Kiel. She was taken into service on 19 July 1941 and carried out a total of ten war patrols, all but one in the Mediterranean during which she sank a total of seven enemy ships totalling some 22,700 tons. She was sunk on 30 July 1943, lost with all hands.

In this shot, the crew of U-552 have just presented the commander, Kapitänleutnant Erich Topp, with a hand made 'Knight's Cross' to celebrate his decoration with this award in June 1941. Note that in the centre of the cross the men have painted the boat's prancing devil emblem rather than a swastika. Topp's contribution to the U-boat war was enormous and he was one of only a handful of U-boat commanders to win the Oakleaves with Swords to the Knight's Cross.

Type VII and Type IX boats, and were thus, initially at least, in a better position to escape the attentions of Allied warships if discovered. These boats, however, were not to become operational until the spring of 1942.

During 1941, there were some 30 specific operations against Allied convoys. Of these, 17 saw the U-boats either fail to make contact or make contact but fail to achieve any sinkings. The vastness of the Atlantic, the small number of U-boats available, leaving huge gaps in the areas patrolled, and the interception of German radio traffic, allowing Allied shipping to be directed away from the waiting U-boats and through these huge gaps, meant that pickings for the U-boats were becoming slim indeed. During 1941, U-boats sank a total of 445 enemy ships totalling around 2,171,000 tons. During the same period 38 U-boats were lost, but 202 new U-boats joined the fleet. The U-boat arm had begun the year with a total of 94 boats on strength and ended with 247.

Fortunes were about to change once more for the U-boats, however. On 7 December 1941, Japan launched an attack on the US naval base at Pearl Harbor, and this was followed shortly afterwards by a German declaration of war on the USA. The German Navy had of course made plans for a possible conflict with the USA but were nevertheless shocked when the day arrived. Only five of the six boats destined for use against US shipping were actually available when war was declared, the sixth being in dry dock. This tiny handful of boats was, however, to have an effect out of all proportion to its size. Code-named *Paukenschlag* (Drum Beat), this first operation began on Christmas Day 1941 and involved U-66 (Zapp), U-109 (Bleichrodt), U-123 (Hardegen), U-125 (Folkers) and U-130 (Kals). These few

U-boats and others rapidly dispatched to American coastal waters were to wreak havoc against Allied shipping in the weeks and months to come.

1942

Despite having seen the effect of U-boat attacks on Allied shipping over the preceding two years, America retained an incredibly blasé attitude towards its own anti-submarine defences. The designated U-boats arrived off the US coast in mid-January 1942. They were astounded to find virtually no precautions being taken: no black-out restrictions were in place and the coastline was ablaze with light. U-boats were able to operate safely on the surface within sight of land, being able to fix their positions with complete accuracy from well-illuminated landmarks ashore. Lying low in the water, they were able easily to spot their victims, backlit by the lights on shore and fully lit themselves. Within just two weeks, these five U-boats had sunk 20 enemy merchant ships totalling over 150,000 tons. In the period between January and May 1942 the total number of U-boats operating off the US coast reached 30. These boats sank a total of 360 enemy ships during this period, representing around 2,250,000 tons. Only eight U-boats were lost during this phase, which became known to the Germans as the 'Second Happy Time'. From May onwards the US finally began to appreciate the need for the implementation of escorted convoys for its coastal traffic and the free-for-all ended.

The Germans once again began to feel that victory in the war against Allied shipping was within their grasp. U-boat strength had also improved, with over 330 U-boats

U-20, a Type IIB operating out of Constanza, carried out 17 combat war patrols and sank 15 enemy ships totalling some 38,500 tons. Though small, the Type II made a valuable contribution to the war effort. A lucky boat, she suffered no casualties amongst her crew, the boat being eventually scuttled when the Germans were forced to evacuate the Black Sea.

This view of U-109 shows the conditions experienced by U-boats operating in Arctic waters, her deck covered with a thick layer of ice. After 17 war patrols she met her fate after being bombed by Allied aircraft on 4 May 1943 in much warmer climes, in the waters north-east of the Azores.

now available. Subtracting those on training duties or otherwise unavailable, over 140 were available for operational duty and 50 on patrol at any time.

On 29 March 1942, the U-tanker U-459 sailed for American waters under the command of Kapitänleutnant Wilamowitz-Möllendorf, arriving in her patrol area in mid-April. Between 19 April and 5 May, U-108 (Scholtz), U-98 (Schulze), U-333 (Cremer), U-582 (Schulte), U-571 (Möhlmann), U-751 (Bigalk), U-107 (Gelhaus), U-572 (Hirsacker), U-558 (Krech), U-566 (Borchert), U-594 (Hoffmann) and U-564 (Suhren), a total of 12 U-boats, were all replenished with both fuel and food, including fresh-baked bread from U-459's on-board bakery, and, though U-459's fuel load was now expended, U-253 was provided at least with additional fresh food supplies if not fuel.

A second refuelling mission in late May saw the minelaying Type XB U-boat U-116 (von Schmidt), which had been converted to a tanker, refuel six more U-boats at sea (U-94, U-96, U-106, U-124, U-569 and U-590), all without incident. The U-tanker concept appeared to be proving itself a great success. A second trip by U-459 in June saw her refuel 16 U-boats at sea whilst her newly commissioned sister U-460 (Schaefer) attended to the needs of 14 other U-boats before returning safely to port. U-tankers U-462 and U-463 were dispatched to the western Atlantic to refuel boats employed in Caribbean waters. In all, ten Type XIV tankers were commissioned and between them carried out 36 war cruises. The first to be lost was U-464 (Harms) which was caught on the surface by an Allied bomber to the south of Iceland and sunk on 20 August 1942. Fortunately, 53 of the crew were saved.

Unfortunately for Germany, however, American shipbuilding expertise and construction capacity was now coming into play. America alone was more than capable of producing an annual rate of new builds far in excess of what Germany was able to sink. Nevertheless, there were some significant successes. During August a pack operating under the code-name *Lohs* attacked Convoys SC94, SC95, SC100 and ON122. This pack comprised up to 19 boats including U-135, U-174, U-176, U-256, U-259, U-373, U-410, U-432, U-438, U-569, U-578, U-593, U-596, U-604, U-605, U-660, U-705 and U-755. Twenty-two enemy ships were sunk or damaged. In the same month, SC94 was attacked by the *Steinbrinck* pack comprising U-71, U-176, U-210, U-379, U-454, U-593, U-597, U-607, U-660 and U-704. During this attack 11 enemy ships were sunk and one damaged, but two U-boats were lost and three damaged.

In November SC107 fell victim to an attack by the *Veilchen* pack, when 15 ships were sunk and two damaged by 15 U-boats including U-71, U-84, U-89, U-132, U-381, U-402, U-437, U-438, U-442, U-454, U-521, U-522, U-571, U-658 and U-704. Two, U-132 and U-658, were sunk during the attack. In these three attacks alone, 48 enemy ships were sunk for the loss of five U-boats.

In October 1942, U-559 was forced to the surface in the Mediterranean. British sailors were able to board her before she sank and before her secret papers could be destroyed. Amongst the treasures gained by the British were code books used to compile messages before they were encrypted using the Triton ciphers. Within two months, British Intelligence were once again able to read the current German naval codes. German intelligence had also cracked the Royal Navy's codes so that even as the British were deciphering German signals warning them of the wolf packs gathering for the attack, the Germans were deciphering Allied signals detailing convoy sailing times and assembly points.

In the second half of 1942, the Kriegsmarine had introduced the Metox receiver which detected the 1.7m wavelength radar emissions of the British ASV II radar. This allowed the U-boat to detect the approach of an aircraft using radar and dive in plenty of time to avoid being attacked. The device, however, was extremely crude. It consisted of a wooden cross (known colloquially as the *Biskayakreuz* or 'Biscay Cross') onto which wires were strung to make a very basic antenna. The whole contraption, with attendant cabling, had to be laboriously carried up through the hatch onto the conning tower and rotated by hand. It was prone to damage, especially if it had to be rapidly disassembled and taken inboard at the approach of the enemy.

The British, however, were developing a new 10cm wavelength radar, which was being installed in warships by late 1941. The airborne version, ASV III, did not see widespread use until 1943 but, when it did, it was most effective. The radar was used in conjunction with the 'Leigh Light'. Once the radar had guided the aircraft to within close proximity of the U-boat, undetected by Metox, the Leigh

The *Pennsylvania Sun* burns furiously after being struck by a torpedo from U-571 on 16 July 1942 in the waters to the west of Key West, Florida.

Light was switched on illuminating the scene and exposing the U-boat on the surface. The Germans were fooled into believing that it was the Metox equipment itself, which did indeed radiate a signal, which was in turn being detected by the Allies and used as a 'homing beacon' for them to locate the U-boat; in August 1943, Dönitz ordered that its use be ceased. In the same way as the Metox system was introduced to detect the long wavelength emissions of the ASV II, so the 'Naxos' system to detect 10cm wavelength ASV III emissions was developed. The main disadvantage of Naxos was its extremely short range, some 5,000m. By the time an enemy aircraft was close enough to be detected, it was almost too late. Continued developments in radar left the German continually trying to catch up and design new radar detection equipment to foil each new British system.

The introduction of *Schnorchel* equipment on submarines in 1944 meant that U-boats no longer needed to surface to run their diesels in order to charge their batteries, and were thus relatively safe from detection from the air. Radar had difficulty in picking up an object as small as the head of the *Schnorchel* device, though detection was by no means impossible. Although *Schnorchel* brought the bonus that it was no longer necessary to surface in order to charge the boat's batteries, it was not the panacea to all the U-boat commanders' problems and indeed brought along several new problems of its own. The level of noise made by the diesels made the hydrophones impossible to use, and therefore meant that the periscope had to be used to keep watch whilst the *Schnorchel* was raised. The raising of the periscope in turn brought its own issues, in that the boat could not proceed at much more than 5–6 knots for fear of excessive vibration to the periscope. When,

In order to plot the boat's position accurately it was necessary to take accurate readings whenever possible. In storms or bad weather boats could drift off course, so an opportunity was taken to do what the Obersteuermann here is doing and put the sextant to use.

in rough seas, the head of the *Schnorchel* dipped below the surface a special valve automatically closed and meant that the diesels then, being unable to draw air from above the surface, drew it from the boat's interior. If this continued for any length of time, the crew would suffer ill-effects, perhaps even asphyxiation.

Another device used with some success was the anti-sonar material Alberich, already referred to, which was used to coat the hull of the U-boat. Although the material itself worked well, the Germans were unable to produce a wholly satisfactory adhesive with which to fix the tiles of anti-sonar material to the hull. Those which came loose, but not detached, caused excessive noise and made the submarine easier rather than more difficult to detect! Attempts to produce a suitable adhesive continued throughout the war and tests with Alberich-coated hulls continued through into 1945. The radar decoy device Aphrodite, consisting of metal foil strips suspended from a balloon, also made a useful contribution.

By May 1942, the initial outstanding successes of Operation *Paukenschlag* had tailed off dramatically as US anti-submarine defences grew stronger and more organised. The U-boats then turned their attentions towards the waters of the Caribbean, and between June and December of that year embarked on one of the most successful of all U-boat campaigns. Although it almost seems as though this campaign has been confined to the sidelines of the history of the U-boat war in favour of the Battle of the Atlantic, U-boats operating in these waters were the most successful of all in statistical terms. A total of 97 U-boats operated in the

Although small and carrying only five torpedoes, the Type II boats gave good service in the Black Sea theatre. Note the twin 2cm flak guns on the conning tower, a relatively heavy armament on this type of boat.

Caribbean (59 of them the long-range Type IX, the remainder Type VIIs). Only 17 U-boats were lost in these waters (though a further seven were sunk either on their way to, or return from, the Caribbean), and when compared to the numbers of Allied ships sunk, this gives a phenomenal average of 23 Allied ships lost for every U-boat sunk. No other theatre of the war at sea achieved such a level of success. In addition to German U-boats, six Italian submarines also operated in these waters.

The first phase of the campaign was code-named Operation *Neuland* and ran from February through to March 1942. The first group of boats directed into the Caribbean consisted of U-67 (Müller-Stockheim), U-129 (Clausen), U-161 (Achilles) and U-502 (von Rosenstiel). On 15 February, U-156 attacked the harbour at San Nicholas in Aruba, torpedoing the tankers *Oranjestad*, *Pedernales* and *Arkansas* at their moorings and turning the harbour into a blazing inferno before turning her attention to the nearby oil refinery. Unfortunately, the intention of shelling the refinery with U-156's 10.5cm deck gun was thwarted when the sailor responsible forgot to remove the tompion from the muzzle before the gun was fired. The shell detonated in the barrel, the resulting explosion killing two men. The damaged end of the barrel was sawn off with hacksaws and a renewed attempt at shelling with the shortened gun was made but by now the defences were on full alert and returned fire, forcing U-156 to withdraw.

On the same evening U-67 attacked the port of Willemstad in Curacao. Unfortunately for her commander, the first four torpedoes fired were duds so two tankers which suffered direct hits were spared. The torpedoes fired from the stern tubes, however, worked perfectly and the tanker *Rafaela* was soon ablaze. Meanwhile, out in deeper water, U-502 had sunk the tankers *Tia Juana* and *San Nicholas*. Two days later Albrecht Achilles in U-161 entered Port of Spain and sank the *Mokihana* and the *British Consul*. The U-boat war had come to the Caribbean with a vengeance.

The first of six Italian boats (the submarines *Luigi Torelli*, *Guiseppe Finzi*, *Enrico Tazzoli*, *Leonardo da Vinci*, *Pietro Calvi* and *Morsini*) that were due to operate in these waters also began operations in the second half of February, *Luigi Torelli* sinking the *Scottish Star* on 19 February and *Guiseppe Finzi* the *Melpomere* and the *Skane* on 7 March. U-126 (Bauer) had also just arrived and on that same day torpedoed and sank the *Barbara* and the *Cadona*. *Uniwaleco*, a huge 9,750-ton tanker, fell to U-161 on the same day. Two days later the 9,970-ton *Hanseat* was also sent to the bottom by U-161, before Achilles turned his attention on St Lucia where he took U-161 right into the anchorage, torpedoing the *Lady Nelson* and the *Umtata*.

The operation lasted for just four weeks, after which 41 enemy ships, many of them large tankers, had been sunk, representing some 222,650 tons. A further 11 ships had been damaged. No U-boats had been lost.

A second wave of U-boats, U-66 (Zapp), U-108 (Scholtz), U-130 (Kals) and U-154 (Kolle), began to depart for the Caribbean whilst the first group were still en route for France on their return. U-125 (Folkers) and U-507 (Schacht) joined them soon afterwards. The second phase of the campaign here began on 4 April when the *Comol Rico* was sent to the bottom by U-66. During the course of the month, 14 merchants were destroyed, accounting for over 90,000 tons. May

U-108, a Type IXB, was a particularly successful and 'lucky' boat. She survived an impressive 22 war patrols during the course of which she succeeded in sinking 25 enemy vessels. She survived intact until 24 April 1945 at which point she was scuttled in port at Stettin to avoid capture. Her last commander was Oberleutnant zur See Matthias Brünig.

U-161, a Type IXC boat. Commanded by Korvettenkapitän Albrecht Achilles, she carried out 11 successful war patrols , sinking 19 enemy ships and damaging a further three until being sunk herself by enemy aircraft east of Bahia on 27 September 1943.

was even more successful, as more U-boats were committed to this sector and 78 merchants sunk.

Operating in Caribbean waters during June 1942, Karl-Friedrich Merten in U-68 alone sank a total of seven ships representing almost 51,000 tons in just one patrol. Merten was to be the most successful of the commanders operating in these waters, though U-129 was to be the most successful boat. Under three different commanders, she accounted for 23 ships totalling over 107,000 tons. Twelve of the U-boats operating in this area each accounted for in excess of 50,000 tons of enemy shipping.

June was a disastrous month for the Allies, with U-107 (Gelhaus) beginning the scoring on 1 June by sinking the *Bushranger* near Grand Cayman. By the end of the month a further 63 ships had joined her on the bottom. This meant that more ships had been sunk in the Caribbean than in the Atlantic. Despite this level of success, however, Dönitz was having problems of his own. The extremely long voyage to these good hunting grounds meant that U-boats had to spend a considerable time travelling to and from the area of operations. There were just not enough U-boats available to keep sufficient numbers on station long enough to sustain the degree of success which was being achieved. Allied countermeasures were also, at long last, beginning to have some effect. U-153 (Reichmann) became the first U-boat to be lost when she sank with all hands after a depth charge attack by both aircraft and surface warships on 13 July.

By August things were becoming difficult for the U-boats, as merchants in the Caribbean began to travel in convoy and were given far better protection both by air and by escort warships. U-boat losses grew and by the beginning of December, only four U-boats were still operating in the Caribbean: U-129 (Witt), U-154 (Schuch), U-163 (Engelmann) and U-508 (Staats). The latter was the only boat to achieve any sinkings during that month, adding the *Trevalgan, City of Bath, Solon II* and *Nigerian* to her score. Two further sinkings, *Treworlas* and *Paderewski*, were achieved by U-124 which arrived on scene in mid-December, giving the U-boats a total for the month of just six kills. The year had been exceptionally successful overall, however, as far as these waters were concerned, some 337 enemy ships being sunk, totalling some 1,870,000 tons. The glory days were over for the U-boats in the Caribbean, however, though a few isolated but spectacular successes were still to come and the U-boats would remain in these waters for the remainder of the war.

During 1942, the Mediterranean theatre saw nine boats pass through the Straits of Gibraltar. U-565 (Franken), U-371 (Neumann), U-97 (Bürgel), U-77 (Hartmann), U-74 (Friedrich) and U-133 (Mohr) all returned for their second cruises with new commanders. Two new boats, U-73 (Rosenbaum) and U-561 (Bartels), joined them. Throughout the course of the year, however, 15 boats were lost, so there was no significant increase in German strength here.

This year also saw the beginnings of U-boat operations in far distant waters. In August a first group of four U-boats, U-172 (Emmermann), U-504 (Poske), U-156 (Hartenstein) and U-68 (Merten), together with the U-boat tanker or *Milchkuh* U-459 were sent into the waters around Cape Town in South Africa. These were

U-504, shown here carrying a typical splinter-style disruptive camouflage scheme, was a Type IXC commanded by Kapitänleutnant Wilhelm Luis. A successful boat, she had sunk 16 enemy ships over 13 war patrols before being caught by British warships north-west of Cape Ortegal and sunk on 30 July 1943.

all larger Type IXC boats, with a much greater operational range than the smaller Type VII which formed the backbone of the U-Bootwaffe. This first group, known as the *Eisbär* boats, was swiftly followed by a second comprising U-177 (Gysae), U-178 (Ibbeken), U-179 (Sobe) and U-181 (Lüth). These were improved boats of Type IXD with an ever-greater operational range. These boats found that shipping in the area was still travelling independently and, although not having the protection of being in a convoy, these lone ships were not always easy for such a small group of boats to find. Despite the advantages of these boats, and even with U-tanker support, their time available in the target area was limited and in many cases boats were required to head home because of low fuel stocks before having the opportunity to expend all their torpedoes.

En route, U-156 was involved in an incident that was to have far-reaching consequences. On the evening of 12 September 1942, U-156 encountered a lone ship. She was the 20,000-ton Cunard liner *Laconia*. The ship was a perfectly legitimate target, being employed as a troopship and armed with two 4.7in. guns, six 1.5in. anti-aircraft guns and four Bofors anti-aircraft guns. She was officially designated as an Armed Merchant Cruiser. What Hartenstein did not know was that as well as a few hundred British military personnel, she was carrying nearly 1,800 Italian prisoners of war and a small number of women and children. *Laconia* had set sail for England from Cape Town on 1 September. U-156 encountered her on 12 September steaming northwards some 250 miles to the north-east of Ascension Island. At just after 8pm, *Laconia* was struck by two torpedoes from U-156. It quickly became obvious that the ship was beyond saving and within minutes the order to abandon ship was given.

U-boats were under instructions to try to identify the ship's master or other responsible officer amongst survivors so as to confirm the identity of the ship. Accordingly, Hartenstein steered towards the sinking vessel and was shocked to identify a number of his Italian allies amongst the survivors, and even more shocked to find women and children amongst them too. He was now in a quandary. The enemy ship might have sent out a distress signal which could bring enemy warships swarming to his position. Staying in the area could endanger his boat and its crew. On the other hand, he could not bring himself to abandon so many people to their fate. As his men began to drag survivors out of the water onto the U-boat's deck, he ordered a signal sent to BdU: 'British Laconia sunk by Hartenstein. Unfortunately with 1,500 Italian prisoners of war. Ninety rescued so far. Request instructions.'

Dönitz responded by ordering U-156 to remain on site and further ordered two of the other *Eisbär* boats, U-506 (Würdemann) and U-507 (Schacht), to break off their mission temporarily in order to give assistance. Vichy French warships were also ordered to assist. Hartenstein then sent off a signal in clear: 'If any ship

The captain at the periscope. This photograph shows Kapitänleutnant zur See Kurt Diggins. He is at the navigation periscope in the *Zentrale*, which allows the commander to check that the sky and seas around the boat are clear before surfacing. The attack periscope was located in the commander's battle post in the conning tower.

will assist the shipwrecked Laconia crew, I will not attack her provided I am not being attacked by ships or aircraft. I have picked up 193 men. 4° 52' south 11° 26' west. German submarine'

Meanwhile, U-156 did her best to help, taking wounded on board for first aid and offering hot drinks and cigarettes to survivors crowded onto her decks. The submarine cruised amongst the lifeboats, offering jugs of hot coffee and soup to the disconsolate British survivors as Hartenstein tried to reassure them, in perfect English, that help was coming. Survivors are on record as commenting that the U-boat men treated them with kindness and respect throughout the entire incident. On 15 September, U-506 arrived on the scene and took on 130 survivors. U-507 arrived in the area shortly afterwards and began taking on survivors. Again, great kindness from the Germans is reported by the survivors, who were given hot food and drink.

On 16 September a B-24 Liberator bomber arrived on the scene from the base on Ascension Island and circled U-156, noting that it was towing two lifeboats. U-156 was also displaying a large, unmissable, Red Cross flag on her conning tower. On requesting orders, the B-24 was given instructions to attack. Two passes were made with two bombs dropped each time. Though they missed the U-boat, one lifeboat was hit and the other overturned. Many of the survivors on U-156's deck were blown into the sea by the blast. Hartenstein was forced, reluctantly, to submerge his boat to avoid further attacks. Hartenstein thereafter returned to base, being replaced in the *Eisbär* group by U-159 (Witte).

The archetypal U-boat commander, leather coat, scarf at the throat, white-topped cap and a few days' growth of beard. At sea, U-boat officers shared the same privations as their men and inevitably ended up looking just as scruffy.

The attack resulted in an understandable message from BdU, in which U-boat commanders, disturbed at having to abandon the survivors to their fates, were warned: 'You are in no circumstances to risk the safety of your boat. All measures to ensure safety of your boat. All measures, including abandonment of rescue operations, to be ruthlessly taken. Do not rely on the enemy showing slightest consideration.' Dönitz also advised his boats not to bother flying the Red Cross flag as this was not recognised international procedure and would not afford them any protection.

Later that day, the B-24 re-appeared and this time U-506 was to be its target. The U-boat crash dived, escaping damage but leaving the *Laconia* survivors on board badly shaken. The crew of the aircraft were decorated for having sunk two U-boats. In fact both U-156 and U-506 were undamaged and the only casualties had been among *Laconia*'s survivors. A combined effort from the French warships *Gloire, Dumont D'Urville* and *Annamite* and the Italian submarine *Cappelinni*, which had arrived in the area, saw the survivors still on board the U-boats, together with most of those still in lifeboats, being finally picked up. Those survivors with U-156 when it had been forced to dive to avoid the bombs from the B-24 had a more arduous time. One lifeboat reached the African coast on 9 October and another was picked up by a British convoy on 21 October. Of 2,725 people on board the *Laconia* when she was struck by torpedoes from U-156, around 1,500 were eventually saved.

As a consequence of the attacks on his U-boats whilst clearly undertaking humanitarian actions, Dönitz issued what was to become known as the 'Laconia Order':

1) No attempt of any kind must be made to rescue members of ships sunk and this includes picking up persons in the water, putting them in lifeboats, righting capsized lifeboats and handing over food and water. Rescue runs counter to the most basic demands of warfare for the destruction of enemy ships and crews.
2) Orders to bring in captains and chief engineers of enemy ships remain in force.
3) Shipwrecked persons may only be rescued if their information is important for the submarine.
4) Be hard. Remember that the enemy has no regard for women and children when he bombs German cities.

Given the risks any U-boat took by surfacing when Allied use of radar and growing air power meant more and more U-boats were being caught on the surface and destroyed, Dönitz's exhortations to his U-boats not to put themselves at risk to rescue enemy survivors seem perfectly reasonable, if regrettably harsh.

This shot shows the vast girth of the minelaying Type XB U-boat. Shown here is U-117, commanded by Korvettenkapitän Hans-Werner Neumann. She carried out nine war patrols before being sunk off the Azores on 7 August 1943.

Unfortunately for him, prosecutors at the Nuremberg trials sought to interpret his orders as deliberate instructions for his U-boats actually to murder survivors from ships they had sunk. This attempt failed, with many senior Allied naval figures admitting they had carried out similar policies and in many cases had themselves actually machine-gunned enemy shipwrecked survivors.

In December 1942, a second group of Type IXC boats, U-160 (Lassen), U-182 (Clausen), U-506 (Würdemann), U-509 (Witte) and U-516 (Wiebe), collectively known as the *Seehund* group, was dispatched to the waters around the Cape. This group was to find things rather more difficult, with shipping now grouped into convoys and routed as close to land as possible.

In 1942, over 1,090 ships were sunk by U-boats representing some 5,819,000 tons of shipping, for 88 U-boats lost. Some 238 new U-boats joined the fleet. The year began with 259 U-boats on strength and ended with 397. During the year, some 40 actions against specific, targeted convoys were mounted (with in some cases packs being directed against more than one convoy) and an additional seven operations mounted in the form of general patrol lines.

Although most late-war U-boats boasted a fairly formidable complement of anti-aircraft weaponry, the chances of a U-boat fighting off an air attack were slim. There are a number of recorded cases of U-boats successfully escaping after shooting down an attacking aircraft, but in most cases, the U-boat dared not leave itself defencelessness by recalling its gun crews in order to dive, and so was forced to remain on the surface if the aircraft's pilot merely remained out of range of the U-boat's flak guns. The aircraft could then call up reinforcements. The few successful occasions where U-boats shot down enemy aircraft tended to be when the aircraft attacked alone before support arrived. (Artwork by Ian Palmer © Osprey Publishing)

1943

1943 was a difficult year for the U-Bootwaffe. It began the year with a strength of 413 boats and ended with 442. Although 290 new boats were commissioned, 245 were lost. U-boat construction was now only just keeping up with losses. Nevertheless boats could be replaced, if only barely, but experienced crews were now being lost at an alarming rate. Just over 450 enemy ships were sunk during 1943, totalling some 2,395,000 tons. During this year, at least 46 operations were mounted against specific targeted convoys, plus at least 31 general patrol operations involving packs of boats. In some cases a general patrol group would then be directed to attack a specific convoy. Of the specific operations, a total of 20 recorded no contact with the enemy or failed to make any sinkings. Although some, such as the attacks on Convoys HX229 and SC118, did score some significant successes, in general the rewards bore no relation to the massive efforts expended and were only being won at an alarming cost in U-boats lost.

The numbers of boats being destroyed on the surface, even at night in attacks by radar equipped aircraft fitted with Leigh Lights, was becoming a major cause for concern. The aircraft often were upon the submarine before it had time to dive safely. U-boats were at their most vulnerable during the early stages of the dive. With their upper decks cleared and anti-aircraft guns unmanned they were at the mercy of an attacking aircraft until they reached a safe depth. The successful shooting down of attacking aircraft on a number of occasions encouraged Dönitz to order boats in such circumstances to remain on the surface and fight it out with attacking aircraft. The order *Ständiger Kriegsbefehl 483* was issued on 1 May 1943 and remained in force for just over three months. In that time the Kriegsmarine was to lose a further 26 boats in such engagements with another 17 seriously damaged. In many cases the aircraft would simply circle the boat at a safe distance whilst surface warships were called up to deal with it. Once the aircraft was in range, attempting to dive would leave the U-boat at the mercy of the aircraft, whilst not to dive would merely postpone the inevitable once enemy warships arrived. U-boats travelling on the surface in the company of other boats could give each other cover but, inevitably, if one sought to escape by diving while covered by fire from the other, the boat left on the surface to provide covering fire would be left in mortal danger once alone. Experiments were also attempted with so-called *Flakboote*, U-boats which were given much heavier than normal anti-aircraft armament, in the hope that Allied aircraft tempted to try to sink them would be lured into approaching too closely and shot down. The experiment was not successful.

In these battles, 28 attacking aircraft were shot down. However, aircraft were far easier to replace for the Allies than U-boats were for the Kriegsmarine. In any event, this played directly into the hands of the Allies, who did not mind losing a few aircraft in such engagements if it resulted in more U-boats remaining on the surface where they were easy targets.

This interesting shot of a Type XIV tanker shows a special flak pedestal constructed on the after deck to carry a 2cm *Flakvierling* giving her enhanced anti-aircraft capability. A small walkway between the U-boat's *Wintergarten* platform and the additional pedestal can just be seen.

In the south-west Atlantic, the U-boats which had been so successful in their operations in the Caribbean were forced to look further afield for their victims as, once again, enemy anti-submarine measures gradually began to increase in their effectiveness.

The year began well enough for the Caribbean U-boats. Convoy TM1, having sailed from Trinidad on 27 December 1942, heading directly for Gibraltar, was intercepted by a pack of 12 U-boats. The convoy consisted of 12 merchant ships, nine of them large tankers, protected by just four escorts. The first victim, on 3 January 1943, was the 8,000-ton *Vigilance*, which was sunk by U-514 (Auffermann). The 6,400-ton *Olthena* and 8,000-ton *Albert L Ellsworth* were both sunk by the same spread of torpedoes from U-436. U-522 then claimed the 6,800-ton *Minister Wedel* and the huge 10,000-tonner *Norvik*. The 9,800-ton *Empire Lytton* was claimed by U-422 and finally the 6,900-ton *British Dominion* fell to U-622. The convoy was all but decimated, losing seven tankers totalling over 56,000 tons. So few were the escorts, that none felt able to leave the remaining merchants to pursue any of the many attackers for fear of leaving too large a gap in the defences through which the other 'wolves' could penetrate. It is reported that one escort, in utter frustration, signalled a U-boat trailing the convoy on the surface, asking it to go away. The U-boat is said to have ominously signalled a response saying it couldn't leave, as it still had a 'job to do'.

Meanwhile, U-124 (Mohr) was about to carry out a solo attack on Convoy TB1 heading from Trinidad to Brazil. Twelve ships made up the convoy, of which five were tankers. Despite suffering excruciating breakdown problems due to sabotage of both the fuel supply and the distilled water supplies for the batteries, U-124

A Type VII moving at speed on the surface. Although far more cramped and uncomfortable than the larger Type IX, the Type VII could dive faster and many crewmen felt that the greater potential for a successful escape from the enemy made the lack of comfort worthwhile. (Author's collection)

began her attack on 9 January 1943, torpedoing the 7,000-ton *Broad Arrow*. The boat then surfaced and carried out the rest of her attack on the surface, unspotted by either the victims or their escorts. The 6,200-ton *Collingsworth* was the next victim. *Birmingham City* at 6,000 tons followed, at which point the remaining ships began to panic. *Minotaur* at 4,500 tons was the U-boat's next victim before engine breakdowns and the final spotting of the U-boat by the escorts caused U-124 to dive. By the time her engines were repaired, the remnants of the convoy had long gone. Four ships sunk, totalling 23,700 tons, in a surface attack at this stage of the war, in a boat suffering chronic damage from sabotage, was a tremendous achievement by any standards.

On 22 February, UC1, a convoy of empty tankers dispatched from the UK to fill up with oil, was intercepted by a pack consisting of U-66, U-202, U-382, U-522, U-588 and U-569 and four of its tankers were sunk, with a further three seriously damaged.

On 8 March, it was the turn of BT6, a convoy of empty vessels on their way from Brazil to Trinidad, to come under attack. Once again a solo effort, from U-510 (Nietzel), caused havoc. Seven ships were hit by torpedoes from U-510: the freighter *Kelvinbank* was sunk and *George Meade, Tabitha Brown, Joseph Rodman Drake, Mark Hanna, James Smith, Thomas Ruffin* and *James K Polk* all so seriously damaged that their crews lost no time in abandoning them. Although some of the abandoned ships were later salvaged, this was still a tremendous achievement on Nietzel's part. Even as Nietzel was wreaking havoc with BT6, however, one of the great Caribbean aces, Werner Hartenstein, in U-156, had been located and sunk by US aircraft in the waters to the north-east of Trinidad.

By now, however, these successes were few and far between, and from this point onwards the focus of operations moved to the waters around Brazil. The 'happy days' were over, and from here until the end of the war the presence of the U-boats was more of a harrying tactic, tying down enemy naval forces in protecting their merchant shipping. The days of the massive tonnage scores in the Caribbean were gone.

The Allied landings in North Africa, Operation *Torch*, had drawn away many warships from the North Atlantic leaving this area weakened whilst defences in the Caribbean had been strengthened considerably. Dönitz therefore refocused his attention back to the North Atlantic and was rewarded with considerable successes. In the first three weeks of March alone, 95 merchants were sunk, albeit with the loss of 15 U-boats. By May, however, with the *Torch* landings over, Allied anti-submarine forces were back up to strength in the Atlantic, ready and waiting for Dönitz to launch his next wave of attacks. This was to become the U-boats' darkest hour, and indeed became generally referred to as 'Black May'.

May 1943 saw the loss of the second of the Type XIV U-tankers or Milk Cows. U-463 (Wolfbauer) was caught on the surface by an Allied bomber and sunk. She had carried out four successful patrols. This was her fifth. There were no survivors.

Realising that he had suffered a serious defeat in the North Atlantic, Dönitz once again turned his mind to the warmer waters around the Caribbean area. Not the Caribbean itself this time, but the waters around the coast of Brazil. A veritable fleet of U-boats departed port during June for new operations in the Western Atlantic, including a number of boats commanded by experienced aces. The first to depart was U-572 (Kummetat), followed by U-510 (Eick), U-759 (Friedrich), U-590 (Krüer), U-84 (Uphoff), U-732 (Carlsen), U-134 (Brosin), U-653 (Feiler), U-415 (Neide), U-615 (Kapitsky), U-634 (Dalhaus), U-68 (Lauzemis), U-155 (Piening), U-159) (Beckmann), U-564 (Feidler), U-185 (Maus), U-406 (Dieterichs), U-662 (Müller), U-359 (Förster), U-386 (Albrecht), U-466 (Thäter) and U-155 (Piening).

The boats experienced considerable difficulty even making it across the Bay of Biscay, let alone all the way across the Atlantic. U-134, U-159 and U-415 came under attack but escaped serious damage. U-68 and U-155 suffered so much damage in attacks by enemy aircraft that they were forced to turn back. U-564 and U-185 also came under heavy attack and U-564 suffered serious damage, forcing her to turn back and run for port, with U-185 escorting her. Her damage was too severe, however, and she eventually sank, allowing U-185 to be redirected westwards once again. On 1 July, U-628 (Hasenschar) and U-648 (Stahl) set off to join their comrades, followed by U-514 (Auffermann) on 3 July and U-607 (Jeschonnek) and U-614 (Sträter) on 10 July.

German operations in the far west began to build up again in July. On the 7th of that month U-510 intercepted Convoy TJ1 en route to Rio de Janeiro. This was a large convoy of 20 ships supported by five escorts. Eick torpedoed and sank the *B P Newton* at 10,300 tons before turning his attention to the *Everago*. The *Eldena* at 6,900 tons was his third victim. Meanwhile, U-185 had engaged convoy BT18, sinking the 7,000-ton tanker *Willliam Boyce Thomson* and the freighters *James Robertson* and *Thomas Sinnickson*, and damaging a second tanker, the 6,800-ton *S B Hunt*.

Operations were to be severely curtailed, however, by the loss of the U-tankers (actually converted Type X minelayers rather than the Type XIV U-tanker proper) U-118 and U-119. Many of the boats now operating in these waters were Type VIICs without the long range capacity of the Type IX, and which depended on the refuelling obtained from the U-tankers to allow them to remain on station. Dönitz was forced to order some of the operational boats to become *de facto* tankers and transfer part of their fuel to their fellows, thus further reducing the number of available boats. July also saw the loss of four more Milk Cows. U-487 (Metz) was sunk by Allied aircraft on 13 July near the Azores, though 32 crew members were saved. On 25 July U-459, the original Milk Cow, was sunk on her sixth patrol when she was caught to the west of the Bay of Biscay by Allied aircraft. Her commander died but 44 crew members were saved. Then a double disaster occurred on 30 July when both U-461 (Steibler) and U-462

U-515, one of a small number of boats which were captured almost intact by the Allies. A successful boat with 11 patrols under her belt, during which she had sunk 23 enemy ships and damaged a further four, U-515 was forced to the surface after a heavy depth charge attack on 9 April 1944 and captured. Her commander, Werner Henke, was shot during a suicidal attempt to escape from captivity in Fort Meade, USA in June 1944.

(Vowe) were sunk by Allied aircraft crossing the Bay of Biscay. U-461 had completed six cruises and U-462 five. The former boat had 15 survivors and the latter, more fortunate, boat 64.

By mid-July, over 30 boats had been allocated to the Caribbean region, of which eight had been sunk and four so badly damaged they had been forced to return to base. The force available had been virtually cut in half and those that did remain were faced by ferocious anti-submarine actions from both surface and, in particular, air attack. Recent orders by Dönitz that those U-boats with beefed-up anti-aircraft armament should remain on the surface to fight it out when attacked from the air had not proved useful. U-159 was sunk in a textbook attack by US aircraft on 15 July 1943. U-662 successfully drove off two separate attacks by US bombers, the planes suffering heavy damage on both occasions. U-415 and U-662 also successfully fended off aerial attacks, but the enemy soon began to adapt their tactics. In the case of U-662, the enemy aircraft had been driven off but it had been able to drop its depth charges, which did inflict damage on the U-boat. A second attack on the weakened boat, now low in anti-aircraft ammunition, succeeded and U-662 was sent to the bottom. Only the commander and one crew member were eventually saved. U-67 and U-527 were sunk by enemy aircraft as they attempted to depart the Caribbean on their way home. U-466 engaged an aircraft in combat and although the U-boat inflicted a huge amount of damage on the aircraft, driving it off, the U-boat itself was sufficiently damaged to force it to turn back and head for home. U-759 was sunk with no survivors after an attack by US aircraft. U-359 was also sunk by depth charges after an intense battle with a US aircraft which saw the aircraft severely damaged. During July, over 30 battles between U-boat and aircraft had been fought and, although the U-boats had put up sufficiently intensive defensive fire to ensure that virtually every attacking aircraft had suffered damage, the U-boats themselves had also taken punishment. By the end of the month five U-boats had been sunk in such actions, plus another five sunk on their way into the region and two more on leaving for home. Tonnage sunk was negligible.

During August, the greatest of all the U-boats' battles with aircraft occurred when U-615 (Kapitsky), a Type VIIC with enhanced anti-aircraft armament, came under attack. During the initial attack, U-615 suffered serious damage but managed to shoot down its attacker. Subsequently, more aircraft were vectored in on the stricken U-boat which astonishingly withstood a total of 12 concerted attacks by six different aircraft, fending off each attack and inflicting tremendous damage on several of the enemy planes. The boat was becoming more and more damaged, however, and its captain was severely wounded by enemy strafing fire. Nevertheless, using the cover of heavy rain squalls, the boat managed to avoid its attackers until the pumps finally failed and, unable to deal with the level of flooding, the commander, dying from loss of blood, ordered her abandoned.

A Type XIV *Milchkuh* carries out a refuelling operation at sea. In a shot taken from the receiving boat, the fuel transfer pipe can be seen played out over the stern of the Type XIV.

U-615 sank on 7 August. Of her crew, 43 were eventually picked up by the enemy, who were not yet aware that U-615 had sunk, her final demise being unnoticed in the poor visibility of the rainstorm.

By mid-August, all U-boats had been withdrawn from this theatre of operations as Dönitz once again transferred his attentions to the North Atlantic. From now on, only nuisance attacks were made by U-boats in the Caribbean, intended to tie down as much enemy naval resources as possible in protecting these waters and away from the main battleground in the North Atlantic. August also saw the fleet of U-tankers dwindle even further when U-489 (Schmandt) was sunk by Allied warships. There were no survivors. Two months later, U-460 (Schnoor) suffered the same fate. This left Dönitz only two Milk Cows remaining from his original ten.

Dönitz had high hopes for renewed success in the North Atlantic. His U-boats now had greatly enhanced anti-aircraft capabilities, the new T5 Zaunkönig acoustic torpedoes were available and improved radar search equipment had been fitted.

On 21 September, a combined convoy consisting of ON202 and ONS18 came under attack from a pack of 22 U-boats. In the battle that ensued, three enemy escort warships were sunk, three more seriously damaged and six merchantmen, totalling around 36,000 tons, were sunk. Any optimism created by this result was soon dashed, however, when on 15 October an attack on Convoy ONS20 resulted in six U-boats being sunk for the loss of just one freighter of around 6,600 tons. Losses such as these for such meagre gains could not be sustained: the north-west

This view of U-377 is an excellent example of a typical mid- to late-war Type VIIC. Note the deck gun is no longer carried, the tower has had additional plate welded to the upper sides to give the crew added protection against fire from enemy aircraft and the defensive flak armament has been greatly enhanced. (Jak P. Mallmann-Showell)

Atlantic was finally abandoned and the majority of U-boats concentrated in the north-east where their patrol lines would be shorter and time on station extended.

During the final part of the year, a smaller new group of boats arrived in the Caribbean: U-123 (von Schroeter), U-518 (Offermann), U-218 (Becker), U-161 (Achilles) and U-214 (Stock) followed by a second group comprising U-154 (Kusch), U-516 (Tillessen), U-129 (von Harpe), U-193 (von Paukstadt) and U-530 (Lange). So strong were the anti-submarine defences, however, that, other than minelaying operations, virtually nothing was achieved by these boats during September or October. On 11 November, however, U-516 caused some panic when it sank the freighter *Pompoon*, followed six days later by the schooner *Ruby*. On 23 November the *Melville E Stone* and tanker *Elizabeth Kellog* were both torpedoed by U-516. Allied beliefs that they had cleared all of the U-boats out of the Caribbean were being proved wrong. U-170 (Pfeffer) and U-190 (Wintermeyer) arrived in December, but still U-516 was the only boat achieving sinkings. On 3 December U-193 sank the 10,000-ton tanker *Touchet* and on the next day U-129 sent the freighter *Libertad* to the bottom.

U-516 continued its rampage, sinking the freighter *Colombia* on 8 December and eight days later sending the 10,000-ton tanker *McDowell* to the bottom. U-530 joined the scoring on 25 December when it torpedoed the tanker *Chapultec* off Panama. At the end of 1943, Dönitz could look back at over 45 war patrols carried out in these west Atlantic waters with only 31 ships sunk. This was less than 10 per cent of what had been achieved in the glory days of 1942. Nevertheless, successes like Tillessen's sent a sombre message to the Allies that the U-boat could still inflict serious damage and that it was still necessary to maintain considerable naval and air resources in the area to defend against potential U-boat attacks.

During 1943, 11 additional boats made the passage through the Straits of Gibraltar. U-97 (Trox), U-431 (Schöneboom), U-453 (Lührs), U-596 (Nonn), U-380 (Brandi) and U-565 (Henning) entered the Mediterranean for their second patrols, this time under new commanders. They were joined by U-224 (Kosbadt), U-303 (Heine), U-414 (Huth), U-410 (Fenski), U-616 (Koitschka), U-409 (Massmann), U-223 (Wächter), U-450 (Böhme), U-642 (Brünning) and U-230 (Siegmann) who all successfully passed into the Mediterranean. Two others were sunk making the attempt and one was forced to turn back.

The greatest challenge for the Mediterranean U-boats was to halt the Allied seaborne invasion of North Africa, Operation *Torch*, in November 1943. Targets available to the U-boats included three aircraft carriers, one battleship, seven cruisers, 17 destroyers, 40 merchants, 15 tankers and a number of smaller craft. In the event, only six merchantmen and two destroyers were sunk. During December, however, the destroyers *Partridge, Porcupine* and *Blean,* the 16,000-ton troopship *Cameronia* and the 24,000-ton troopship *Strathallan* were also torpedoed and sunk.

When out on operations, and in relatively safe waters where any attack from the enemy was considered unlikely, boats would occasionally seek to supplement the food rations by fishing. Here, one of the officers from U-461 is using the boat's MP40 machine pistol to shoot sharks in South Atlantic waters.

Further afield, in late January and early February of 1943, the *Seehund* group of boats had arrived in the waters around the Cape. Although traffic here was now grouped into convoys sailing close enough to shore to be afforded cover by land-based radar, these boats did score some successes. In waters near Durban on 3 March, a convoy was intercepted and four ships sunk. Operations here ended in early April, however, and the group headed home, U-182 (Clausen) being sunk on the return journey. A second group of Type IXD boats had been dispatched in March/April comprising U-177 (Gysae), U-178 (Dommes), U-180 (Musenberg), U-181 (Lüth), U-195 (Buchholz), U-196 (Kentrat), U-197 (Bartels) and U-198 (Hartmann). These boats were ordered to patrol even further afield, rounding the Cape and operating in the waters around Madagascar.

It is also interesting to note that it was one of these Type IXD boats, U-177, which carried the experimental 'Bachstelze' mini helicopter. This flimsy one-man 'microlite' helicopter was towed behind the U-boat, its cable acting also as a means of communication between the helicopter and the boat. The height achieved by this device gave the U-boat a much greater field of vision in its search for victims. In the event, it appears that only one enemy merchantman, the *Eithalia Mari,* was actually detected using the Bachstelze.

After patrolling the waters around Mauritius, Mozambique and Madagascar, the majority of these boats headed for home, having achieved only very modest results. The exception was U-178 which was ordered to the port of Penang in Malaysia. Here the commander, Wilhelm Dommes, would become the Chief of U-boats in the Southern Seas (Chef der U-Boote im Südraum). The German naval base established in Penang would also control other facilities at Singapore,

U-183, a Type IXD, is about to refuel at sea from a German tanker. The ability to refuel either from a tanker or from one of the *Milchkuh* submarines greatly extended the length of time a U-boat could remain on patrol. U-183 carried out 13 war cruises before herself being sunk by the US submarine *Besugo* on 23 April 1945.

Jakarta and Surabaya as well as at Kobe in Japan, all of which were provided courtesy of the Imperial Japanese Navy.

The suggestion of U-boats operating in the Far East had originally come from the Japanese and been rejected by Dönitz who felt that better opportunities for success were offered by operations in the Atlantic. However, as U-boat losses in the Atlantic grew in step with improved Allied anti-submarine measures, the opportunity to operate in Far Eastern waters came under consideration once again. Accordingly, as well as Dommes with U-178 being directed to Penang to establish the base there, U-511 (Schneewind) set off for Japan on 10 May 1943, to be exchanged with the Japanese for a supply of rubber. On arrival, and after handing over U-511 to the Japanese, its crew were to move to Penang to provide spare crew resource for boats which would operate from there. On its way to Japan, U-511 scored a number of successes, sinking two 7,100-ton freighters, the *Sebastiano Cermeno* and the *Samuel Heintzelmann*.

From mid-June to late July 1943, a number of Type IX boats set off for Penang. Scheduled to arrive in the area just after the end of the Monsoon season, this group inevitably became known as the 'Monsun' boats. The original group included U-168 (Pich), U-183 (Schafer), U-188 (Ludden), U200 (Schonder), U-506 (Wurdemann), U-509 (Witte), U-514 (Auffermann), U-516 (Tillessen), U-532 (Junker), U-533 (Hennig) and U-847 (Kuppisch). Unfortunately, a number of boats were lost in transit, U-200, U-509, U-506 and U-514 all being sunk in attacks by Allied aircraft en route. Unfortunately, of the two tankers assigned for refuelling the group, U-462, was badly damaged and forced to return to base and U-487 was sunk. As an expedient, two Type IX boats, U-155 and U-516, the latter itself one of the *Monsun* boats, were used to provide emergency fuelling for the others. After depleting his own bunkers providing fuel to U-532 and U-533, Tillessen in U-516 was no longer able to continue the journey and had to return to base in France. Only five boats, therefore, U-168, U-183, U-188, U-532 and U-533, made it safely to their new area of operations where they were further refuelled from a tanker sent out from Penang. U-168

U-219 at sea. One of a small number of Type XBs built, this boat served in Far East waters, and was still based in Penang when Germany surrendered. Taken over by the Imperial Japanese Navy, she was renumbered as the I-505. Note the raised casing forward of the deck gun indicating the position of the forward mine-carrying shafts.

thereafter operated in the waters off Bombay where she sank the *Haiching* in early October. U-183 patrolled the area between the east African coast and the Seychelles but found no successes. U-188 operated in the Gulf of Oman where she sank the *Cornelia P Spencer* in late September and the *Britannia* in early October. U-532 was active off the south-west coast of India where she sank the *Port Longueuil* and the *Banffshire* in late September and the *Tahsinia*, the *Jalabala* and the *British Purpose* in October, all on her way to Penang. U-533 was herself sunk whilst operating in the Gulf of Aden. All four surviving boats reached Penang safely by early November.

U-178 (Spahr) had departed Penang in late November to return to France, sinking the *Jose Navarro* en route and arriving back at Bordeaux in May 1944. It was an eventful voyage, however, the boat being attacked and severely damaged by Allied aircraft and barely making it back to base in one piece.

Because of the losses suffered by the first group en route, reinforcements in the form of U-219 (Burghagen), U-510 (Eick), U-848 (Rollmann), U-849 (Schultze) and U-850 (Ewerth) were dispatched in the autumn and early winter of 1943. Of these five boats, U-219 was recalled for other use, and U-848, U-849 and U-850 were all destroyed during attacks by Allied aircraft when running on the surface. Only Alfred Eick in U-510 reached Penang. The facilities in Penang were in any case rather limited and only five boats could comfortably be accommodated here.

1944

If 1943 had been a difficult year for the U-boats, then 1944 was disastrous. Only 131 enemy ships were sunk, representing some 700,000 tons. The force began the year with 447 boats and ended with 408. U-boats were now being sunk faster than new builds could be commissioned. Wolf pack tactics against Atlantic convoys proved ineffective. During the first part of the year, only 11 ships travelling in convoy were sunk (some 71,000 tons) whereas attacks by individual U-boats against ships travelling independently netted 42 victories (representing around 245,000 tons). During the same period, however, more than 100 U-boats had been lost to enemy action.

On 26 April 1944, the Type XIV tanker U-488 (Studt) was sunk by Allied warships, taking all hands to the bottom with her.

In June 1944, the Allied invasion of Normandy presented the U-boats with a vast fleet of troopships as targets. Unfortunately, Allied air cover by now was virtually unchallenged, and over 50 escorts were ploughing back and forth over the waters off the French coast to keep the U-boats at bay, which they did with great success. Even the use of *Schnorchel*-equipped boats that did not have to surface and thus offer themselves as potential targets to enemy aircraft did not fare well.

June also saw the last of the Milk Cows destroyed when U-490 (Gerlach) was attacked and sunk by Allied warships in the mid-Atlantic. There were, however, 60 survivors. Between them, the unarmed (apart from defensive flak guns) Type

Oberschreibmaat Walter Gerhold is seen here in the cockpit of his 'Neger' manned torpedo. These 'vessels' were probably more dangerous to the men who crewed them than to the enemy. Gerhold was awarded the Knight's Cross of the Iron Cross for his bravery as an *Einmannfahrer*.

XIV tankers had carried out a total of 36 cruises bringing essential fuel and supplies to combat U-boats which allowed them to remain at sea for far longer than would otherwise have been possible. Interestingly, these huge beasts also managed to shoot down six enemy aircraft during attacks on them. Unfortunately for them, Allied cracking of the German codes allowed aircraft and warships to lie in ambush for them at the designated rendezvous points so that not only the Milk Cows were lost, but also combat boats they were due to replenish.

In the period between June and December 1944, some 35 enemy ships travelling in convoy were sunk (around 178,000 tons), together with a further 36 travelling independently (162,000 tons). U-boat losses were heavy, however, with over 140 being lost.

During 1944, U-371 (Fenski), U-407 (Korndörfer), U-596 (Kolbus), U-223 (Gerlach) and U-230 (Eberbach), returned to the Mediterranean with new commanders and were joined by U-952 (Curio), U-343 (Rahn), U-455 (Scheibe), U-969 (Dobbert), U-586 (Götze), U-421 (Kolbus), U-466 (Thäter), U-471 (Kloevekorn) and U-960 (Heinrich). A total of 62 boats served in the Mediterranean during 1944, every one of which was lost before the end of the year.

In the Caribbean, U-154 (Gemeiner) and U-218 (Becker) returned to the area, joining U-518 (Offermann) to provide just three U-boats in this once busy theatre. On 6 March, U-518 torpedoed and sank the tanker *Valeria*. It was the only sinking achieved before all three boats returned home in April, though some minelaying operations were also carried out. In June, U-539 (Lauterbach-Emden) entered the Caribbean. On 2 June he torpedoed the freighter *Pillory*. Nine days later a surface attack on a tanker was interrupted by the appearance of a US aircraft which was driven off by heavy flak fire from the submarine. The tanker

A rare shot of U-295 acting as a mother ship for two of the 'Biber' class mini-subs carried on her decking. The Biber was not a particularly successful weapon, but this shows once again the great adaptability of the Type VIIC U-boat.

U-2017, a Type XXI, in dry dock. The workers on deck and the dockyard staff standing under her rudder give a good impression of how big these boats were. Their interior was far more comfortable and spacious than any other U-boat type. Thankfully for the Allies, these excellent boats did not see service soon enough to affect the course of the war.

escaped, however. At the end of June U-516 (Tillessen) re-appeared, now refitted and featuring a *Schnorchel*. On 6 July, he torpedoed the 10,000-ton tanker *Harrisburg*. It was to be the last merchantman to be sunk in Caribbean waters before the war's end.

During 1944, an additional nine U-boats successfully penetrated the Straits of Gibraltar, three others being sunk during the attempt. By the time the final U-boat operations in the Mediterranean ceased, U-boats had sunk 119 Allied ships, of which 24 were warships, including a battleship and two aircraft carriers.

On Christmas Eve of 1944, the U-boat arm scored one notable success when the *Schnorchel*-equipped U-486, lying in ambush off the port of Cherbourg, torpedoed the troopship *Leopoldville*. Despite her taking a considerable time to sink, the sheer lack of organisation on board resulted in the deaths of over 760 US soldiers who were still on board when she finally sank or had been killed in the blast when the torpedo impacted.

By the end of 1944, Germany had lost all of its operational U-boat bases in occupied France and was left with bases in Germany and Norway, plus a few boats operating in the Far East from Japanese bases in Malaya. The convoy war was all but over and most U-boats were lucky to return from a patrol alive, let alone score significant successes against Allied shipping.

The *Monsun* boats were relatively active in 1944. U-168 (Pich), operating first out of Penang and then out of Jakarta, sank the *Salviking* and the *Epaminonas C Embinocos* and damaged a Norwegian freighter but was herself sunk on 6 October of that year. U-183 (Schneewind) accounted for the *Palma*, the *British Loyalty* and

243

This shot shows the relatively spacious after deck of U-188, a Type IXD, as her crew muster during her commissioning ceremony. Although she carried out only six war patrols, she succeeded in sinking 16 enemy ships. She was scuttled on 20 August 1944 to prevent her capture. U-188 was commanded by Kapitänleutnant Siegfried Lüdden.

the *Helen Moller* and survived the year still operating from Penang. U-532 (Junker) dispatched the *Triona*, the *Walter Camp* and the *Tulagi* and also survived the year. U-188 (Ludden) was particularly successful, sinking the *Fort Buckingham*, the *Fort La Maune*, the *Saruda*, the *Samouri* and the *Olga E Embinicos* in January 1944, and the *Chung Cheng* and the *Viva* in February.

The so-called *Monsun* boats caused great concern to the Allies, tying down significant numbers of ships in attempting to keep the Pacific and Indian Oceans safe from these predators. Here U-178 is welcomed back from a successful cruise. She carried out three long-range patrols in the South Atlantic and Far East, sinking 13 enemy ships totalling some 87,000 tons.

Three of the boats, U-183, U-188 and U-532, were ordered to return home, taking essential war materials obtained from the Japanese, in order to load up with supplies of torpedoes and essential spares for the base at Penang. Particular problems were being experienced with torpedoes due to lengthy storage in such humid tropical locations. In the event, the sinking of the supply tanker *Brake*, based at the Penang facility, left the U-boats short of fuel and only U-188 was able to return to France.

In the early part of the year, between January and April, a total of 14 additional boats were ordered to sail for the Far East. Unfortunately eight of them, U-177 (Buchholz), U-198 (von Waldegg), U-801 (Brans), U-851 (Weingärtner), U-852 (Eck), U-859 (Jebsen), U-860 (Buchel) and U-1059 (Leupold), were sunk before reaching Penang. U-198 and U-859 did reach the Indian Ocean, where they were active and did score some sinkings but were sunk before ever making it to their new base. U-181 (Freiwald), U-196 (Kentrat), U-861 (Oesten) and U-1062 (Albrecht) reached Penang safely, whilst U-537 (Schewe) and U-843 (Herwartz) put in to Jakarta. A second batch of boats set off in the second half of the year: U-180 (Reisen), U-195 (Steinfeldt), U-219 (Burghagen), U-490 (Gerlach), U-862 (Timm), U-863 (von der Esch) and U-871 (Ganzer). U-180, U-490, U-863 and U-871 were sunk, with U-862 reaching Penang and U-195 and U-219 reaching Jakarta. Of the boats which did make it through to their new bases, two were lost in action soon afterwards, U-196 and U-537, both being destroyed in early November 1944.

1945

The final major convoy battle of the war came in April 1945, when Convoy RA66 came under attack by a pack of 14 U-boats. The convoy was a fairly large one consisting of 24 ships. The U-boats managed to sink only one, the frigate HMS *Goodall*. One of the U-boats involved set a record of its own, surviving the most intensive depth charge attack of the war when it suffered an incredible assault of 678 depth charges over a sustained period.

On 4 May 1945, Dönitz sent out the following radio signal to his U-boats:

> All U-boats. Attention all U-boats. Cease-fire at once. Stop all hostile action against Allied shipping.

Though the war would not officially be over for several more days, as far as the 'Grey Wolves' were concerned, their fight had come to an end. A second, more personal signal followed:

> My U-boat men! Six years of submarine warfare lie behind us. You have fought like Lions! A crushing material superiority has forced us into a narrow

The diminutive Type XXIII U-2329 sits alongside a larger Type IX. One of a small number of this type to see combat action, under the command of Oberleutnant zur See Heinrich Schlott, she carried out an attack on Allied shipping, damaging one enemy vessel. She was surrendered at Stavanger, Norway in May 1945.

area. A continuation of our fight on the remaining basis is no longer possible. U-boat men! Undefeated and unblemished you lay down your arms after a heroic battle without equal. We remember in deep respect our fallen comrades, who have sealed with death their loyalty to Führer and Fatherland!

Comrades! Preserve your U-boat spirit, with which you have fought courageously, stubbornly and imperturbably through the years for the good of the Fatherland.

Long Live Germany!
Your Grand Admiral

During the period from January to May 1945, only 71 enemy ships were sunk, representing some 332,000 tons. Only 93 new U-boats were commissioned but nearly 400 were sunk. Only 102 operational U-boats remained by May 1945.

In the closing months of the war, a number of the *Monsun* boats tried to reach home, often carrying loads of critical war materials. U-843 ended a long voyage begun in Jakarta on 10 December 1944 when she reached Bergen safely on 3 April 1945. She was subsequently sunk whilst trying to make the last leg home to Germany. U-861 also reached Norway safely on 18 April 1945. U-510 succeeded in adding a last victim, the *Point Pleasant Park*, on 23 February 1945 on her run homewards. She surrendered on 24 April 1945 having run out of fuel and thus being unable to reach home. U-183 was sunk by the American submarine *Besugo* on 24 April 1945 near Jakarta. U-195 remained at Jakarta at the end, her condition too poor to make the long trip home. U-181 also remained

at Jakarta. U-532 sank the *Baron Jedburgh* and the *Oklahoma* on her return trip carrying a cargo of tin. She never reached Germany, however, surrendering at Liverpool on 10 May 1945. The remaining boats in the Far East, U-181, U-195, U-219 and U-862, were seized by the Japanese on 15 July 1945 but never saw further operational use. U-181 and U-862 were scuttled at Singapore in 1946.

At the end of the war in Europe, the German Navy executed Operation *Regenbogen* (Rainbow) where, on receipt of a coded message, U-boat commanders scuttled their boats to prevent their falling into enemy hands intact. During this operation a total of 219 boats were scuttled. These included 20 Type II, 68 Type VII, six Type IX, 85 Type XXI and 32 Type XXIII boats. Many of these were boats which had been completed by their builders and taken into the Kriegsmarine but were still working up or under training. By no means all were fully operational combat-ready boats.

In all, the Kriegsmarine lost 805 U-boats. Of these, 663 losses were due to enemy action, the vast majority of them in attacks by enemy aircraft or warships. The remainder were non-combat losses such as those destroyed in bombing raids, scuttled at the war's end, lost in accidents, etc. In total some 65 per cent of all U-boats were lost. Of those remaining (some 376 in total) at the time of Germany's surrender, over 200 were scuttled to prevent their seizure by the enemy.

THE END – OPERATION *DEADLIGHT*

By the time of the German surrender in May 1945, around 150 functional U-boats survived. Despite a number being sabotaged or scuttled by their crews in the final hours, a substantial number of U-boats, including the new Type XXI and Type XXIII models, were now available to the Allies for examination.

U-234, a Type XB U-boat with long-range capability, was commanded by Kapitänleutnant Johann-Heinrich Fehler. She surrendered to the US Navy on 19 May 1945 shortly after the war ended, having been en route to Japan carrying a cargo of uranium and a number of Japanese naval staff who committed suicide rather than surrender to the Americans.

Several U-boats were allocated to Allied nations for their own use and for disposal as they saw fit. In some cases these boats saw actual operational service in their navies. U-995, for instance, was passed to the Danish Navy which operated the boat as the *Kaura*. When it was of no further use to them, it was presented back to Germany, into the hands of the Deutsche Marinebund, and now sits on a concrete pedestal on the beach near to the German Naval Memorial at Möltenort, a permanent memorial to the men of the U-Bootwaffe. Other navies, including the British, the US, the Canadian, the Danish, the Soviet and the French, operated U-boats for a short period, mainly for evaluation purposes. Over the years that followed, most of these were scuttled or used as targets during training exercises. Some did see operational use in peacetime, however. U-2518 became the *Roland Morillot* of the French Navy and served until 1967; U-926 was renamed *Kya* and served with the Royal Norwegian Navy until 1964; U-995 and U-1202 also served with the Royal Norwegian Navy as the *Kaura* and *Kinn* respectively.

For the bulk of the captured U-boat stock, however, there was no further use. At the end of the war, those U-boats still operational were instructed to surface and, flying a black flag, to sail for Allied ports. Boats surrendered were gathered at Lisahally in Ireland and at Loch Ryan in Scotland, often after being toured around UK ports to be shown off. After these boats had languished at their moorings for some time while they were being stripped of any useful material, the decision was taken to have them sailed into deep water and sunk. This operation was given the code-name *Deadlight*. Some boats were simply scuttled whilst others were used for target practice.

A total of 115 U-boats were sunk during this operation, 93 of them 'regular' boats and 22 of them the so-called 'electro-boats', Types XXI and XXIII. The last of the U-boats to be disposed of under Operation *Deadlight* were sunk on 12 February 1946. A number of them have subsequently been 'found' once again by marine archaeologists and dives have been made on several. It is known that salvage contracts have been issued for some of them because of their scrap value so some may well see the light of day once again at some time in the future.

PART V
CONCLUSION

Any reader with a keen interest in the subject of U-boats will be well aware that the number of books written on the subject over the years since the end of World War II seems almost legion. Of particular interest is how the image of the U-boats, their crews and their commander-in-chief, Karl Dönitz, has changed during this period.

At the end of the war, the perception amongst the Allies, despite the fact that they must have known how relatively 'cleanly' the U-boat men fought their war, seemed to be that captured U-boat men were a 'dangerous' breed. Unlike many regular sailors at the end of the war who were swiftly demobilised and allowed to return to civilian life (or in some cases, such as the men of the German Minesweeping Administration, actually continuing to serve but under British control), a considerable number of U-boat men were held in captivity for many months or even years after their fellow sailors had been released. The last U-boat men to be released from captivity were not allowed home until 1949.

Early books often show a tendency to demonise the U-boat. U-boats are considered a dastardly weapon, crewed by unpleasant, almost piratical Nazi fanatics. Emphasis tends to be on the fate of the victims, with little mention of the horrific fate that

Sadly, this was to be the fate of 75 to 80 per cent of Germany's U-boat men: a death at sea, commemorated by their family in such cards issued to friends and family at the funeral service. (Author's collection)

250

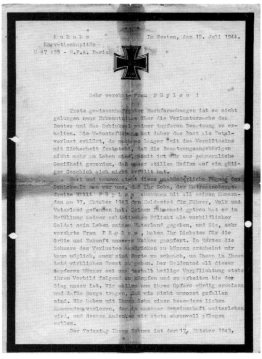

befell so many U-boat men. As the years passed, grudging credit began to be shown for the astonishing achievements of the U-boats and their crews, though the overall image remained a negative rather than a positive one. This despite the fact that by the early 1950s German writers were already beginning to produce detailed works on the U-boat war which accurately reflected the realities of life in the U-boat arm. Whilst such works were admired and respected by U-boat veterans, the former 'enemies' were still unwilling to see the average U-boat man as anything other than a hardened Nazi killer. In 1955 the creation of the West German Bundesmarine saw many former Kriegsmarine U-boat men return to the service of their country, including several of the great 'aces'.

In the 1970s, interest in World War II and military subjects in general mushroomed. The novel *Das Boot*, written by Lothar Günther Buchheim and published in 1973, was to be a turning point. A former naval war correspondent, Buchheim was able to call upon his own experiences when he had undertaken a combat patrol with the famed U-96 under Heinrich Lehmann-Willenbrock. The book was made into a successful TV mini-series and then into an equally successful movie. At last, U-boat sailors, instead of being demonised as Nazi fanatics, were shown as human beings, subject to the same hopes and fears as sailors of any other navies. Although the book, and film, drew considerable

ABOVE LEFT

U-boats were no different from other vessels in that it was common for a mascot to be adopted. This Oberleutnant zur See posing with his boat's mascot hardly fits the typical image of the hardened killer that Allied propaganda would seek to portray.

ABOVE RIGHT

A rather sad memento of the U-boat war. This is a condolence letter sent by Korvettenkapitän Kuhnke at the Naval Personnel Office in Paris on 15 July 1944 giving his condolences to a Frau Päplow on the death of her son Willi on 17 October 1943 when his boat, U-540, was lost with all hands. Such a long gap in time between a boat being lost and the family receiving a formal letter was not uncommon, the unfortunate sailor being posted as 'missing' for some time before this was changed to 'fallen'. (Author's collection) levels of criticism from some U-boat veterans, others, including famous U-boat aces Erich Topp and Peter 'Ali' Cremer, leapt to its defence.

The U-boat memorial at Möltenort features large bronze panels on which are recorded the names of every U-boat sailor killed in action during World War II. There are 28,748 such names. This figure represents approximately 65 per cent of all those who had served at some point in their career with this branch of the navy, a terrible rate of sacrifice by any standards. As a percentage of those who specifically served on front-line operational boats, the so-called 'Frontboote', it is even higher. It is estimated that somewhere around 7,000 front line U-boat crewmen were still alive at the war's end.

If time has brought with it a mellowing of public perception of the image of the U-boat man – now more willingly accepted as being a sailor pretty much like a sailor in any other navy – the degree of interest in the U-boats which has developed has led to much more critical analysis of their effectiveness and successes. Post-war research in official records, both German and Allied, has led to a reappraisal of many of the claims made by U-boat commanders of tonnages sunk. Even when revised downwards, however, the scores remain impressive and certainly the averages are much higher than those attained by the submarine commanders of any other nation.

The general perception held of Karl Dönitz has also come under attack in recent years. Attempts have been made, generally unsuccessfully, to portray him as a Nazi sympathiser. The fact that his U-boats acted in at least as chivalrous a manner, if not more so, than most of their Allied equivalents and his attempts to keep his U-boat service free from political interference do, however, tend to suggest that any pro-regime speeches he may have given were the result of a senior officer paying 'lip-service'. In any case, though Dönitz may not have been perfect, he certainly paid for his misdemeanours with a ten-year jail sentence which many senior Allied figures considered exceedingly harsh. Though there are some in the U-boat veteran community who would criticise Dönitz for continuing to send his U-boats into action long after the point had been reached when there was little or no chance for them to achieve any success, the majority of those who served under him never lost their admiration for Der Löwe.

Whilst the U-Bootwaffe failed in its attempts to blockade the United Kingdom into submission, a failure for which we should all be grateful, and whilst how closely it came to achieving this goal is still hotly debated, no other submarine force in history has ever come near to equalling its achievements or sacrifices, to say nothing of the technological advances made within the U-boat branch of the Kriegsmarine which had such fundamental influences on post-war submarine development.

GLOSSARY

Akkumulatorraum Battery store

Bassin Basin

BdU (Befehlshaber der Unterseeboote) C-in-C U-Boats

Beton Concrete

Bug Bow

Büro Office

Caisson Cofferdam

Decke Ceiling, roof

Deckenträger Roof support

Dreherei Turning shop (lathe workshop)

Electro-Werke Generator room

Fangrost System of interlacing concrete beams above a bunker's roof to create a protective layer and prevent bomb damage

Feindfahrt War cruise

FdU (Führer der Unterseeboote) Flag Officer U-Boats

Flak (Fliegerabwehrkanone) Anti-aircraft gun

Flakstand Anti-aircraft station, gun position

Funkraum Radio room

Geleitzug Convoy

Hafen Harbour

Heck Stern

Heizwerk Heating works

Innenhafen Inner harbour

Kai Quay

Kesselhaus Boiler house

Kommandant Commander

Kran Crane

Lager Store

LI (Leitender Ingenieur) Engineering Officer

Luftschutzbunker Air-raid shelter

Magazin Magazine

Matrose Seaman, Sailor

Mechaniker Mechanic

Nassbock A 'wet' pen

OKM (Oberkommando der Marine) Naval High Command

Panzertor Armoured door

Ponton Pontoon

Pumpenraum Pump room

Rammpfähle Pile-driver

Ruder Rudder

Sauerstoffanlage Oxygen plant

Schraub Screw (Propeller)

Sehrohr Werkstatt Periscope workshop

Schiffs-Reparaturwerk Ship repair works

Schleusse Lock

Sperrballon Barrage balloon

Steuermann Helmsman

Tauchretter Submarine escape gear

Tiefgangruder Diving planes

Tischlerei Carpenters' workshop

Torpedolager Torpedo store

Trockenbock A dry-dock-capable pen

Turm Conning tower

UZO (U-Bootzieloptik) Targeting binoculars

Wabo (Wasserbomb) Depth charge

Werft Shipyard

Werkstatt Workshop

WO (IWO or IIWO) Wachoffizier First/Second Watch Officer

Zentrale Central (control room)

Zerstörer Destroyer

BIBLIOGRAPHY AND RECOMMENDED READING

Angolia, John R., and Littlejohn, David, *Labor Organisations of the Third Reich*, R. James Bender Publishing, San Jose, 1999.

Fröhle, Claude, and Kühn, Hans-Jürgen, *Hochseefestung Helgoland*, Fröhle-Kühn Verlagsgesellschaft, Herbolzheim, 1999.

Hadley, Michael L., *Count Not the Dead*, McGill-Queens University Press, Montreal, 1995.

Kaplan, Philip, and Currie, Jack, *Wolfpack*, Aurum Press, London, 1997.

Kelshall, Gaylord T. M., *U-boat War in the Caribbean*, Naval Institute Press, Annapolis, Maryland, 1994.

Kurowski, Franz, *Die Träger des Ritterkreuzes des Eisernen Kreuzes der U-Bootwaffe 1939–45*, Podzun Pallas Verlag, Friedberg, 1987.

Mallmann-Showell, Jak P., *U-boat Commanders and Crews*, Crowood Press, Wiltshire, 1998.

Mallmann-Showell, Jak P., *U-boats under the Swastika*, Ian Allan, Surrey, 1998.

Mallmann-Showell, Jak P., *German Navy Handbook*, Sutton Publishing, Stroud, 1999.

Mallmann-Showell, Jak P., *U-boats in Camera*, Sutton Publishing, Stroud, 1999.

Mallmann-Showell, Jak P., *Enigma U-boat: Breaking the Code – The True Story*, Naval Institute Press, Annapolis, Maryland, 2000.

Mallmann-Showell, Jak P., *U-boats at War: Landings on Hostile Shores*, Ian Allan, Surrey, 2000.

Mallmann-Showell, Jak P., *Hitler's U-boat Bases*, Naval Institute Press, Annapolis, Maryland, 2002.

Mallmann-Showell, Jak P., *U-boat Warfare, the Evolution of the Wolfpack*, Naval Institute Press, Annapolis, Maryland, 2002.

Mulligan, Timothy P., *Neither Sharks Nor Wolves*, Naval Institute Press, Annapolis, Maryland, 1999.

Neitzel, Sönke, *Die Deutschen Ubootbunker und Bunkerwerften*, Bernard/Graefe Verlag, 1991.

Rössler, Eberhard, *The U-boat: The Evolution and Technical History of German Submarines*, Arms & Armour Press, London, 1981.

Rössler, Eberhard, *The Type XXI U-boat (Anatomy of the Ship)*, Naval Institute Press, Annapolis, Maryland, 2002.

Schmeelke, Karl-Heinz, and Schmeelke, Michael, *German U-boat Bunkers –
Yesterday and Today*, Schiffer Publishing, Altglen, 1999.

Schmidt, Dieter and Becker, Fabian, *Bunker Valentin*, Edition Temmen, Bremen,
Rostock, 1996.

Sharpe, Peter, *U-boat Fact File*, Midland Publishing, Leicester, 1998.

Stern, Robert C., *Type VII U-boats*, Arms & Armour Press, London, 1991.

Tarrant, V. E., *The U-boat Offensive, 1914–45*, Naval Institute Press, Annapolis,
Maryland, 1989.

Taylor, J. C., *German Warships of World War Two*, Ian Allan, London, 1966.

White, J. F., *U-boat Tankers, 1941–45*, Airlife Publishing, Shrewsbury, 1998.

Wynn, Kenneth, *U-boat Operations of the Second World War Vol. 1*, Chatham
Publishing, London, 1997.

Wynn, Kenneth, *U-boat Operations of the Second World War Vol. 2*, Chatham
Publishing, London, 1998.

After the Battle magazine, Battle of Britain Prints, London, No. 55 (1995)
contains excellent information and photographs of the U-boat bases in
France. No. 111 (2001) contains an in-depth feature on the demolition
of the Hamburg U-boat bunkers.

ONLINE RESEARCH RESOURCES

UBOAT.NET
Without doubt the single most important online resource is the superb Uboat.net
run by Gudmundur Helgasson with the assistance of a number of dedicated
enthusiasts. There is very little about the U-boat war which does not have some
level of coverage on this excellent site. http://www.uboat.net

UBOOTWAFFE.NET
A newer site and one that complements uboat.net well. It contains much statistical
data on sinkings, war patrols and crew lists. http://www.ubootwaffe.net

THE U-BOAT WAR
This site provides an excellent general history of the U-boat service, with data on
U-boat types, the U-boat flotillas, etc. http://www.uboatwar.net

UNTERSEEBOOTE
The author's website, detailing the uniforms and insignia of the U-Bootwaffe
from 1914 to the Bundesmarine of today. http://www.unterseeboote.co.uk

U-BOAT BASES
This site provides information, statistics and photographs of the French U-boat
bases. http://www.uboat-bases.com/

APPENDIX 1

VISITING FRENCH U-BOAT BASES AND BUNKERS TODAY

For a convenient starting point, travelling from the UK has been assumed. The nearest ferry port for a trip to the U-boat bunkers would be Roscoff: the directions that follow are based upon travelling by road from there.

BORDEAUX

One of the so-called 'Walter' boats running at speed on the surface on the river Elbe in 1944. An amazing vessel with a revolutionary Walter turbine engine, the type never saw action. This boat was scuttled at the end of the war but raised and taken over by the Royal Navy where she underwent extensive testing.

The U-boat bunkers at Bordeaux stand pretty much as they did in 1945. The bunkers are now in private hands and permission to visit them can be arranged. Be aware that maintenance work has not been carried out over the years: some parts of the bunker complex are now somewhat dangerous and entry is forbidden. A bus service runs from the main railway station in Bordeaux right to the banks of the Garonne, just a few minutes' walk from the bunker complex. A good view of the interior of the pens can be had from the quayside.

From the ferry port of Roscoff, follow the signs for St Pol (D769), then on to the D58: follow this until the junction with the D173, where you should bear right onto the D19. Follow this route until the junction with the N12. A large portion of the journey, some 186km, is on this road: follow it until the junction with the N136. After 7.5km, follow the signposts for Nantes on the N137. Around 95km further on, join the A844/N844/D844 until Junction 48 and join the A83 at Porte des Sorinieres. Follow this road for about 146km before changing on to the N148, following this briefly before joining the N11 and the N150 at the junction with the Niort Southern Bypass. Leave this road at the junction with the N248, and just over 2km later join the main A10/E5. This route takes the driver to within 5km of Bordeaux: leave the motorway at Junction 4 and travel along the N210 into the city.

BREST

Following their capture by Allied forces at the end of the war, the U-boat bunkers at Brest were found to be relatively intact. Some damage had been done, though none of it fatal to the structure. Lumps of concrete dislodged by bomb blasts had fallen into the water around the pens and the Germans, before surrendering, had sunk blocking ships in them to prevent their use by the enemy, as well as dumping considerable amounts of unexploded ordnance into the water. In time, all of this debris was removed and the pens brought back into use.

The U-boat pens are still in use by the French Navy, and so cannot be accessed by the public. The area directly to the rear of the bunker complex is still accessible by public road (Route de la Corniche) and the condition of the bunker makes this a worthwhile visit even if the interior itself cannot be seen.

From Roscoff, follow the signs for St Pol (D769), then on to the D58. Follow this road until the junction with the D10 and take the D788 exit. Follow the D788 until the junction with the D69 at the edge of Plouvorn. Following the signposts for Brest will bring you to the junction with the N12 which will take you all the way to this historic port.

LORIENT

The bunkers were taken over by the French Navy after the war and continued to accommodate one of its original inhabitants, U-123, now known as S-10 *Blaison*. Keroman III was used as a dry-dock facility by nuclear submarines. Fortunately, however, the French authorities have appreciated the historical significance of this site and the public interest therein, and from the middle of June to the middle of September guided tours of the Keroman complex are available. It is still possible to approach quite close to the bunker exteriors in many cases.

Both *Dom* bunkers are still in existence, one having been abandoned and the other still in use by a civilian boat-building firm. These bunkers, being outside the naval base, may be approached without problem. The Scorff bunkers are now used to house surface vessels: access to these bunkers is prohibited. The former mansion at Kerneval, employed by Dönitz as headquarters of the *Befehlshaber der U-Boote*, is used by the French commanding admiral.

Follow the route given for Brest as far as the N12 junction, but turn off on to the D30 and follow this until meeting the D764. This route in turn should be followed to the junction with the D18. Follow the D18 until the junction signposted for Quimper, joining the N165 which can be followed all the way to the outskirts of Lorient: the final 3km of the route are along the D29.

LA PALLICE

The bunker at La Pallice is still owned by the French Navy but is not in military use: two of the original pens have been leased out for civilian use. Nature has achieved what the bombs of the RAF and USAAF failed to do: the bunker, lacking the requisite maintenance, is now in poor condition and considered too dangerous to be kept in use. The bunker lies close to the quay from which the ferries run to the Île de Ré, and an excellent view into the pens can be had from the long jetty which runs out between Pens 7 and 8. Access to this jetty is not restricted. Access to the rear and sides of the bunker complex is also possible. The bunker was used for location shots for the film *Das Boot*, which also provides fine views both internal and external of this site.

ST NAZAIRE

The St Nazaire complex fell into Allied hands intact with one of its inhabitants, U-510, in reasonably good order. After minor repairs, U-510 served with the French Navy. The bunker is still in good condition today although, having been abandoned as naval establishments, the pens were allowed to silt up and some have even been infilled. The bunker complex at St Nazaire is in an entirely civilian area and may thus be approached without problem. Notices point out that access is prohibited, although this is because the bunker is still used by commercial firms for storage as opposed to military use. Clear views into the pens may be had from the opposite side of the basin.

Follow the same route as for Brest, but from the D69, turn onto the D764 at the junction with the N12 – signposted Quimper. Follow the D764 until its junction with the D18, and the D18 until its junction with the N165/E60. Follow this main route past Junction 17 and turn onto the D773 which is signposted St Nazaire. Follow this to its junction with the N171, and then follow the N171 for about 10km until reaching the N471, which leads into the city. Follow the same route as for Bordeaux as far as Junction 7 on the A83/E3. Here, turn on to the N137 and follow this to the junction with the N11 some 43km further on. Here, turn on to the N11/E601. La Rochelle/La Pallice is only 10km from here.

MUSEUMS AND COLLECTING

The finest single repository of data of any type on the U-boats of both world wars is without doubt the U-Boot Archiv in Cuxhaven. Under the guiding hand of its director, Horst Bredow, himself a U-boat veteran, this has become the world's foremost source of U-boat information.

The Archiv is located in a large detached villa and, as well as containing a sizeable museum collection of original U-boat artefacts, it has a massive photographic and documentary collection, much of which was donated from the photograph albums of surviving U-boat crewmen, including a large amount of material on the various U-boat bunkers and bases. The facilities of the Archiv are available to those who wish to visit in person, but prior arrangements must be made. The Archiv is a registered charity. No fee is charged for entry and the Archiv depends on its visitors making a suitable donation after their visit. The Archiv will also, on payment of a suitable fee, carry out research on behalf of those who cannot visit.

At Laboe, near Kiel, the Type VII U-boat U-995 has been taken from the water and mounted on a concrete plinth on the beach just by the German naval memorial. U-995 is open to the public and a trip on board is a real eye-opener as to just how cramped the conditions were on a typical U-boat. U-995 was taken over by the Royal Norwegian Navy after the war but, once her active service days were over, she was returned to Germany and accepted as a memorial by the German Naval Association (Deutsche Marinebund). She was refurbished and repainted in her original wartime finish.

In Bremerhaven, the Type XXI U-boat *Wilhelm Bauer* (formerly U-2540) is also open to the public at the German Maritime Museum. This boat was salvaged after the war and used as a test bed for submarine equipment. Her original conning tower was heavily reworked, changing her appearance considerably. When her working life was over, she was converted back to wartime specification (though only externally) and her original conning tower configuration restored. A visit to this highly advanced late-war U-boat makes an interesting contrast to U-995.

Also on public display is the wreck of U-534, which was raised from Danish waters in 1993 and put on display at Birkenhead, Merseyside, in England. It is now possible to go on board her and partial restoration work has been carried out to rebuild her missing conning tower. There is also a realistic mock-up of part of a U-boat at Bletchley Park, near Milton Keynes, England, which was used for the making of the film *Enigma*.

On the other side of the Atlantic, another Type VII, U-505, is on display at the Museum of Science and Industry in Chicago. She is open to the public, and like U-995 offers the visitor a fascinating glimpse of what life was like on a combat U-boat. U-505 is now undergoing a multi-million-dollar restoration.

COLLECTING

Unfortunately, as with most types of Third Reich memorabilia, almost anything connected to the U-boats has been widely reproduced, often to such high quality that even experienced collectors have been fooled. Most commonly faked are the U-Boat War Badge and U-Boat Front Clasp. There is little or no variation in the appearance of the originals manufactured by the prestigious Berlin firm of Schwerin, and pieces which do not match those illustrated in this book should be treated with caution.

Kriegsmarine headgear is also widely collected and original pieces fetch very high sums indeed. Care must be taken to avoid early post-war Bundesmarine caps, which have been retro-converted by the addition of wartime insignia, the basic headwear itself being almost identical. Look for the use of plastics or modern materials which look identical, but are of much later origin. The use of a blacklight (a small hand-held UV strip light used for detecting forged banknotes) may highlight modern threads which use artificial whiteners. Unfortunately, neither of these points is foolproof, as very early Bundesmarine peaked caps used leather peak binding and some original wartime material used dyes which do react to a blacklight. Kriegsmarine cap ribbons are also being re-manufactured, but so far the author has not noted any U-boat ribbons.

The small traditional badges worn on the side of the cap by most U-boat men are highly sought-after collector's pieces. As the originals were often crudely hand-cut from scrap metals, they are equally easy to forge and artificially age. Treat everything with caution unless fully satisfied as to an item's provenance, and only buy from reputable sources which offer a lifetime money-back guarantee of authenticity.

Large numbers of replica sets of the grey leather U-boat clothing have been manufactured for film use and their accuracy is remarkable. Only the lack of 60 years of natural ageing is likely to raise suspicions, and clever forgers will have no problem artificially ageing such garments.

U-1406, a Type XVII one of Germany's last-ditch efforts in introducing high-tech new submarines which it was hoped would turn the tide of war. She never saw action and was scuttled on 5 May 1945 in Cuxhaven. She was eventually raised, taken to the US and used for testing before finally being scrapped in May 1948.

It is in the field of medals and awards that the forger's 'art' has reached its peak. Modern laser die-cutting methods make the manufacture of dies a much more feasible proposition for the forger. With U-boat awards, two particular pieces have been hit hard in this respect. The early quality U-Boat War Badge, manufactured by the Schwerin firm in Berlin, has been heavily reproduced and the quality of many of the copies is quite astounding. Originals were finished in mercuric fire gilding, a practice no longer carried out in Europe for safety reasons. The lack of this finish used to be a useful indicator as to an item's provenance, but unscrupulous dealers now send copy badges to the Indian sub-continent where fire-gilding is still carried out.

The U-Boat Front Clasp is also heavily reproduced. Originals were pressure die-cast in zinc and given a bronze- or silver-plating as appropriate. Over time the plating reacts to the zinc base metal to give fine pinhead bubbling to the surface, a useful indicator of true ageing. In fact, the most recent copies of this award are better made than the originals, itself a possible indicator of their true age.

For those with access to the internet, there are a number of forums and newsgroups which deal with such militaria. Highly experienced collectors will happily give advice to those who are unsure of the originality of an item they have purchased, or are considering purchasing.

One such resource, which is highly recommended, is the Wehrmacht Awards Forum which may be found at http://wehrmacht-awards.com.

INDEX